P9-CAO-943

A Life With Horses

A Life With

Horses

A memoir of a woman's life journey
in the company of horses.

Sharon Gates

Order this book online at www.trafford.com
or email orders@trafford.com

Most Trafford titles are also available at major online book retailers.

© Copyright 2010 Sharon Gates.
All rights reserved. No part of this publication may be reproduced, stored in a retrieval
system, or transmitted, in any form or by any means, electronic, mechanical, photocopying,
recording, or otherwise, without the written prior permission of the author, except by a reviewer,
who may quote passages in a review.

Photo Credits:
Cover photo by Sharon Gates
Racing photo (Pas Paul Pas) by Ralph Morgan
Barrel racing and Undecorating photos by Rick White
Barrel racing photo Canadian National Finals by Ken Marcinkoski
Reining photos by: Sharon Latimer, Diane Nicholson
Working Cowhorse photo by Tracey Eide
Other photos by Verna Allinson, Penny Ogasawara, Slim & Florence Gates, Cindy Collins, Lana Morrow,
Dave Harley, Don Williams, Sharon Gates.

Quotes by: Marsha Norman, Napoleon Hill, C.S. Lewis, Tony Robinson, Monica Dickens, Robert Smith
Surtees, William Kittridge, Jerry Schulman, Mark Helprin, Xenophone, Nicholas Evans, Leslie Desmond,
Will James, Sharon Ralls Lemon, The Koran, Karen West, L. McGuire, Vicki Hearne, Lucy Rees, Monty
Roberts, John Masefield, William Ogilvie, Florence Gates, Sharon Gates.

Printed in Victoria, BC, Canada.

ISBN: 978-1-4251-7987-8 (Soft)
ISBN: 978-1-4251-7988-5 (e-book)

*Our mission is to efficiently provide the world's finest, most comprehensive
book publishing service, enabling every author to experience success.
To find out how to publish your book, your way, and have it available
worldwide, visit us online at www.trafford.com*

Trafford rev. 2/17/2010

 www.trafford.com

North America & international
toll-free: 1 888 232 4444 (USA & Canada)
phone: 250 383 6864 ✦ fax: 812 355 4082

For all the horses I have known;
For all the ones that now have gone;
For every one that carried me
And all the horses yet to be.

ACKNOWLEDGEMENTS

In memory of my parents, Slim and Florence Gates, and my grandparents, Leslie and Gertrude Giauque, who set me on a path with horses on it.

Thank you to Rick and Cindy Wilker, who encouraged me to write, then reminded me until I did.

Special thanks to Mae Ranger, Mandy Blais and Verna Allinson, whose faith in A Life With Horses and me inspired me to finish.

Thank you to the many owners of the horses I have trained and shown. You trusted me and my training program enough to place your horses in my care. Several have provided content for this book.

And thank you to *my* horses for enriching my life and guiding me when I lost my way.

CONTENTS

Part 4
HORSES AND TRAINING IN BC

Part 5
RIDING FULL CIRCLE

Introduction

In my bookshelf is a book of horse stories friends gave to me for Christmas five years ago. Inside is the inscription, "For a woman who could (and should) write her own collection of horse stories". They told me the same thing every time I launched into a long tale about a horse, but that note motivated me to start. For the next several weeks, I carved at least an hour out of each day to sit at my computer. At first, my ramblings were not a book, only random stories giving voice to memories, but as the words poured out, I embarked on a wonderful trip. I wandered down back trails until I was in the present in the past. I was *there*—on the prairie, on the mountain, with my parents, brother, friends, with my horses. I laughed, cried, rejoiced and regretted. Many times horses were the heart of the emotion. Their stories were my story, *A Life With Horses,* a book.

Three reasons motivated this work. First, there was my desire to write, a desire quieted for too long. Then there was my need to recognize the horses that had influenced my life. Lastly, and maybe most importantly, there was the hope that my story might carry a bigger one about the dignity, grace, patience, courage and humility learned in the company of horses.

Multiple factors determine who we are and who we become. Being born is not enough. Environment, our parents' character and philosophy, fate, and sheer luck all create trails on the road map of our life. I was lucky. I was born to parents with the vision and the wisdom to let me *be me*. They protected without stifling. They taught me to believe in choices, to believe in myself. They allowed me to experience all that life has to offer. For me, that life included horses.

And so this is not only a book about horses but also a book about *living* with horses. It is about gifts received and lessons learned from the horses in my life. There are many.

Though *A Life With Horses* is in no way intended to be a horse training book, my training philosophy and methods have crept into the stories. So has a deeper truth—I have come to believe it is not I who teaches them but they who teach me.

All the stories in *A Life With Horses* are true as I remember them, though my memories may not be another's of the same event. Although happy times far outnumbered sad ones, I shed tears many times as my fingers tapped out my memories. In fact, as I read and re-read the serious passages, I cried every time. I know my readers will empathize. They will laugh and cry at the same places I do. How do I know? Because readers of *A Life With Horses* will have picked it up because they already feel that connection to horses or they want to.

Part 1

Growing Up with Horses

*Dreams are illustrations about the book your soul
is writing about you. ~ Marsha Norman*

The Dream

Cherish your visions and your dreams as they are the children of your soul, the blue prints of your ultimate accomplishments.
~ Napolean Hill

The gelding is impatient. He nudges his young rider with his nose as she opens the gate, dances through, swings around, and bumps her again. The girl brushes him away with one hand as she closes the gate with the other, and then wraps her arms around his neck, slips the reins over and bounces into the saddle. Already he is turning, already walking. Ears pricked forward, eyes bright, head bobbing in time to the soft rhythm of his unshod feet, his step quickens. The girl reaches forward to stroke the silky black neck.

"You know where we're going, don't you?"

As if to answer, the horse breaks into a jog. Gently, she pulls him back.

"Easy. I am not in a hurry today."

The scenery is familiar. She and her brother ride here often. Sometimes they play horseback games; sometimes they follow the old logging road far into the backcountry to round up cattle on the open range[1] with their parents. Today the girl rides alone.

The pair has reached a trail leading into the bush, a trail they both know well. The black turns and they disappear into spruce and pine. A few minutes later, they emerge into a tiny meadow edged by a shallow creek. Giant weeping willows dip green-yellow leaves in the water and shade the secluded patch of grass. Most days the girl crosses the creek to ride under the apple trees in the old orchard but not today. Today she stops beside the water. Shaking her feet free of the stirrups, she wiggles onto her stomach to lie across the saddle, legs dangling. She hangs suspended for a moment, and then slowly slides down the slick leather until her toes touch the ground. Her horse is already stealing mouthfuls of rich meadow grass.

Carefully, she folds the reins into one hand and sinks into the cool carpet beside the black gelding's head. She stretches flat on her back and looks up. Through waving willow branches, the sun blinks back at her. She closes her eyes. The contented munching of her horse and the soft gurgling of the creek could lull her to sleep, but she is thinking, planning, dreaming. . .

Horses are in all of her dreams. She visualizes a fine band— bays, sorrels, chestnuts with flaxen manes, greys, palominos and blacks like the horse she rides now. She imagines every detail of every one. She will live with them, care for them, and train them. It's not the first time she has dreamed this dream.

After a time, the girl opens her eyes. In the reality of midday light, she knows it is a romantic and foolish idea. Her parents are practical people and, though they would never laugh, they would not think "horse trainer" is life work she should be aspiring to. She shakes off her fanciful plans.

I won't tell anyone, she thinks. *It's just a silly dream.*

But she remembers, and many years later, when she is living the life she wished for so long ago, she asks her friends, "How many people can say they are living the dream they dreamed when they were a child?" and tells the story of the girl lying in the grass beside her black gelding planning a life with horses.

*****

---

[1] Open range is unfenced grazing for cattle—expansive, mostly unimproved land of which a significant proportion of the natural vegetation is native grasses.

1. A girl and a black gelding in 1956.

I am the dreamy-eyed girl, of course, eleven or twelve and horse crazy. Though that day is long ago and I certainly did not understand the significance, it is just as real to me today as it was then—the wishing, the fantasizing, the planning . . . and trying to let go. For a while, I didn't have to. I was born into a life with horses. Mom and

Dad used horses every day on the Diamond Dot Ranch. They were tools of the trade and more. They were a life *style*.

The Diamond Dot (now owned by my brother) lays within the Coteau Hills of Saskatchewan, a broad band of grassland extending from south of Saskatoon into the United States. Acres and acres of ranchland insulate the ranch from the flat farmland beyond the rolling hills. Kyle is twenty-four miles west; Beechy is twenty-five miles east.

The ranch buildings are nestled in a wide valley partially encircled by buttes. Trees and caragana hedges surround the house and barn and extend west into the field, offering protection against wind. East of the house, behind a line of towering poplars, a dugout[2] catches spring runoff[3] for the livestock. A 175-acre alkali lake stretches to the south.

Roads through the Coteau Hills were primitive. Motorized travel to the ranch followed roughly bladed fireguards[4] across the rolling prairie through multiple gates and descended into the valley via a rutted coulee trail. When snow filled the coulee and erased the trail, the only way in or out was on horseback. In the winter, riders followed high ridges above the coulee and dropped into the valley over the face of the butte. Wind always blew on the buttes, not the place to be in a blizzard. Mom often told a story of wind so wild on the butte that it almost swept her horse off his feet!

This is where I grew up—in the little ranch house with coal oil lamps, a wood stove, a cellar under the kitchen, and an outhouse.

The Diamond Dot was first known as the Giauque (pronounced "Jake-way") Ranch or the Half Diamond F. In 1917, Mom's parents acquired Coteau Hills lease land that included a quarter section originally homesteaded by Grandpa's brother. Hoy's land had reverted to the government after he lost his life in World War I. Grandpa and Grandma Giauque purchased an adjoining deeded parcel that would be the home quarter of the Giauque Ranch and, in this valley, they settled with their family.

Grandpa bred and raised horses by the hundreds. A superb horseman, he could sit almost any horse in the most difficult of

---

[2] A dugout is an excavation "dug out" in a location to fill with water when the snow melts in the spring.

[3] Runoff is snow that melts and "runs off" the ground, usually into sloughs, lakes or dugouts.

[4] Fireguards are wide trails bladed through the hills by graders to aid in controlling a prairie fire should one occur.

situations, but he saw no shame in being bucked off either.

"The man that says he's never been throwed is the man who never rode," he said.

2. Grandpa riding a bronc.   **3. Grandma, Grandpa, Dad, Mom.**

The following excerpt from an article my mother wrote for the Jonesville Homemakers Club Compilation of History provides insight into Grandpa's cowboy skills and personality:

This chapter might well begin one day in early May in the year 1902 with the appearance of three horsemen on Snake Bite Butte. Their horses were beginning to feel the effects of a long, hard trail, but the men being young, hardy and born in the saddle, were still alert and ready. These three were Andrew Grottier, Jerry La Roche and Leslie Giauque. From their vantage point on the butte, they spotted a band of wild horses grazing on the flat stretch of country, which lay between them and the spot where Beechy now stands. Some excitement and a fresh horse apiece! Quietly, the three slid down the butte and began to fan out, circling the little band. With ropes down and ready, the riders circled closer until the horses broke and ran. Then each rider chose a horse and ran him down. Andrew's rope made the first catch. Les front footed and hog-tied him, then after the fleeing horses, which Jerry still pursued. This time Les' rope tightened around the neck of a little black stallion. He was likewise hog-tied then away again for a mount for Jerry. Then one by one, three wild horses were to be saddled, blindfolded, mounted and ridden to a sweating standstill. Such an incident was only to quicken the blood of cowboys and break the dull monotony of those far-off days when men were men and horses were more than gold".

In the next generation, horses were still "more than gold". My parents, Slim and Florence Gates, depended on horses for their livelihood and often for their life.

My mother grew up in the Coteau Hills. Small and wiry like her father, quick of step and mind like her mother, Mom's riding skills surfaced early in life. Grandpa was pleased. She would have spent all her time on a horse if Grandma had not stepped in with cooking lessons and if Mom herself had not wanted more. A horsewoman, a housewife and school teacher, she could give an English lesson from the back of a horse riding across the prairie and include good old fashioned horse sense in the classroom with equal ease.

4. Mom with Charm and Pride.   **5. Dad with Tex.**

My father grew up on a farm in the Weyburn area of Saskatchewan. Though not born to ranch life, some aspects drew him to the lifestyle. Ropes fascinated him and eventually led to rodeo, where he competed in calf roping and performed as a trick roper. His lean and lanky frame earned him the name "Slim". Few knew his given name was Harold.

Dad and Mom met with a little help from their horses. In 1937, Mom and her brother drove bucking stock to the Rosetown Rodeo, fifty miles from the ranch. Mom rode her favourite mare, Nancy. Apparently, Dad had brought the only trained horse to the rodeo. All the calf ropers and bulldoggers wanted to ride Tex, but there were too many. Besides, bulldogging required two horses—one for the dogger and one for the hazer. The cowboys spotted Nancy and, because Mom wanted to help, she agreed to lend Nancy out for as many runs as she thought the mare could handle. So, Tex and Nancy paired up in the bulldogging event and Dad and Mom paired up for life. A year later, they married. A year after their marriage, they bought the Giauque Ranch and named it the Diamond Dot.

6. Dad calf roping (now called tie down roping) at Calgary Stampede in 1929. He placed second.

7. Dad performing a horse catch. Mom on Pride. In Dad's handwriting on the back of this photo are these words: "An overhead catch made after jumping through a Backward Ocean Wave."

Horses were a necessary part of Mom and Dad's life. They almost lived with them. Horses cut, raked and hauled in the hay. Horses gathered the cattle and brought feed to them in the winter. Horses pulled the sleigh and pulled the stone boat.[5] Horses carried the mail and carried the children. The welfare of Mom and Dad's horses took precedence over their own. I suspect they cared for them better than they cared for themselves. They loved their horses. They rejoiced when they excelled. They cried when they hurt.

It was from this stock I was born . . . with very big shoes to fill if I was to be the horseperson my ancestors were. As I matured, I realized I did not have to try to fill their shoes. I needed only to listen to my heart. Horses were in my blood and bones all right, but horses were also in my soul.

8. Mom performing some trick roping of her own.

9. Dad on Pride in front of the Diamond Dot ranch house.

---

[5] A stone boat is a flat sled on skids turned up in front so it will slide and used for moving stones, firewood, manure, etc.

The Grey Team, Pronto and Trixie

And God took a handful of southerly wind, blew His breath over it, and created the horse. ~ Bedouin Legend

My first memory of horses at all is of a team of grey mares, a wonderful, loyal pair of heavy horses that were part of our family. Dad harnessed The Grey Team almost every day. Big and strong, one quite grey, the other almost white, they stood side by side in a double tie stall in the small dugout barn at night and when they were not in use. Sometimes, while Mom was milking the cow, my brother and I played in the manger in front of them. We giggled and hid under the hay and they paid no attention to us. I can still feel the soft, pink nose of the whiter of the two as she nuzzled around us. I recall she was a bit shyer so I liked her better and spent more time with her.

As far as I know, the mares never had names. I recall pestering Mom until she named them, but I suspect she just tired of me asking, because neither she nor Dad ever called them anything but "The

Grey Team", and now I have forgotten the names she told me.

I have fuzzy memories of The Grey Team hitched to huge racks of hay in summer or to a sleigh bound for a Christmas concert but according to my parents, they came into my life much earlier than I can remember. In fact, they contributed to my survival. The Grey Team brought my mother and me home from the hospital when I was two weeks old, a twelve-mile sleigh ride through uninhabited rolling hills in a Saskatchewan winter. Mom and I snuggled under cowhides in the box of the sleigh while Dad guided the dependable pair over hill after hill of endless white. Two years later, again in winter, The Grey Team sleighed the desolate distance twice more, first to take my pregnant mother and me to the settlement, then to return for us when my brother, Harold, was two weeks old. On the return trip, a few miles from the little ranch house in the valley, a sudden fierce blizzard blew in, stinging Dad and the team with pellets of snow and wiping out the trail. Blinded, Dad fought to keep his bearings, but he was driving his family into a swirling white wall. Finally, he lifted the cowhide covering Mom and his babies.

"We're off the trail," he said. "I don't know where we are." I can only imagine how he must have felt.

Dad had done all he could do. The rest was up to the faithful, reliable mares pulling the sleigh. He loosened the lines to the mouths of The Grey Team.

"Giddap," he said. "Take us home," and that is exactly what they did. With only their sense of "home" to guide them, bowing their heads to driving snow, skirting deep draws and snow drifts that would have crippled the sleigh, they brought their precious cargo— Mom, Dad, Harold and me—home.

The Grey Team worked tirelessly on any task Dad asked them to perform. They cut and raked hay, hauled it home and to the cattle, pulled the stone boat loaded with manure and pulled the sleigh in the winter. I took much of this for granted, having grown up with it, but one task always seemed special to me, maybe because I did not see this one every day. In the spring, when the runoff water was fresh and soft, my mother liked to use it for washing clothes. Dad hooked the team to the stone boat, lifted a wooden barrel on it, and headed over the hill to the nearest slough.[6] He pailed the barrel full and placed a flat piece of wood on top of the water to keep it from

---

[6] A slough is a small lake formed by the runoff water in the spring.

slopping. If I close my eyes, I can still see The Grey Team, Dad on the lines, carefully sliding that stone boat and barrel over rough, uneven ground to the house with Mom's wash water.

The Grey Team has earned a place in my heart.

10. Dad and I behind The Grey Team in winter of 1945.

11. Sharon, teamstress?

For the first few years of marriage, both Mom and Dad spent several hours of every day on horseback. Mom taught school, riding both ways every day to teach eight grades in one room at one of the country schools, and Dad worked for a Community Pasture.

Patrons brought their cattle to "community" pastures and a manager cared for them during the grazing season. In the fall, riders delivered the cattle back to the patrons by herding them from one farm to another and cutting out[7] each farmer's cattle. It was not an easy job and, though I don't know how many cowboys rode on the drive, I can guess the number was inadequate. For sure, every rider needed to ride a good horse and to know what he or she was doing.

Mom helped with the annual drive, which necessitated an adjustment after I was born—she bundled me up and took me with her on her horse. All day, Mom and Dad took turns carrying me as they moved the herd from one farm to the next, stopped and cut out the cattle belonging to that farm. Dad would have been riding Tex, his favourite rope horse. Mom probably rode Pride. How trustworthy these horses must have been! Riding with a baby was risky enough. Add cattle and the work involved moving them around and the risk was considerably greater. There was no choice. There was a job to do so the baby came along. Later, with two babies, Mom could not ride unless someone babysat, but it wasn't long until Harold and I were old enough to ride too. My life with horses had begun.

12. Dad and I on Tex in 1944.

13. Me on Pronto, Mom and Harold on Pride.

The first horse I rode by myself was Pronto, a nondescript brown mare with a kind disposition. She was a horse, not a pony, and I cannot say how tall she was. Since there were no ponies on the ranch

---

[7] Cutting out cattle is separating specific animals from the rest of the herd.

at that time nor had I ever seen one, I thought nothing of riding a full-sized horse. Mom hoisted me up on Pronto when I was five and thereafter I wanted to ride everywhere. I have vague memories of riding around the yard (with supervision, I'm sure) but the clearest memory of riding Pronto is my first "header" off of her!

My parents' herd of horses ran in a pasture north of the house and yard. It must have been a dry summer, because the water dried up in their field so, in the morning, when they gathered in the corner, Mom saddled up and brought them to the dugout by the house to drink. When she opened the gate, they ran flat out to the dugout, splashing themselves in joyful abandon as they lunged belly deep into the water. After they drank their fill, Mom herded them back to pasture.

Every day I watched Mom do this and every day I begged to go. Though reluctant to take me along, she eventually gave in.

"I thought I could keep control riding at Sharon's side," she would say later.

14. Harold and I on Pride, winter 1950.

Oh, the excitement at the prospect of "chasing" the horses to water! I was old enough to ride with Mom on an important job!

The adventure began well. Mom and I leisurely jogged to the gate, no doubt with me chattering a mile a minute. She told me where to stand on Pronto, got off Rocky (more about him later), opened the gate and stepped back. As she mounted and stood beside me, the horses boiled through the gate and ran. We started to walk our horses behind the herd, but, as all horses will, Pronto and Rocky wanted to run too. As the herd gathered speed, Pronto pulled on my five-year-old arms and I could not restrain her. We were running up on the pounding herd and headed straight for the dugout.

I don't remember being scared, probably because I didn't recognize the danger, but my mother knew she had to stop the runaway. Since she was riding a faster horse, she easily caught up with Pronto but when she reached across and grabbed the reins, the mare stopped so abruptly she launched me into the buck brush.[8] I emerged unhurt, dirty, with bits of brush in my hair, a headache and new sense of pride. I could say I had been "bucked off".

A couple of years later, there *was* a pony on the ranch, an adorable paint Shetland mare. I have no idea where she came from, but Mom and Dad bought her for Harold to ride. She was quite a novelty for both of us.

Harold loved Trixie as much as I loved Pronto and together we wiled away many hours. Often we rode bareback, sometimes with a saddle. I have no recollection of how we got the horses ready. Mom must have saddled and bridled for us at first, but I imagine it was not long before we were doing the job ourselves, however badly. We took it for granted our horses would not ever hurt us and indeed, they did not. My parents entrusted their children to the care of dependable babysitters!

As all children do, we liked to play games. Since our ranch was very isolated, we did not see other children often and depended on each other and our imaginations for entertainment. We made up games and many times these games included the horses, in this case Pronto and Trixie. One game was to ride "to the neighbour's place". We heard our parents talking about riding to the neighbour's many times. It was natural we would do the same.

The "neighbour's place" was a fence post of distinction four or five hundred yards from the house. We spent hours at that post "visiting" with the people who lived there (Mr. and Mrs. Jones?), but the return home presented somewhat of a problem if we got off and had ridden bareback. I could jump on Trixie from the fence, but I could not get on Pronto, since she was so much taller. Harold, on the

---

[8] Buck brush is an erect, loosely branched shrub 1-3 meters high.

other hand, could not climb on Trixie, since he was probably five at this time. I could boost him on or he could boost me on Pronto, but it still meant one of us was going to walk home. I tried getting on the fence and moving Pronto over, but she usually moved away. I even helped Harold up and tried to jump on behind so I could get on Pronto from Trixie (counting on the never-ending patience of our horses). Imagine how well that worked! We frequently walked back to the house and we didn't like that, maybe just because we were embarrassed to be walking when we should have been riding. For the rest of my life I have not wanted to walk if there was a horse to ride.

Harold and I spent hours on the backs of Pronto and Trixie. In the spring we rode up and down a long line of caraganas behind the house, weaving in and out of the bushes, inhaling the heady fragrance, plucking the sweet yellow blossoms and popping them open between our fingers to suck out the honey nectar. In the summer, we amused ourselves with our horseback games or, if we were lucky, checking cattle with Mom or Dad. When threshing[9] crews came in the fall, we wandered around the fields on Pronto and Trixie, keeping our distance from the hub of activity around the threshing machine as Dad had warned us. My brother and I were too young to be any help at threshing time, but we loved watching. Dad worked with the crew; Mom spent most of her time cooking for them; we did almost nothing. On our horses, though, we had found a new pastime. Short pieces of string beckoned us from a growing pile of chaff[10] beside the threshing machine, the twine that had tied the sheaves[11] the men pitched into the machine. The tag ends provided Harold and me with hours of entertainment. Our imaginations ran wild, dreaming up projects for the ragged pieces . . . *if* we could reach them. That's where Pronto and Trixie came in handy. From their backs, we pulled out the pieces, being careful not to fall off for we could not get on again, and wove them into wonderful trinkets for our overworked parents.

Pronto and Trixie, patient partners for all of our childhood games and plans, have also earned a place in my heart.

*****

---

[9] Threshing is separation of the kernels of grain from the straw and chaff.
[10] The seed coverings and other debris separated from the kernel when the grain is threshed is called chaff.
[11] Sheaves are bundles in which grain is bound after reaping.

15. Harold and I on Trixie and Pronto in 1952.

I had only one adventure with Trixie as I rarely rode her but, on one of the first mild days of spring, she was the mount Mom chose for me.

Mom was riding to High Point post office (six miles west) for the mail. All winter, at approximately two-week intervals, she made the trip on horseback since the trail was not open to any kind of machine. Now, though the weather was nicer, a car still could not drive out of the ranch. I begged to go with Mom (I did that a lot!), and she finally agreed. This time I rode Trixie.

I welcomed the "alone time" riding with my mother through the Coteau Hills on such a beautiful day. The meadowlarks trilled their cheery spring song; furry-headed, lavender crocuses popped out of any patch of bare ground warmed by the spring sun; water from the melting snow pooled in every low spot. Snowdrifts remained in many of the draws, though, and water ran under the snow. We rode on high ground as much as possible, but once we dipped through a draw and my stirrups skimmed the water since Trixie was so short. I squealed with delight and could hardly wait to tell Dad.

The twelve-mile ride was a little too much for me. Somewhere on the return trail, Mom took me with her on her horse and turned Trixie loose to follow. Instead, she stopped to eat. Mom assured me she would find her way home, but I was worried. I must have slept then. Mom would have passed me to Dad along with the mail before leading her horse to the barn. The moment I woke up in the morning, I thought about Trixie. I ran out to Mom making breakfast in the kitchen.

"Did Trixie come home?"

"Look out the back window," Mom said. There, happily grazing behind the little ranch house, saddle and all, was Harold's black and white Shetland pony.

Worrying about my horses was to become a lifetime habit.

A Life With Horses

Rocky and Pride

No one can teach riding so well as a horse. ~ C.S. Lewis

In 1952, Mom and Dad bought the Orofino Ranch on Meyers Flat in Oliver from my grandparents and moved to British Columbia. They did not sell the Diamond Dot so operated both ranches, a less than perfect arrangement that included traveling back and forth between the two provinces.

We needed horses in B.C. and my parents moved a few, but Pronto and Trixie did not ever reside there with us. I'm not sure what happened to them. Grandma and Grandpa Giauque lived only a few miles from the Orofino and we often borrowed Nell, Grandpa's favourite mare, or her daughter, Babe.

Around this time, I realized horses did not come ready to ride. Someone had to train them to be ridden. I clearly recall my mother starting and riding Boots, gingerly urging the 1948 bay daughter of Pronto to walk around the corral and yard at the Orofino Ranch. It must have made an impression because the concept of "training" a horse intrigued me. Boots may have inspired my dream of becoming a horse trainer.

In 1953, a breeder in Montana introduced my parents to the American Quarter Horse. They often dipped down into the States on trips between B.C. and Saskatchewan (if they were not hauling livestock) and on one such drive, they met the Llewellyns and their Quarter Horses.

The strength, athletic ability, speed and cow sense of the relatively new breed impressed Dad and Mom and they purchased a two-year-old registered stallion. Dad planned to train him for a rope horse and breed mares in both B.C. and Saskatchewan. Copper Red Boy, a rich blood bay glistening with copper highlights that inspired his name, was the "bulldog" type of Quarter Horse. His heavily muscled, short-coupled body contrasted greatly with the lean-muscled Thoroughbred/cowpony cross horses of the Diamond Dot, but he rounded up cattle, cut them from the herd, roped calves—all the ranch tasks they did—with a no-nonsense, almost unflappable

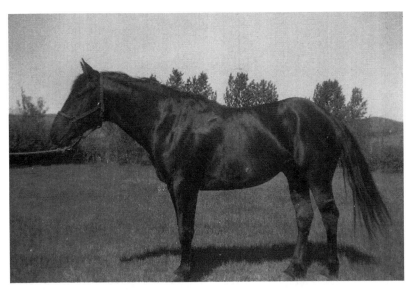

16. Copper Red Boy.

demeanor. His foals possessed powerful hindquarters, quick speed, and cow sense. For the next few years, Red commuted between provinces, usually in the back of a one-ton truck, leaving a legacy of good ranch and performance horses. Mom and Dad's forward-thinking decision to purchase Copper Red Boy introduced some of the first Quarter Horse blood into Canada and introduced me to the breed.

Harold and I schooled in B.C. and spent summer holidays in Saskatchewan. They were long holidays for we did not return to B.C. until on into September. Horses for us to ride were scarce in Saskatchewan with Pronto and Trixie gone. The stallion was very quiet and sometimes we rode him. We also borrowed an Arabian mare, Gara, from friends for a couple of summers, but it was always a challenge to provide horses for both of us. Thus, in the summer of 1953, Mom and Dad discussed bringing in Rocky, a black gelding who had become unsound[12] a few years before. His name was originally Brownie, named so because they thought he was brown, of course. When it seemed he more black than brown, the name changed to Rocky. Neither name showed much imagination.

Dad had bought Rocky when he was four or five and trained him for a calf roping horse, but a mysterious sporadic lameness terminated his rope horse career. He ran the range doing absolutely nothing. When he ran out with the herd, he showed no sign of hurting, so periodically Mom or Dad brought him in and rode him, but he always limped. Not at all hopeful, they told me if I rode him lightly, I might have a horse for the summer. Rocky was fourteen years old. I was nine.

That summer extended into many summers of a very happy partnership. At first, I could not be sure Rocky would remain sound.[13] Mom cautioned me repeatedly to be careful with him or I wouldn't have a horse to ride. One warning made a big impression or I would not remember. I ran Rocky through a draw and buck brush over rough ground and Mom read me the riot act. Thereafter, I took my cues from her as to what I could or could not do with Rocky. I did not want to lose my horse. We kept adding work to Rocky and, when he showed no signs of lameness, Mom pronounced him ready for anything. For the rest of his life he was sound but, in his twenties, white hairs appeared on his right shoulder, which led us to believe the lameness was a slow-healing shoulder injury.

Rocky moved to B.C. in 1953 or 1954 with Pride, daughter of Pronto. Pride was a favourite horse of my mother's, born the year she and Dad married. She was a year older than Rocky and even blacker than he was. These two striking black horses became horses for Harold and me. They would not have been most people's idea of kids' horses.

---

[12] An unsound horse is lame.

[13] A sound horse is not lame in any way.

Rocky was full of fire, which I may have thought was wonderful, but in fact was a little hard to control. He was temperamental and couldn't stand an aggressive rider. He didn't like to walk so he did a little jiggidy-jig that would drive me crazy now but which did not bother me a bit then. Someone had cut his tongue up with a severe bit before Dad bought him and his mouth was extremely sensitive, a fact Dad and Mom reminded me of often from the first time I rode him and which may have accounted for his edgy personality. Mom also told me not everyone could ride him, which I took as a compliment. I suppose it was, but now I think I got along with him because I did not make many demands. For whatever reason, Rocky and I matched. How I loved that horse, his spirit, his never-quit attitude, his speed and heart!

17. Rocky and Pride on the Orofino Ranch.   **18. Rocky and I on the Orofino 1950's.**

Harold rode Pride, also high energy. For her entire life, she had pulled on the bit until she was hard-mouthed.[14] If she ran away, Harold would not have any hope of stopping her, another fact drilled into us, especially me since I was the older, "responsible" child. Fortunately, she was very quiet and the only time running away was an issue if we let her run, which we were not supposed to do.

But we were kids who knew we had fast horses. We devised a plan whereby we could gallop the horses and still get them stopped. Meyers Flat at that time was just that, an open flat. A creek across

---

[14] A hard-mouthed horse is insensitive to pressure from a bit.

the middle was great for jumping, but other than the creek, the flat was wide open. We experimented a little and discovered Pride would slow down if no horse ran beside her, so with plenty of field in front of us, we let them go. Then it was my responsibility to pull Rocky up in time for Harold to stop Pride. It always worked.

Mom never knew about our little races on the flat, but she found out about one piece of foolishness on a ride with my cousin Gloria. We were riding along a side road of Meyers Flat, a semi-open area edged with pine trees. Mom had warned both Gloria and me not to let the horses get out of control, knowing how much Pride and Rocky liked to run, but we let it happen. This time we had to admit poor judgment. The ride did not end well. We let the horses go and Pride, with Harold perched bareback on her broad back, swerved under the pines. The low, craggy branches swiped him off, cutting his face and ear. We took him home with blood all over him. We not only worried about Harold, who at least was talking and didn't seem to have any broken bones, we were more than a little scared of the trouble we would be in with Mom. Gloria would have liked to detour to Grandma's but faced her aunt and the tongue-lashing. Mom spared me because, as she saw it, Gloria, three years older than I, was now the older, responsible child. Harold must have been eight or nine.

Pride and Rocky were our mounts in B.C. from 1954 to 1957 just as Pronto and Trixie had been in Saskatchewan. When we were not riding them, they grazed in a pasture below our house on the side of the mountain. Harold and I could catch them any time we wanted,

19. Rocky in the pasture below the house in B.C.

20. Rocky and I, Harold and Pride beside the house on the Orofino Ranch in 1956.

jump on bareback (by now we could do that with a little help from the fences, stumps or whatever) and ride back to the house or ride around the pasture. Again, we invented games to play on the horses and if we fell off, they waited for us to pick ourselves up and find a way to get on again. We jumped them over creeks, ran them across Meyers Flat, or just hung out with them. Once, only once, we decided four-foot high clover would be a soft place to land if we bailed off the horses into it. Harold knocked the wind out of himself, so we never did it again. We had seen a few movies by that time. I suspect that is where this foolish idea came from.

Rocky and Pride did not belong to Harold and me. Rocky was Dad's; Pride was Mom's. It was time for us to have horses we could call our own. Since Dad and Mom already had a stallion and mares, they promised they would raise one for each of us.

Harold's foal arrived first. In 1953, Grandpa's mare, Nell, presented Harold with a bay filly sired by Copper Red Boy. He named her Neenah. Through unforeseen circumstances, probably mares not getting in foal, my horse arrived three years later in Saskatchewan. I was staying with my grandparents and going to school in B.C. at the time of the foal's birth. Mom and Dad were at the Diamond Dot for spring calving. My foal was the first for a Thoroughbred-Standardbred grulla[15] mare called Cherry and, of course, sired by Copper Red Boy. When I finally got word of the arrival, it was through a letter from Mom. Cherry had foaled, she said, but she could not tell me any more. She had foaled in the hills, as was the practice then, and when Cherry saw Mom riding up to the herd, she flew over the prairie with a little dot glued to her side.

"I think it's brown," she wrote. "I don't know if it's a filly or a colt, but boy can it run! I think you should call it Cheetah."

The foal was a little brown filly named for the fastest animal in the world. I was twelve and for the first time in my life, I owned a horse.

In 1957, my parents sold the Orofino Ranch and moved back to the Diamond Dot. By this time, they owned a single axle, open-topped horse trailer, a wooden box with a tarp stretched on a metal frame over the manger in the front. Into this, we loaded Pride and Rocky, waved goodbye to the Orofino, and left B.C.

I do not remember the trip. I know we probably camped at least two nights on the road with Pride and Rocky tied either to the trailer or to trees. We may have slept in the horse trailer. What I do remember is the final few miles.

Night had fallen long before we turned off the highway onto the road to the Diamond Dot, and a wild electric storm raged. Jagged bolts of forked lightning punctuated by ear-splitting cracks of thunder, briefly lit up an otherwise black sky. Curtains of rain, more than the windshield wipers could handle, crashed to earth and pooled in the ditches, the fields and on the road. Six miles of dirt and

---

[15] Grulla is a colour of horses in the dun family, characterized by smoky or mouse-coloured hair.

another six of prairie trail lay ahead. Dad knew the road, not graveled, would be slick, greasy mud. It could send the outfit in the ditch, especially with the horse trailer. He couldn't risk injury to the horses.

"We'll have to unload," he said. "You kids ride."

The driving summer rain instantly soaked Harold and me to the skin, but Dad boosted us up on the horses' backs and told us to ride across the ditch into the field to the right of the road and stay parallel to the truck. Clinging to the slippery wet backs, we mucked onto a farmer's summerfallowed field into flat black darkness broken only by blinding flashes and the vehicle lights on the road to the left.

The lightning was uncomfortably close, each strike almost immediately followed by deafening thunder, but Pride and Rocky plodded calmly through the fury of the storm. Eager, even energetic, they showed no fear. I had a sense of these fine horses taking care of us. Maybe they welcomed the chance to be out of the trailer. They, like The Grey Team, no doubt knew the Diamond Dot was near. In any case, they were happy and confident slogging through the mud until Rocky stopped and would not move forward. Not a step.

"Rocky won't go," I yelled to Mom and Dad. They could not hear me over the din of the storm.

The next flash of lightning revealed the reason, a coil of barbed wire wrapped around Rocky's front feet. We had walked into an old fence. My horse was smarter than I was. He would not budge.

When Mom and Dad saw we were not moving, they stopped and sloshed through the ditch with a flashlight. Rocky stood, feet ensnared in wire, water pouring off him, while Dad carefully extricated his legs. Only then did he cautiously step ahead. I had grown up hearing and seeing the damage barbed wire can cause, so was thankful he had not been hurt and more than a little impressed with his intelligence. Harold and I crossed over to the muddy road and the remainder of the ride, though wet and miserable, was safe.

A friend from B.C. joined my family at the Diamond Dot that summer. I was thirteen, Kathy twelve. We did everything together, many times with Harold too, who good naturedly put up with two giggling girls. Mom and Dad gave Kathy a horse for the summer— Goldie—and she learned to ride on the pretty, sorrel, part-Arabian mare. She did everything Harold and I did and, looking back, we should not have expected her to. We involved horses in many of our escapades and took chances we should not have (with ourselves, not the horses) and Kathy, though not as accustomed to riding as we were, always took part.

A favourite activity was loping the horses around a narrow lane between a fence and the poplar trees that circled our house. It was almost, but not quite, a race. I'm sure that was the attraction. On this day, when Mom and Dad were away, we all hopped on the horses bareback. Harold and I had made our usual tour around the trees. Kathy, of course, prepared to follow suit. Did I say Goldie had a mind of her own? We all knew Goldie. When she set her mind against doing something, it could be a fight. Goldie had made a decision. She was not going to play.

Enter Sharon, the horse trainer. I cut a switch, jumped on and proceeded to show the mare who was boss. Yes, I got her moving a lot faster than Kathy did. She was practically *running* when she set the brakes and somersaulted me over her head onto sun-baked ground. As I slowly pushed myself to my feet, I knew my back had taken the brunt of the fall. End training session that day. End *riding* that day.

I knew how stupid I had been. *My back will be better in the morning. I won't have to tell Mom and Dad.*

By evening, my back was worse. When I tried to rise out of a chair and could not, I admitted what I had done. The lecture was not what I expected. I suspect they were a little proud of me for trying to school the recalcitrant mare. I minimized the pain, however, and never went to a doctor. My back still reminds me of my training session with Goldie.

Harold and I played another far more risky game on the horses, *always* when Mom and Dad were not home—riding our horses without saddle, bridle or even a string around their neck, allowing them to run around a pen at free will. It was our version of the now-popular "bridleless performance" except we were saddleless too and were not performing for anyone but ourselves. We were testing the limits.

We turned the horses loose in an area around the cattle sheds south of the barn. It was not a small turnout pen but a large, oddly shaped paddock, an uneven piece of ground with a low, boggy draw running through it and a knobby little knoll above the draw. The pen was not in view of the house. This was where Harold and I staged our "freedom rides" (my term).

We first played this game with Pride and Rocky. Clutching

handfuls of mane, legs glued to black hides, we trotted and loped (don't think we walked much!) zigzag patterns around the pen. Loping was the best. I will never forget what those rides felt like. "Freedom" does not completely describe the oneness of horse and rider, the fluid motion, the *freeness* . . . all heightened by a little healthy fear.

When we wanted to end the ride, we slid very carefully down our horse's side as if to get off. The method accomplished what we wanted—to slow down or stop—because Pride and Rocky were trained rope horses. They stopped when the roper dismounted after he roped a calf. Rope horses stop hard, however, so we inched our way down until they slowed, and it worked every time. I would not have been able to stop Rocky without the rope horse training, but I had to be cautious. He stopped exactly as he did everything else— suddenly!

Harold and I may have included Kathy in everything up to this point, but we were not totally stupid. We knew Kathy should not try this stunt . . ., which made her want to take part even more.

By this time, Harold had retired Pride and used Neenah, but I still rode Rocky. As always, I toured the paddock, loping around the perimeter while Kathy watched from the fence. She asked again if she could ride Rocky like that.

Harold and I could be talked into almost anything. I gave very specific directions on how to get Rocky stopped, and then gave her a leg up[16] and off she went.

Kathy was not scared but I may have been. After a very short ride, I directed her to slide down his side as I had shown her. It was time to stop the ride. She complied but she moved quickly. So did Rocky. He screeched to a halt and sent her over his shoulder as Goldie had thrown me. I was not laughing. I was worried. Bruised, but not seriously injured, Kathy picked herself up. She was all right. No one had to know about the freedom rides . . . yet!

Kathy, Harold and I rode together all summer on Goldie, Rocky and Neenah. In the fall, Kathy went back to B.C. for school and I joined her to take my grade eight in Oliver, which meant leaving my family and my horses. It was a family decision. This period of nine

---

[16] "Leg up" is a method of mounting a horse where the rider uses a hand of someone on the ground for leverage to propel himself up on the horse. (Can also mean to condition a horse.)

months was one of only two times in my life when I did not live with horses. I could still ride Grandpa's mare, but mostly I concentrated on classes and my music (violin, orchestra and choir). When school let out in June 1958, I moved back to Saskatchewan and reunited with Rocky. My Cheetah was now two and I rode Rocky while I waited for her to grow up.

*****

21. Rocky and Pride (pair standing fourth and fifth from the right) in their retirement years with the herd in Saskatchewan.

A Life With Horses

High School and Horses

Horses change lives. They give our young people confidence and self-esteem. ~ Toni Robinson

In B.C., Harold and I walked down the mountain from our house and a taxi (Yes, a taxi!) picked us up to take us to school. Attending school in Saskatchewan was a little more complicated. Six miles of prairie trail still separated the ranch from the settlement and the school bus stop. Even though my parents had built a new house on the ranch, we still did not have electricity or phone and still used the outhouse. The Diamond Dot ranch was as isolated as it was when I was born.

I was fourteen years old, Harold two years younger. Harold had started school in Sanctuary the year I finished grade eight in B.C. and, after one more year there, would transfer to Kyle in grade nine. I, in grade nine now, would immediately school in Kyle. Somehow, we both had to meet the school bus.

Harold had already learned to drive. Now I needed to learn and I did. For our remaining school years, we drove ourselves, on the rutted, rocky trail through the hills, to the settlement to catch the school bus. When winter closed the trail and we could no longer drive, we rode the distance, boarding with families at the edge of the hills on weekdays. We left the ranch as late as possible Sunday or very early Monday morning and rode home Friday night for the weekend. If the weather was not good, we waited until Saturday morning. Horses were now more than fun and games. They were survival.

For all of his school years in Saskatchewan Harold used Neenah on the winter trail. I rode Rocky the first year, and then Cheetah. Red was always in the barn for Mom or Dad to ride if they needed a horse. The horses were all equal to the harsh, demanding conditions of winter riding. We never knew how tough the trips would be. Some were quite pleasant; others were torture. Even dressed as warm as we could—parkas, ski pants, hand knit mitts under cowhide ones, hand knit wool socks and scarves over our faces to protect us from the constant wind—we froze much of the time. If the trail was open, we rode at a steady pace; if the trail had drifted over, as it often did, travel was much slower. The wind-packed drifts rarely carried the horse's weight. They plopped a front foot on a drift, heaved the other up, only to have the first one break through . . . and so on. We took turns breaking trail when traveling was tough.

One stretch we rode on ice. Less snow on two lakes we crossed made travel easier for the horses and therefore faster. We picked our way a little, looking for ice with snow stuck on it for traction. I did not like riding (or driving) on ice, but it was easier than wallowing through snow in ravines.

On bitterly cold days, we got off and led our horses to warm our feet, slapping our bulky leather mitts together to increase circulation in our hands at the same time. We learned (and were told!) to get off and warm up before frostbite set in or our core body temperature had dropped. If we faced a wind, or even a breeze, we bowed our heads to protect our faces. Eyes sometimes rimmed with so much ice our vision blurred squinted at the unforgiving landscape from between two wool scarves, one over mouth and nose, another over forehead. When the scarf iced over from our breath, it worked even better.

The horses were as frosty as we were. Tiny icicles hung from their manes, tails, eyelashes and nose. Great clouds of steam rose from their bodies as they slogged on—tough, strong, steady and willing. A long trot was the gait of choice. Loping exhausted the horses and could have damaged lungs; if they walked, we chilled quickly. The horses were a bit more eager returning to the Diamond

Dot, but they knew their "other home" too, and the feed and warm barn waiting for them there. My hands got even colder looking after my horse before going to the house, but I loved knowing she was comfortable. My parents taught me at an early age to care for my horse before thinking of myself.

If Harold and I rode out alone, Mom had no way of knowing we were safe since there was not a phone to the ranch, so sometimes she rode with us, probably for her peace of mind. Then she rode home alone. I kept a diary in 1959. Here are a few entries from that winter:

Sunday, February 15, 1959 *Dear Diary: It's storming today so I guess we won't get out to Anderson's.*
Tuesday, February 24, 1959 *Dear Diary: I had to go back with Daddy tonight to help him carry back some stuff.*
Wednesday, February 25, 1959 *Dear Diary: I rode Rocky out bareback at 7:00 AM this morning. Sure was nice.*
Sunday, March 1, 1959 *Dear Diary: Harold and I rode the north pasture to find the horses so we could all ride out tonight.*

From the matter-of-fact tone of these skimpy entries, I can only believe the circumstances of my education did not seem unusual. Yet, I was the only student in my class to use horses to attend school.

This was the norm for my four remaining years of school. Harold and I drove to the bus in fall and again in spring; in the winter we rode the trail and boarded for school days. Sometimes, before the road completely closed, Dad would try to drive us, but that usually meant a lot of shoveling. It got even more complicated when I started to date. I had to plan my dates carefully and my parents had to know what the plan was. I played basketball too. Sometimes, after a game, dance or other social event, I rode home in the middle of the night, but often I stayed until Saturday morning. A great deal depended on good sense, knowledge of the trail and respect for prairie winters.

In Saskatchewan, Harold and I discovered new games with our horses—horseshows. We had watched a few in B.C. because friends of the family were involved in a local horse club, but Harold and I never took part. I think this was how the interest spread to the prairies though. While I was in B.C. finishing grade eight, Mom and Harold competed in shows on Rocky and Neenah with winning results. When I moved back to Saskatchewan, Mom handed over

Rocky's reins. At first, I competed only in local fairs, then rodeos and the Saskatchewan Cutting Horse Association. The SCHA shows were a lot more than cutting. Barrel racing, pole bending and novelty gymkhanas appealed to me. Harold rode Neenah, truly an all around horse. She even jumped. What fun for Harold to jump Neenah bareback and win! I showed Rocky the summer of 1958 and 1959, but he was getting old.

Harold and I could not have shown our horses without our parents' support, of course. I think now of how it must have taxed their energies to work all week and then load up on Sunday for a horseshow. Usually we returned very late at night and sometimes, if the trail to the ranch was muddy, Harold and I rode the last six miles in the dark while Mom and Dad slipped and slid down the trail to the ranch.

Beechy Fair was a high point of the summer. We often took as many as six horses and rode to Beechy the day before. Usually Mom, Harold and I rode, leading a horse apiece. I think Rocky "jigged" the entire twenty-five miles.

22. Rocky in the Stock Horse class, Beechy, Saskatchewan 1959.

I entered Rocky in every event from Stock Horse to Best Trained Pony, but barrel racing was his best event. He won many, many ribbons and trophies, but the win I was most proud of was the barrel race at Clearwater Lake Rodeo when he was twenty years old. With the money he won, I bought a transistor radio and a plaque that reads "In memory of Rocky". Though Rocky and the radio are gone, the plaque is tucked away in my jewelry box.

23. Rocky and I with trophies and ribbons (1960).

24. My last ride on Rocky (center), a girlfriend on Pride (right), Harold on a young gelding named Kiowa, one of Boots' foals (Summer 1962).

Any horse training I did in my childhood, good or bad, was purely unintentional. I assumed my horse would do what I asked him to and he did . . . because Mom and Dad had trained him that way!

For the most part, my parents trained horses on the job. They did not start riding the youngsters until they were at least three years old (Grandpa brought colts in to ride when they were four or five!) and until that time, they ran the hills. When the work *did* start, it was constant and demanding. They did not spend a bunch of time in a round pen or corral. "He'll be broke when I get back." is a phrase I heard a lot.

By the time Mom and Dad had put a horse through "the program" at the Diamond Dot, he was an all around ranch horse. The horse went *where* his rider wanted *when* he wanted at the *speed* he wanted. He could work cattle or rope a cow. He could carry a calf draped over his neck in front of his rider or a deer carcass strapped *to* the saddle. He would lead off another horse or pull a young one along to teach him to lead.

Inevitably, the time came when my parents expected Harold and me to help with "breaking" the new ones. I did not like this term even then and have since taken it out of my horse training vocabulary, but around our house "breaking" a horse meant training him to ride.

By the time Harold and I "started" (the term I use now for introducing a horse to riding) our own horses, someone had decided three years old might be older than necessary to begin training. The new program included bringing in the colts from the range the fall they were two-year-olds, saddling and riding them for a couple of months, and turning them out until they were three.

Although Dad rode and trained his own horses, especially rope horses, he was not as interested or committed to the task as Mom was. She loved everything about the process, and she encouraged Harold and me. She involved us in the training. We first worked with the colts in their yearling year, at which time we taught them to lead. We roped the colt or ran him into a chute to fit a halter on, tied him to a snubbing post[17] and let him fight it out until we could approach him without him flying backwards. When he stood for petting, we untied the shank and tried to lead him. A sore nose (the colt) and insightful handling (the person on the shank) encouraged the colt to

---

[17] A snubbing post is a large post, usually in the middle of a corral, used to tie a horse, especially if the horse is wild or not trained to a halter.

follow. Knowing when to quit for the day was probably the most important element of the lesson. It always amazed me how good the colt behaved the next day if we ended the session after he had taken only a step or two. Halter training yearlings who have run out all their lives was not easy on horse or cowboy, but the colts led well.

After halter training, we turned the colt out for at least a year. When the young horse came in for saddle training, he was wild again. We had to rope him to put a halter on, but after considerable thrashing around, a light bulb flickered and he remembered his experience with people as a yearling. After a refresher course in haltering and leading, he was ready to ride.

Thank goodness the day was gone when cowboys saddled and mounted the horse with someone earing[18] him down and riding to a standstill—or not. Thank goodness, also, for the corral. Grandpa mounted up in the open! It was still pretty western though. The two-year-old, big, strong and not accustomed to people, had run with the herd all of his life except for a brief time in his yearling year. He was herd bound[19] and scared.

First, the rider sacked out[20] the horse. When he could place the saddle blanket on his back and it stayed there, he carefully saddled, tightening the cinch enough to ensure the saddle would not slip during the explosion sure to follow. Then the cowboy stepped away. Usually, the colt stepped away too and felt, for the first time, the constricting cinch around his girth. Usually, he bucked, sometimes violently, until tired. Then the rider got on. Sometimes Mom or Dad saddled a trained horse to pony[21] the green horse[22] if they thought riding was too risky. There was more control this way, and, if the colt bucked, the rider on the other horse could dally up[23] and keep the bucking horse's head up. My parents believed in the method, but I was never comfortable ponying if I was the one on the colt. I wanted the horse to throw me clear if he bucked me off, not between two horses.

---

[18] To ear a horse, the cowboy holds the ear and pulls steadily. The horse does not usually fight if he is eared.

[19] A herd bound horse is not comfortable away from other horses.

[20] "Sacking out" is a process of systematically rubbing or flicking a sack or blanket on every part of a horse's body to desensitize him to objects on or around him prior to saddling the first time.

[21] To pony a horse is to lead him from another horse.

[22] A green horse is an untrained horse.

[23] To dally up is to wrap the lead shank around the saddle horn.

After the rider felt he could stay on top of the colt in some fashion, maybe even jog around the corral, he rode the "trainee" out the gate and over the hills and prairie. Regular ranch work provided the venue for further education.

This "training on the job" method is how we introduced Diamond Dot horses to saddle, bridle, rider and ranch life. Though I didn't know it, I was apprenticing for my life work.

Cheetah 5

Let us ride together, blowing mane and hair, careless of the weather,
miles ahead of care, ring of hoof and snaffle, swing of waist and hip,
trotting down the twisted road with the world let slip.
~ Anonymous, Riding Song

Harold's Neenah had turned into a wonderful little mare. Harold showed her what to do and she would try to do it. They roped calves, barrel raced, jumped a little. She excelled at every task. Cheetah, on the other hand, was a challenge.

Mom must have started Cheetah under saddle the fall she was two, as I have no recollection of me saddling and riding her first. She did not buck nor did she mind people doing things around her. I started riding her almost right away, which may have been a mistake.

At only 14.1 hands and fine-boned, the little brown mare possessed a toughness that belied her size. Short cannons, strong hocks, and good flat bone stood up to the abuse she heaped upon herself. She had inherited the powerful hindquarters of her sire, Red, and the long underline of a racehorse from her dam. Mom's assessment of Cheetah's speed was accurate. Not only *could* she run, she *loved* to run! The combination of speed and heart was exactly what I needed for my next barrel horse *if* I could control that speed. I set out to train her.

25. Cheetah at 1 year.

26. Cheetah at 2 years.

27. Cheetah at 3 years.

Though Cheetah did not buck, she unloaded me several times another way. She spooked—at anything or nothing! She threw me more times than I care to remember. She could displace herself twenty feet to the left or right faster than any horse I have ridden since. I was at first disappointed, then mad, then determined.

Next time, Cheetah will not dump me!

Harold and I still loped the circle around the house, on Neenah and Cheetah now instead of Pride and Rocky. We had done it many times, but one time, when Cheetah and I popped out of the trees, Tuffy, our little black terrier cross, ran out. Excuse enough. Cheetah's forward motion switched to a sideways sweep to the left.

*I will **not** fall off. . .*

Well, I tried. Harold said it looked like a slow motion scene in a movie as I desperately grabbed for, and missed, the saddle horn. Leather slipping through my hands, I dropped to the ground into a perfect headstand, balanced for a few seconds and toppled over. Harold laughed. Score another one for Cheetah.

Since Cheetah always ran off after she was rid of me, the day she "spooked" me off on the ice of one of the lakes we rode over to school, I held on to a rein. I was not going to walk! I skidded across the ice on my stomach until she stopped, much to Mom's enjoyment, but I still had a horse to ride.

Mom may not have been so amused when Cheetah left *her* walking on a winter ride. Through a set of circumstances I have forgotten, Cheetah was at the ranch and I was in the settlement. On a spring-warm day, Mom saddled her to bring a suitcase of clothes to me. Maybe Cheetah's winter hair itched under the saddle. Maybe the snow looked too inviting. For whatever reason, half way through the hills, Cheetah, without warning, lay down to roll—with Mom on her.

"Didn't have a hand to take the rein and slap her!" Mom said later. (She carried the suitcase in her right hand.)

Of course, Cheetah left the scene and ran all the way to the farm where I boarded. When the school bus dropped me off, everyone was running around in a frenzy. Understandably, they were worried when Cheetah ran into the yard riderless, but no one wanted to get on to ride back. Quickly, I donned winter clothes, mounted up, and headed down the back trail to the ranch. I did not have to go far. Mom was "hoofing it" (her term for walking) suitcase in hand, unhurt and laughing. I told her Cheetah had scared everyone with her wild-eyed, mad dash into the yard and everyone had waited for me to come home from school to ride back and look for her. We chuckled. Cheetah looked more dangerous than she was.

Yes, she made me work, even frustrated me, but I loved her still. She had the same courage and tenacity of Rocky and I admired her for it.

28. Cheetah and I at the Diamond Dot in 1961 (Buttes behind).

I rode Cheetah the summer of 1959 and for the rest of my high school years she took Rocky's place on the winter trail and all riding on and off the ranch. Not ever a great cow horse, I appreciated her talents best barrel racing, flat racing and any time I needed a horse tough enough to finish something I started.

*****

Remember the bridleless, saddleless rides my brother and I took on Pride and Rocky in the big paddock behind the cattle shed, how we grabbed the mane and let them run wherever they wanted? This game would lose its appeal.

Spring had arrived at the Diamond Dot, one of the first warm days after a long cold winter. Neenah and Cheetah relaxed in the sun in the cattle shed paddock; Harold and I leaned over the fence petting them. We couldn't stand it any longer. Most of the snow in the paddock had melted. A bit of the bare ground was drying up. We had to ride.

29. Harold on Neenah after he roped a calf for branding. Dad flanking.

The two high-strung blacks we depended on for our "freedom rides" had been retired. Harold had used Neenah the summer before, but Cheetah was only three and firecracker hot. We discussed the wisdom of me riding Cheetah, who would run. I did not know how I would stop her—a rope horse she was not! Score one for the kids this time. We decided using Cheetah would be madness. We would take turns on Neenah.

The paddock was quite a mess, not ideal ground for our riding event. The cattle, out to pasture now, had wintered there so remnants of hay, straw and cow pies "seasoned" the mud. Spring seepage, yellowed with manure, trickled down to the alkali lake through a boggy draw in the middle. Across the draw, the ground rose sharply to the only dry area in the pen, a low knoll beside the corral.

The tricky part was getting on, trying to hold Neenah still without a halter while one of us helped the other on. Though normally calm, she felt the spring air. I had some difficulty keeping her in one spot long enough to help Harold up. Eventually, we got organized and Harold trotted and loped her around the pen, came back to the fence and got off. My turn.

This time Neenah did not stand well at all. Harold legged me up on her, but before I could slide my leg over her back, Neenah walked away. I lay across her back on my stomach as she mucked, almost trotting, across the low spot. I looked down at the mud and manure.

I'll wait to sit up. I don't want to fall off in that.

That's the last thing I remember until I sat perched on a stool at the breakfast counter in the kitchen of our house. Groggy and hurting all over, I tried to answer Mom's questions, but Harold supplied most of the information.

According to Harold, I tried to right my position on Neenah when she strode out of the draw. At the exact moment I turned to bring my leg over her back and sit up, she kicked high in the air, as horses full of good feeling will, and sent me over her right shoulder onto mine, which connected with the hard ground on the knoll. I have no recollection of walking to the house cradling my right arm. I had blacked out.

My arm was broken, a complicated, extremely painful break close to the shoulder joint. The local doctor tried to set it but sent an x-ray to University Hospital in Saskatoon when I was still in pain. The x-ray revealed a muscle pinched in the fracture and five days after the accident I underwent surgery in Saskatoon.

I never knew the reckless abandon of riding a bridleless, saddleless Cheetah with the wind in my hair. We were busted.

I have always liked to ride alone. My horse relates to me better and, without a companion, my mind can wander wherever it wishes, allowing freedom of thought and formulation of new ideas.

One spring and summer, with my parents' approval, I rose at five o'clock almost every day for solitary rides on Cheetah. Often I rode the pastures of the Diamond Dot, but sometimes the Community Pasture, only a mile east, beckoned. One of my morning rides there saved a life.

The day was perfect. The sun, barely above the horizon, warmed my face. In the distance, antelope grazed the skyline, aware of the horse and rider but not spooked. In no particular rush, Cheetah and I walked through endless prairie wool,[24] her feet deftly avoiding gopher and badger holes.

---

[24] Prairie wool is a wild grass native to the prairies.

No cattle grazed the hills. I pondered this fact briefly, and concluded the pasture manager must have moved the herd. Then I heard a sound I knew well, the plaintive bawl of a very young calf. As I scanned the grass and brush for the origin of the cry, an all-red calf struggled to his feet in a small patch of buck brush not a hundred yards from Cheetah and me.

The calf was a newborn. His mother should be near. I looked around. Not a cow in sight.

What do I do now?

Either the cow was dead or she had stashed her calf here to return later. If riders had rounded up the field, she may never be able to come back for him. I decided I should take him home . . . on Cheetah. Could I lift him up, hold him there and get on?

Cheetah, for once, was patient as I struggled to hoist and push the little baby on my saddle, but he slipped back every time I tried to get on with him. Finally, I gave up. I would return home and ask Dad to come and get him.

As I started to leave, the calf tried to follow. I had an idea.

"Come on." I called. "Come on, little guy."

It worked. On wobbly legs, he followed Cheetah, the closest he had seen to his mother in a day or so. I coaxed him for a mile, stopping often, looking back, and calling, "Come on." At the gate to our ranch, he lay down and would not get up. He could go no further.

Quickly, I trotted home and told my story. Dad returned for the baby, brought him back in the truck and volunteered the milk cow for a surrogate mother. As soon as we could, we phoned the pasture manager, told him we had found a calf and asked if he had a cow looking for one. He had indeed rounded up the field but didn't know which cow the calf belonged to, so he gave him to me. I named him "Come-on".

I had driven cattle, rode the hills winter and summer, and rode to school, but I had never been on a trail ride. I didn't really understand the *concept* of a trail ride. Most of my family's time on a horse was necessary, with purpose and destination. Packing a horse with only the goal of riding, unpacking, and camping, was quite foreign. In fact, we did not own a pack saddle or packing equipment.

Jeanette and I had become friends through our horse interests. She attended the same school in Kyle and was a year and a grade older. She and her brother rode and showed their horses just as Harold and I did.

Jeanette's family owned a farm south of Kyle within riding distance of the South Saskatchewan River. In October of 1959, construction on Gardiner Dam had just begun. In the next few years, the low land on both sides of the river would be flooded. Cottonwood groves dotting the banks would disappear under the water of a huge reservoir, Lake Diefenbaker. The river breaks would never be the same. For this reason, Jeanette and I wanted to ride over the land that soon would be no more. We decided to make it an overnight trail ride, complete with all the items trail riders take.

The adventure was one of those ideas kids come up with that is more trouble than it's worth for parents. We would ride to the river, camp overnight, then on to the Matador[25] summer camp the next day before heading home, a simple plan with plenty of complications. Jeanette's mare, Nipper, had a foal, and he would have to go with us. We did not have a pack horse either, but Harold came to our rescue. He gave us permission to use Neenah. The mare had never packed, of course, but she had always been quiet and agreeable to anything anyone asked of her.

We made a list of provisions and mapped our trail. Jeanette knew this area better than I did, so she prepared the itinerary.

October 2, 1959 *Dear Diary: Mom hauled Cheetah and Neenah down to McCries for me. Jeanette and I are going to camp in the river breaks tomorrow. Neenah will be our pack horse.*

The Great Pack Trip began. A pack saddle would have been handy, but we improvised . . . with our parents' help. We saddled Neenah with a regular western saddle. All of our saddles had long strings front and back for tying packages on, so with help from Jeanette's father and my mother we packed sleeping bags, food, and even oats for the horses on Neenah. It was a very awkward load, but we were sure it would hold together long enough for us to get where we were headed. We slowly started down the trail from Jeanette's farm, two excited girls on horseback with a foal and an oddly packed pack horse trailing behind.

I led Neenah and she was not happy. A quarter mile from the farm, she shied at the load on her back, pulled away from me, and jumped a fence to return to where we had started, Jeanette's yard.

---

[25] The Matador is a very large community pasture southeast of Kyle, Saskatchewan.

Our camping supplies, now grotesquely askew, stayed on her back and Neenah was unscathed. Her jumping ability held her in good stead. Even with the pack, she cleared the barbed wire fence.

Take two. We repacked the load and started again. This time all went well. Neenah, true to her character, did not fight the inevitable. At a respectful distance, she willingly followed Cheetah for the duration of the ride. Nipper's palomino colt, Tango, scampered along beside us, in front of us, and around us until he tired enough to follow. When he wanted to nurse, he blocked Nipper and we stopped until he had drunk his fill. Jeanette and I, carefree and happy, were going to be on our own for a day and night. Our biggest responsibility was the horses, all four of them.

We found the perfect grove for our camp, tied the horses to trees, made a campfire and ate. If I did not have my diary, I would not remember *what* we ate.

October 3, 1959 *Dear Diary: We rode down early, made camp and had dinner (hamburgers and half-cooked potatoes) . . . had a cold supper.*

After supper, horses grazing, we talked by the fire until dark, and then fed them some of the oats. We had not brought a tent, so rolled our sleeping bags out on the ground. We didn't tie Tango, of course, and we discussed how to hide the grain from him. The perfect spot seemed to be in the bottom of my sleeping bag. With horses tucked in for the night, we snuggled down too. The weather was cool but pleasant. We had no apprehension about animals bothering us and were soon fast asleep. I slept so soundly, in fact, that, for a moment, I didn't know why I woke up. Something was yanking at the foot of my sleeping bag . . . and pulling me along the rough ground! My eyes popped open. When they adjusted to the inky dark, I spied the culprit. Tango. He had smelled the oats and tried to shake both the grain and me out of the sleeping bag!

October 4, 1959 *Dear Diary: When we woke up this morning it was raining so we went right home instead of riding to summer camp . . . sure had a ball!*

Weather cut the ride short, but we didn't care. What was important was the time we had spent together and with our horses.

Note: In 1966, my husband and I joined a group to ride the river breaks one last time before Gardiner Dam slowed the mighty South Saskatchewan River for Lake Diefenbaker. Although it was a wonderful day spent with wonderful people, the experience did not compare with the exhilaration of two teenage girls overnighting under the cottonwoods with their horses.

A girl never forgets her first date. I certainly haven't forgotten mine . . . or the part horses played in it!

My parents did not allow me to date until I turned sixteen, but in December of my fifteenth year, I met the son of a rancher and he asked me to the New Year's Eve dance in Beechy. He lived at the edge of the Coteau Hills and my parents knew his parents. I was hoping, since my sixteenth birthday was only a month away, Mom and Dad would reconsider.

The date would actually be a double date. Friends living only a mile apart on ranches had asked Jeanette and me to the dance. We wanted to go badly but were not sure our parents would agree. No doubt, the parents talked at length, but they said we could go, with one condition. Harold had to go with us.

Getting permission was not the only problem. Getting to the dance was the other one. With all roads to the ranch closed, my date would not be able to pick me up. His parents' ranch lay twice the distance in a completely different direction than the trail I rode to the school bus. Our parents had a plan.

Jeanette would come to our house (by horse, of course, one of ours), and from the ranch Jeanette, Harold and I would ride to meet our dates.

During my short lifetime, I had ridden every direction from the ranch, but never this one in midwinter. Even so, I do not recall any uneasy feelings about the ride. . . I really wanted to go to that New Year's Eve dance!

December 31, 1959 *Dear Diary: I rode out to Jean's (Anderson) for Jeanette at 9:00 this morning and at 2:00, we left for Smiths.*

I spent a few hours on my horse that day—two hours to pick up Jeanette and bring her to the ranch, another two riding to my date's ranch. Unlike me, riding the hills in winter was new to Jeanette, but she never once said she wanted to back out!

Packing for the dance must have been a challenge, but like the ride itself, I remember nothing about it. I do not remember what we wore to the dance either, but I'm sure we packed party clothes—dress, heels, nylons, and makeup. I cannot imagine how we packed it all on horses.

The three of us dressed for winter riding, our heads filled with thoughts other than horses this time. The layers went on: parkas, wool pants, heavy socks and boots, mitts and scarves. We didn't look like we were going dancing.

Bundled up and mounted, we stood outside the barn door for a photo—Jeanette, Harold and I on Cheetah, Neenah and Rocky. A glimmer of doubt crossed Mom's face. No farms or ranches lay between the Diamond Dot and our destination. No phone lines either. She would not know if we had arrived until we returned. She may have wanted to change her mind. . .

30. Jeanette on Cheetah, me on Rocky and Harold on Neenah in front of the barn at the Diamond Dot before riding across the hills to go to the New Year's Eve dance in Beechy (December 31, 1959).

My date met us at his parents' ranch and cared for the horses while we hurried to the house to warm up. Then we dressed in our packed-behind-the-saddle finery, piled into his old car or truck (Can't remember anything about the vehicle. . .), drove to Beechy and danced in the New Year, 1960!

Riding home in the middle of the night in midwinter was not an option. My parents had arranged for all of us to stay overnight at the family ranch after the dance. The next day, we switched back to parkas and mitts, climbed up on our horses, and faced the snow-covered hills once more. Head filled with the excitement of my first date, I remember nothing of the ride home either.

After I discovered Rocky could run, fast horses attracted me. Even in B.C. I wanted to race. Two young men goaded Harold and me into a race once (which Mom understood but could not condone) down a gravel road on Pride and Rocky. After that, horse racing was on my mind.

Mom liked a horse race too. She told many times of a match race[26] she had run on Red. The stallion was quiet to the point of being lazy, and she did not like lazy horses, but he won her over with this race. The owner of a long, lean Thoroughbred-type gelding challenged Red and, in spite of her misgivings about the stallion's speed, she accepted. She knew the Quarter Horse was named for speed at short distances, but she didn't think Red had a chance against the long legs of the racy-looking sorrel.

"Red is too lazy to run," she said.

Red surprised her. When Dad yelled, "go", he left the starting line like a bullet and won the race. Thereafter, Mom could not say enough about the quick speed of the Quarter Horse, although she didn't change her mind about Red's laziness.

Obviously, I did not fall far from the family tree. I, too, loved a horse race, especially if *I* rode. After the family attended the Calgary Stampede, I wanted to be an outrider for chuckwagon races. Oh, the thrill of flying around the track with the thunder of hooves in my ears! My parents tolerated my ridiculous babbling. They did not try to discourage me, though they may have wanted to. Luckily, I did not pursue this craziness. I was twelve.

For good reason, my parents prohibited racing on the ranch. A horse that races against others all the time soon will not behave himself on everyday rides. Cheetah already had "run" in her head, so I knew I should not encourage her. I certainly remember when she cold-jawed[27] running back to the house yard and hit a four-strand barbed wire fence. I resisted pulling on the reins and rode it out. She

---

[26] A match race is a race between only two competitors.

[27] A horse "cold jaws" if he becomes insensitive to pressure from a bit.

hit the fence square with all the force of the runaway it was, snapped the top two strands, stumbled, slammed me to the ground so hard my legs numbed, and kept running. My legs would not hold my weight for a few minutes, but when the circulation came back, I staggered after my horse, terrified of what I would find. She was not injured, the only sign of her misdemeanor a tiny prick of blood on her chest. Yes, when she ran, she thought of nothing else and that was not acceptable around the ranch.

However, racing suited both Cheetah and me. Fairs and horseshows scheduled flat races, so we could run there. For the next few years, I raced Cheetah on several tracks with outstanding results. Mostly I ran her bareback to spare her the extra pounds. There were no rules stating the horse had to be saddled.

Races at horseshows ran, for the most part, on half-mile tracks, which every fairground had. The distance was a shade too much for Cheetah. She was sired by a Quarter Horse with early speed and Thoroughbred breeding gave her *some* staying power but not enough to finish a half mile well. Most times, it didn't make any difference. She gained a lead early and the field could not catch up. One time, though, it didn't happen that way...

Whitebear horseshow hosted Chuckwagon races and an outrider had entered his horse, a lanky, bay Thoroughbred gelding, in the flat race. Still confident, I lined Cheetah up with the rest and she burst off the starting line just as she always did. At the quarter, we had opened up a considerable lead. I looked over my shoulder, expecting to see horses struggling to keep up. Instead, I saw the Thoroughbred gobbling up the track with long ground-eating strides. Shocked that any horse could run faster than my Cheetah, I could only stare as he so effortlessly passed us. This horse taught me a lesson in humility: my mare was best at a quarter mile; sometimes a faster horse would cross the finish line in front of her.

Occasionally my parents made an exception to the "No racing except at shows" rule, like the time Jeanette's brother challenged Cheetah and me. He bet five dollars his mare could run faster than mine; I was sure she could not! The parents approved a race, set it up on a dirt road, lined us up and started us.

The race was not as much fun as I thought it would be. Cheetah outdistanced his mare so badly in the first few strides I pulled her up. Embarrassed for both of us, I did not want to take his money, but his father insisted. I got the distinct impression he knew his son was not going to win and sought to teach him a lesson.

During the summer of 1961, I dated Garry Collins. In between "normal" dates to drive-ins or dances, we rode. Garry and his sister, Sharon, worked at the Beechy Community Pasture ten miles from the Diamond Dot. In the course of the summer, four of us—Garry, Sharon, Harold and I—rode back and forth many times, visiting and generally goofing off. Good-natured bantering went on all summer between guys and girls, everything from baking pies to racing horses. The pie-baking contest didn't get off the ground (the boys chickened out), but we ran a match relay race with Mom and Dad's permission.

A relay race on horseback is like a relay race on foot. A rider starts with a baton, runs a leg of the race[28] and passes the baton to the next rider within a set distance, who passes to the next rider, etc., until the last rider races to the finish line. Usually the race runs on a track. We improvised.

The grain field by the house was swathed[29] and ready for harvest. The field was a half-mile long and, though not perfectly flat, was at least free of gopher holes. Plump swaths of golden grain lay in parallel rows the length of the field, lanes for our race.

Dad was the official starter. He lined Garry and Sharon up at the predetermined starting line. They each held a stick to pass to Harold and me on Neenah and Cheetah, waiting a few hundred yards down the field between the same swaths as our partner. Sharon was a little shaky at the start, having not spent as much time on a horse as the rest of us, but with a little weaving down the field, she made the pass to me. Harold and I raced to the finish and Cheetah's exceptional speed saved the day. It was not a long race, maybe a quarter mile total, with field left to stop the horses safely. After all the planning, the race was over in a few seconds. The girls won. The guys cried "foul" because Sharon veered out of her swath lane into Garry's.

The relay race at the ranch was not the only relay race I ever ran. Beechy Fair was an annual event, one I never missed. One year the fair board planned a relay race as the feature event of the show, each team to consist of three riders, each rider to run a segment of the race and pass a baton to the next rider in an allotted space.

---

[28] A leg of a race is one portion of a race.

[29] A swathed field is a field of grain that has been cut into rows.

Harold, Colin and I were one of three teams. Harold would run first on Neenah, pass to Colin, who would pass to me on Cheetah to finish the race . . . in first place we hoped. A piece of wood about a foot long served as the baton. The total distance of the race was a half mile on an oval track regularly used for harness races. Officials separated the track into three sections, each of which would be a leg of the race. Each rider would run his prescribed distance and pass to the next. Heavy cable separated the track from the barns and show arena and cars pulled up to the cable on what would be the final turn of the race. People lined the track between cars. As riders took positions on the track, Mom took *her* position on top of a car, the better to see the entire track.

I, on Cheetah bareback, watched my team's first rider leave the start line from my station at the third leg of the relay. He had a slight lead when he passed to our second rider, but Colin's horse lost a little ground on the turn. As he rolled toward my now-agitated mare, I knew Cheetah would have to run her best to win the race for our team. I reached for the baton . . . and came up empty handed. He had used the stick to bat his horse and had broken it! I held Cheetah up to stay within the "passing section" and the final rider for one of the other teams (none other than Garry on a buckskin gelding I knew was not as fast as my Cheetah) flashed by. Just in time, I grabbed the truncated baton. The buckskin rump sprayed us with dirt, but I leaned over Cheetah's neck into the final turn. She would not have a problem passing! We were closing the gap rapidly when I knew I was not in control. Cheetah had drifted to the outside of the track and had frozen on the bit. I could not turn her and the cable was coming to meet me. I had only one choice for the safety of all. I released the reins. Cheetah straightened, jumped, and sailed over the cable between cars and people scrambling to safety. Miraculously, I did not fall off, was not hurt, and did not harm anyone else. Mom, when she caught up with me, said, "That's the last time you race bareback."

I did not see any reasoning to the rule since I stayed on, but at least she did not say there would be no more racing.

It was not the last time I raced. There were to be many more horse races and, after I left home, some were without a saddle.

A Life With Horses

Chiquita and Life on the Ranch

*You and your horse. His strength and beauty. Your knowledge and
patience and determination and understanding and love. That's what
fuses the two of you onto this marvelous partnership. . . .*
~ Monica Dickens

As a working ranch, a cow-calf operation, the Diamond Dot
handled cattle on horseback. Horses rounded up and
separated the herds, checked fence and fields, and dragged calves to
the branding fire. Harold and I were part of the team. We joined
Mom and Dad in early morning roundups before school and long
days branding at the corral. If we found a cow, calf, or yearling in
trouble when we checked fields, we cut the animal away from the
herd and brought it home. Our horses became skilled in ranch work
and I soon learned a good cow horse made the difference in getting
the job done or not. Cheetah, as noted, did not have a love of ranch
work, but eventually I owned a horse that did. Her name was
Chiquita.

Chiquita was a full sister to Cheetah but built differently—taller and shorter coupled but with the same powerful hindquarters. A pretty head, short ears, and wide-spaced eyes set off her colour. She gleamed golden buckskin, complete with black points.[30] I had admired her since she was born in 1959.

31. Chiquita as a yearling in 1960.

Chiquita belonged to Dad and I waited for him to ride her but, at three years old, still he had not saddled her. Concerned that the beautiful mare would spend her life running with the herd untrained, I considered broaching the subject to him, but he had already found a solution. Soon I would graduate from high school and he knew exactly what to give me—a buckskin mare named Chiquita!

Thrilled with my gift, I immediately started working with Chiquita. She had an advantage—three years running the prairie building muscle, legs, heart, lungs, and spirit—but Mom and I sacked her out and saddled her in the corral. Not surprisingly, she bucked. That was a problem. I had started only one horse before, a mare called Sierra, and she had bucked me off a couple of times. I had no wish for a rerun. Chiquita bucked around the corral until she tired and we could walk up to her. I did not want to get on.

I think we repeated the sacking and saddling for one or two days more. Then it was time to ride. Mom knew I might be in trouble with

---

[30] A horse is said to have black points if his mane, tail and bottom portion of his legs are black.

the mare, so this time she did not insist I go it alone. Dad would pony Chiquita and me off Red. As I said, I was not completely comfortable ponying but not in a position to argue either. If it must be, I could not think of anyone I would rather have on the lead shank than Dad on Red.

After Chiquita "warmed up" in the corral with the now familiar pattern of bucking until she quit, Dad snubbed[31] her to his saddle horn, I mounted and, after a few rounds in the corral, we left in the general direction of a big field east of the house. Dad led us up the slope from the corral, past the dugout and onto the field, Chiquita scrooching along beside Red and me tense in the saddle. Dad wanted to trot to loosen the mare up and wear off some energy, but when we did, she lurched ahead and bucked me off between her and Red (my fear in the first place). I scrambled to my feet, got back on, and we finished a very short ride with limited success, still snubbed to Red. The next day I was on my own.

Either Chiquita *liked* to buck or she *learned* to buck, because she threw me two or three more times. Once she bucked the saddle *and me* over her head. Chiquita's training was going in the wrong direction. By not being able to ride through the buck, I had encouraged a bad habit for the tough mare, a habit she needed to lose. Mom told me I needed to "camp on her" or, in Grandpa's words, "pull a lot of wet saddle blankets off of her". Chiquita needed more riding than I could give her on the Diamond Dot.

Extra rides for my determined buckskin mare were closer than I knew. Rangeland south of the Diamond Dot belonged to a ranch that summered cows there but whose owner lived in Kyle, not a good arrangement because he could not check the cattle as often as he should. Mom and I considered his dilemma and offered a solution, a solution for all of us. We asked for a job. We would ride the pastures and check their cattle, a summer job for me, and miles of riding for Chiquita! The rancher accepted our proposal immediately.

Checking cattle in huge fields of several sections each provided the perfect venue for a horse that needed a lot of work. Long regular rides would accomplish what my shorter ones did not. We were going to be riding a half-day or more every time we left the barn.

We struck an agreement for bi-weekly rides of the rancher's fields, but the job was more time-consuming than we anticipated.

---

[31] A horse is snubbed when he is dallied to the saddle horn or a post with a very short rope.

Many cows required various treatments. We trailed them to our corrals, treated them there, and took them back to pasture. To care for the herd well, we made extra rides to check up on a patient or a cow that had just calved. What began as twice weekly extended to daily, hours and hours of riding! At first Mom and I kept up with the fast-paced schedule, but soon both Dad and Harold helped—Harold with riding and Dad with vet work. We were on horseback most of every day and I used Chiquita almost every time. She developed a back sore, but I cut out a piece of the saddle pad and kept riding her. It was exactly what she needed. By the end of the summer, Chiquita was not only "broke" but also an experienced ranch horse. She could single-handedly bring in a range cow and her calf and not use a bunch of extra steps doing it. I would need and appreciate Chiquita in a few years.

32. Chiquita and I (leading Cheetah); Harold on Arrow (leading Neenah).

A riding job I loved above all others at the ranch was rounding up horses. Our horses sometimes ran in the School Section, which was just that, 640 acres. The School Section lay straight north of the house, past the funny post where Harold and I "visited the neighbours", through the gate Mom and I had opened to water the horses when Pronto threw me, and over the butte. More often, the horses ranged in a two-section field known as the North Pasture, north and east of the house. There, too, I climbed out of the valley, via either a coulee or a trail up the face of a butte. A fence below the buttes separated the North Pasture from fields around the house and I always closed the gate until I returned. I maintained better control if the horses did not stampede through ahead of me.

Once on top, I crisscrossed the pasture until I spotted the herd, rounded them up, and turned them toward home. Horses chase easily once started, and always run when they are driven, so the herd gained distance on me by the time they reached the buttes above the valley. They never used the coulee trail to the gate, though, which would have been the easiest route. Every time they ran along the ridge, stopped at the brow of the butte, milled around a few minutes as if deciding who would lead, and then, as one mass, dropped over the top. It was a spectacle—mares, foals, and sometimes a stallion skidding down the face of the butte in a haze of dirt! My horse (especially if I rode Cheetah) pulled at the bit as I slipped and slid down behind, and then ran wide open to circle them into the corner so I could open the gate. I will remember the "feel" of those rides— the shifting, moving muscle under my seat and legs as my horse adjusted her weight over her hindquarters and skidded—forever. I "see" yet the herd heaving in the corner, crowding through the gate, dashing madly to the corral. Heads swinging side-to-side, swerving, bucking, kicking. Delightful, delicious freedom.

Every girl who loves horses dreams of taming a wild one. I was no different.

At least once every summer my mother visited her friend south of the Diamond Dot on horseback. Mrs. Merrison, a widow, lived alone on a large ranch south of the road between Beechy and Kyle. On this day, I tagged along.

The trail we took across the hills was the same one we had ridden to the Clearwater Lake Rodeo where Rocky won money for my transistor radio. This time, instead of riding west to the lake, we crossed the road to the Merrison ranch. It was then Mom told me about the wild horses.

Merrison horses had gone "wild" on the ranch and had run the hills for years. Wild horses already fascinated me. Now I hoped I could see one. Though I had never thought of owning or taming one up to this time, the persona of the wild horse intrigued me.

Merrison Ranch grassland looked exactly like the Diamond

Dot—rolling hills of prairie wool with sloughs or "potholes" in low spots. If a road existed (I'm sure it did.), Mom and I were not on it. We cut across the hills to the little ranch house.

Then I saw *the one*. On a not-too-distant knoll, a stallion shuffled nervously in a small circle, stopping only a few seconds, looking, pacing, stopping again. I thought for a moment he might run to us, but instead, he froze. Liver chestnut hide gleaming, flaxen mane thick, long and luxurious, he warily watched, silently studied. We had pulled our horses up, quite in awe of the picture he presented— proud, haughty, magnificent, *and wild.* He was not there long. With a toss of his head, he turned and disappeared down the backside of the hill and out of sight.

I looked for him on the return trip to no avail. All the way home, I babbled on and on.

"Can we buy him?"

"Do you think we could train him?"

My enthusiasm was infectious because by the time we got home Mom was just as excited as I was. She was sure Mrs. Merrison would sell him to us. We would geld him and she would help me train him. She said it was possible. He would be our "project" and I would have a fabulous horse.

Dad was not as easily swayed. He said it was "a damn fool thing to do" and that was the end of it. Usually Mom would have argued a little, but I suspect she agreed.

The Diamond Dot was isolated to be sure, but I could not imagine living anywhere else. I loved the cattle, the horses and the lifestyle.

As we grew up, Harold and I played less and worked more with our horses. We saddled up to check cattle, round up, or bring a cow in from or out to the pasture. Dad taught both of us to rope, and I spent some time throwing a rope at a cream can.[32] Harold learned to rope well, but I did not practice enough to be proficient. Dad also taught us rope tricks and I spent more time with trick ropes than calf ropes. I even performed rope tricks at a rodeo with Dad once or twice.

I roped from a horse only once. I rode Red that day with Garry on one of his twice-weekly checks of the Community Pasture fields. If he found an animal that required treatment, he roped it and gave

---

[32] A cream can is large metal can used for shipping cream.

penicillin or topical medications. I helped him spot sick animals or handed him supplies, but mostly I watched him work. Finally, I offered to help.

"I'll rope the next one," I told Garry. A Hereford calf needed treatment for pinkeye.

Red is a trained rope horse. He will put me in position. It can't be that hard.

Off we went, Red running over uneven ground pocked with gopher and badger holes. In only a few strides, Red caught up with the calf and I threw my loop, but the attempt was pathetic. The loop fell far short of the running calf.

Not that easy after all.

I gathered the rope up, coiled it, made another loop and kicked Red into a lope after the retreating calf but Red would not have any part of it. I understood. He had done his part the first time and I had not. He was not going to make the effort again. My calf roping career, like my wild horse dream, ended as quickly as it began.

*****

Mom had spent most of her life in the Coteau Hills. As we rode, she pointed out old homesteads, buffalo wallows, teepee rings and a gravesite marked with stones at head and foot. She named wild flowers, bushes, trees, birds and animals. We rode all times of day and night.

I liked to ride at night, especially to "The Hog's Back", a ridge in the North Pasture. Mom showed us how, in just the right place on The Hog's Back, on a clear starry night, we could see the lights of seven towns. It was the highest point on the ranch. I loved to ride to the top, rest my horse, count the towns, and try to name them. I scanned the night sky for the Big Dipper and found the North Star from it as Mom had shown me. Often, The Milky Way whitened the sky or, in the fall, Northern Lights danced with the stars. The heavens wrapped me in such stillness that, even today, the memory comforts me. I still search for high ground and the sense of peace I found on the Hog's Back.

Often, if we visited in the settlement to the east, west, north or south, we rode home in the dark. We did not ever worry for the horses were sure-footed and dependable. Besides, we could not always finish a task by nightfall. We rode in the dark so much I have no reason to remember any of the rides . . . except one.

Mom and I had a purpose to this ride. We needed to log some miles on our long two-year-olds.[33] Barely started under saddle, we were anxious to step up their training before winter. I rode Sierra, a pale yellow-sorrel mare out of the Goldie mare who hurt my back; Mom rode Arrow, a flashy, red sorrel gelding with four white stockings and a star in his forehead.

It was mid afternoon when we saddled our young horses and struck out south from the ranch. A long ground-covering trot took the edge off the colts' freshness and they soon settled down. I cannot remember if we planned to visit the Smiths, but that's where we ended up—twelve miles across the hills, the same twelve miles Jeanette, Harold and I had ridden in the winter to attend the New Year's Eve dance. We chatted with Mrs. Smith for a few minutes, intending to turn around and ride home, but she insisted we eat supper with the family. We knew the long ride home would be in the dark if we stayed, but the horses were good, the weather warm and pleasant, and the food tempting. We accepted the invitation.

It had been a wonderful evening. Hunger appeased, happy with our young horses, we laughed and talked all the way home. As we topped the last hill before dropping into the valley and home, we stopped. Headlights on the trail, headed our way. A lone vehicle drove slowly toward us on the trail out of the ranch. We looked at each other. Dad had come looking for us.

He knew we should not have been that late. Not happy about us taking the colts out together in the first place, he worried when we were not home by dark. Now that he had found us, he was mad. He reminded us again that we were riding green horses. It was another one of his "damn fool things to do" moments. Mom, though she knew he had a right to worry, said softly, "Both of us would not have been bucked off."

"Why not?" Dad said.

I did not think about the long ago dream of a life with horses any more. Education pre-empted dreams. In the fall of my eighteenth year, I left for the University of Saskatchewan in Saskatoon.

I still had not chosen my life work. I changed my mind several times, and eventually chose the Arts program. I hoped I would be certain of a career choice after a year of university. Mom had instilled in me the value of an education from the time I was very

---

[33] Long two-year-olds are horses in the fall of their two-year-old year.

young, so continuing my studies was not an option but a life plan. Still, leaving the ranch for the city was very difficult. This was the second, and last, time I would live apart from horses. I rode Cheetah bareback to the pasture to turn her with the herd, slid off her warm, brown back, brought her head to mine, and slipped the halter off. Without a backward glance, she spun away from me and ran up the butte. At the top, she stopped briefly to look back at me, and then disappeared over the top. Slowly, I turned and walked back to the house where I wrote this poem:

To A Horse
On winged hooves thou fairly fly
Until thou pause with head held high
Give haughty toss of head and mane
But careless, proud and free again
Alone thou art!
Would that I could see thee now
And forever keep a vow
To never leave thy side again
Remain together sun and rain
And never part!

I did not want to leave, but my path led another direction. It would be months, maybe forever, until I lived at the ranch again. A chapter of my life had closed and another opened. I moved to Saskatoon for my first year of university.

I enjoyed classes but missed the Diamond Dot, bussing home every other weekend and skipping Saturday classes when I did. In the winter, my parents or brother brought a horse to the edge of the hills so I could ride in to the ranch as I had done all my high school years. I loved every minute of it. When university closed in April, I was back with Cheetah and Chiquita, rounding up cattle, working the job at the adjoining ranch, living the life I so loved. I did not go back to university, but I didn't stay at the ranch either. Garry and I had split up during my grade twelve year but, during that summer, we dated again and, in the fall, married. My horses and I moved away from the Diamond Dot.

A Life With Horses

Part 2

Family and Horses

There is no secret so close as that between a rider and his horse.
~ Robert Smith Surtees

Marriage, Babies and Horses

*Our most urgent social and political question is how to live in right
relationship. In learning to pay respectful attention to one another
and plants and animals, we relearn the acts of empathy, and thus
humility and compassion - ways of proceeding that grow more and
more necessary as the world crowds in.*
~ William Kittridge, in Places of the Wild

Married at nineteen, my life changed from one of carefree
dreams to one of responsibility. Although my husband and
I had hardly a dollar in our wallets, I faced each challenge with the
naivety of the child I still was. We had each other . . . and our horses.
Cheetah and Chiquita joined Garry's two on the Beechy Community
Pasture.

Garry had been hired as a rider on the pasture prior to our
marriage. At the close of the grazing season, the manager resigned
and the Department of Agriculture offered Garry the position, an
opportunity he eagerly accepted. On the pasture headquarters, Garry
and I would be living only ten miles across the Coteau Hills from
Mom and Dad. In fact, the Community Pasture adjoined the

Diamond Dot. We would have the country life we loved, pasture for our horses and a few cows, and I would still be close to my family.

Garry's employment was seasonal, April 1 to October 31, so he would not be drawing wages until spring. Until then, we needed a roof over our heads and income. Perrin Ranching Company offered such temporary employment. When we returned from our honeymoon, we moved a few of our belongings to the old ranch house beside the South Saskatchewan River. Garry worked with three other men; I cooked and cleaned for them.

The men fed cattle, cleaned barns, and milked cows, all the various chores of a working ranch in winter. Daily, they gathered the calves from a treed island on the frozen river that provided natural shelter for the calves and brought them to the feed yard for grain. The ride, though short, was often nasty. Most days the wind whistled off the river, blasting icy fingers into man and beast.

January came in with record-setting low temperatures. The men checked the thermometer every morning before they left the house hoping for a break and complained as the mercury dipped even lower. I, on the other hand, wished I could go with them. One of the men teased me every day.

"You are so lucky," George would say over breakfast. "You can stay in where it's warm."

Finally, I could stand it no longer. Every day I cleaned up after the men left, washing stacks of dishes and the cream separator while they were on horseback.

"Fine," I said. "You do my job and I will do yours." George good naturedly agreed. It was forty degrees below zero.

I was elated. I could leave the kitchen and get on a horse! I short-listed household chores for George to do, layered clothes on my body, hands and feet, ran to the barn, saddled, and joined the men.

Riding was as cold as George had told me it would be. Although the air was calm by the barn, a breeze slipping off the river smacked us in the face when we rode away from the yard. My head ached the moment the wind hit my forehead. Frost bit my cheeks; my nostrils pinched together. I pulled the wooly red scarf over my nose and mouth and drew the fur-edged hood of my parka tighter until only my eyes, glasses rimmed with frost, faced the wind.

So you wanted to ride. . .

Chiquita, too, felt the biting cold. Under a stiff, cold saddle, she rounded her back, reminding me of past behaviour but, instead of bucking, she picked up a quick trot. We would be warmer in the shelter of the trees on the island and, with the wind at our backs, the ride home with the calves would be more comfortable. The men and I extended the trot, rising and sitting in rhythm, warming our bodies. The calves knew why we had come and what waited for them at the barnyard. They gathered easily and strung out across the ice. When they had buried their noses in grain, I unsaddled, hurried to the house, and burst into the cozy ranch kitchen, face aglow. George stood at the sink, still washing dishes.

Our employer had allowed me to keep Chiquita and one other at the ranch for the winter, a weanling colt I called Tonka Wakon. Tonka had appeared unexpectedly in September of the year before. Mom and I discovered the little bay colt on a ride in the North Pasture, a "catch colt"[34] born to Cheetah. My cousin's horse, Comanche, was the sire. When I moved my horses from the ranch, three-month-old Tonka was too young to wean, so I left Cheetah and him with Mom and Dad. In January, Garry and I brought Tonka to Perrin Ranch with Chiquita to make the weaning process easier. I could provide extra care for him if he was living with me.

33. Chiquita "nursing" Tonka.   **34. Tonka and I in the house.**

I loved having Chiquita and Tonka with me at our winter job. The two of them had full run of the yard around the house, a wide-open area extending to the river. I often watched them from the kitchen window as I cooked or washed dishes. Tonka was a joy. He tagged along after Chiquita, or me if I was outside. Chiquita

---

[34] "Catch colt" is a term given to a foal that arrives unexpectedly from an unplanned breeding.

mothered him until she produced milk even though she had never had a foal. We finally had to separate them because he was nursing her. Tonka would follow me anywhere, even up the concrete stairs into the house! He learned easily, a character trait I took advantage of the following summer.

Between spending time with Tonka, cooking, housework, knitting and embroidery for me, and ranch chores for Garry, winter days at Perrin Ranch did not seem long, but we were anxious to be on our own. We welcomed the move to Beechy Community Pasture headquarters the end of March. I was four and a half months pregnant.

In April, Garry, as pasture manager, accepted cattle for summer grazing to the Community Pasture, forty-two sections of Coteau Hills grassland owned by the Saskatchewan Department of Agriculture. All summer, he cared for the herds, and then sorted them for pickup in the fall. He needed good strong horses for long days checking, treating and rounding up and he owned two—Cheevo (a full brother to Cheetah and Chiquita) and a big bay gelding. He also used "government" horses, horses of dubious parentage and training, which belonged to the Department of Agriculture and resided on the pasture. This was the remuda.[35]

My pregnancy was relatively easy, more awkwardness than anything. I rode until I was not comfortable in a saddle. With the baby due to arrive in August, beautiful warm summer days passed me by. I missed riding.

Maybe I can try something new.

A few years before, I had read a "how-to" article in *The Western Horseman* and had written down some notes. Pregnant and armed with those scribblings, I headed for the barn. Tonka was going to be a trick horse.

Tonka liked to learn because he liked to be with people. Overjoyed to be getting so much of my attention, he welcomed our lessons. For the next few months, as my belly got bigger and bigger, Tonka learned to say "yes" and "no" in response to my questions, to bow, to pray, and to respond to voice commands ("come", "stop", "turn" and "back"). He even placed his front feet on a pedestal and tried to balance all four feet on it (with limited success). The very best trick, though, was the mathematical problems he solved.

---

[35] The remuda is the herd of horses from which a cowboy selects his mount.

"Tonka, what is two times two?" I asked, and he would paw four times. I used a cue, of course, but even so, it was amazing how he never, ever, made a mistake. As long as I could do the math, he "pawed" the solution, the cue so subtle no one noticed. I had a lot of fun with Tonka and was with him daily. We were a funny pair—a runty yearling colt and a pregnant woman.

Gloria loved him as much as I did since his sire was her own Comanche, but she became concerned as I was neared my delivery date.

"That baby's going to be born at the barn!" she scolded.

Later that year, I sold Tonka to Gloria. Our baby was not born at the barn, of course, but he definitely changed my life style.

Shayne arrived in mid-August and I adjusted to motherhood and the responsibility of a new baby. With no running water or sewage in the house, managing my time took on new meaning. I used much of my day caring for Shayne, hauling water in and out, cooking, and cleaning. We had a milk cow, chickens and a vegetable garden, all of which added to my work schedule. I baked all our bread, churned butter and canned. For a few weeks, I did not have any time left over to spend with my horses or to ride. That would change. Garry needed extra hands for fall roundup and I wanted the job. I knew the work and, more to the point, we needed extra income. With Shayne a month old, I hired on, working full time. I cooked for the crew, cared for Shayne and rode.

Garry needed four or five riders for fall roundup. Sometimes Harold or one of Garry's brothers helped. Sometimes a rancher rode for us. More often than not, though, Garry rode with an all-girl crew. Verna and Lois were regulars. I had met Verna at horse shows before I married and Lois shortly after. Both women were experienced, dependable and could ride the long hard days required.

"Why is it," their husbands would say, "these girls will get up at five o'clock to ride at the pasture? They aren't that enthusiastic about getting up early to ride the tractor!" Those demanding, sometimes frustrating, sometimes exhausting, but always memorable, days no doubt cemented the friendship we already had. Much has changed in the ensuing years, but the friendships have not.

My schedule for fall roundup started at five o'clock (if I don't count feeding the baby at two in the morning), and ended with the last call for Shayne before midnight. Without most modern conveniences, cooking and housework consumed many hours. On "off days" I baked bread, pies and cookies, cooked meals ahead and washed clothes the old-fashioned way—I carried in water from the rain barrel if it was full or the well (down a hill), heated it on a wood stove and transferred it to the wringer washer. At least I didn't have to use a washboard.

On riding days, Garry jingled[36] horses in the dark for the day's work while I packed dinner for at least five riders and planned supper so it would be ready when we finished at night. Then he rode four miles to the corrals leading extra horses. I drove with food, supplies and, if the weather cooperated, Shayne in a basket on the seat beside me. All day I worked cattle with the other riders at the corrals. When it was warm enough, Shayne slept in the basket on the front seat of the truck parked by the herd and on those days, Garry and his riders rounded up the herd before I arrived. On colder days, I hired a babysitter but, since I was breast-feeding Shayne, commuted to the house every four hours or so.

The Beechy Community Pasture breeding herd numbered fifteen to sixteen hundred animals (cows plus calves) and the dry field[37] about six hundred. We sorted all animals into four main herds, which we placed in separate fields. Later, we rounded each herd up and sorted them for delivery back to the patrons. We cut each main herd into individual owner's herds, penned them and recorded information about each animal that left the Community Pasture. It was a big job, not unlike Mom and Dad delivering cattle to the farmers so many years before, but with one difference. We didn't deliver the herd to the door!

Two or three riders held the herd in the corner of a large wire pen and two cut cattle out of the herd. Garry and I did most of the herd work, reading brands to identify each animal, then pairing up[38] cow and calf and keeping the pair together to the edge of the herd where the other riders helped us separate them. When we had cut out all or most of a brand, at least two riders held the main herd while the others penned the ones we had cut out.

Working days were long, usually extending far into the dark by the time we had tended to cattle and horses. Often we ate supper at ten o'clock. As fall progressed, the weather could be uncertain and

---

[36] "Jingling" horses is rounding up the herd of horses for work that day.

[37] The dry field is a field for animals without calves (steers and/or heifers) or those that will not be bred.

[38] A cowboy "pairs up" a cow and calf by matching the calf and the calf's mother.

cold. Our riders rode long, sometimes miserable and frustrating days in the saddle without complaint, but we shared many laughs too.

Here are a few I remember:

- The day we filled tin cans with staples to rattle at the cows when they wouldn't move (spooked our horses more than the cows)
- The day two of us collided turning back a cow that had run out of the herd (Garry didn't think that was funny, just plain stupid!)
- The morning three out of five riders got bucked off in the fog before the round up began (Garry didn't laugh this time either. He was one of them. I got the blame because I loped my horse down the hill first.)
- The teacher who rode two days but begged off the third (He said he must mark papers . . . found out later he saddle-sored and his boot top had rubbed a hole into his leg.)
- The day we built a little bonfire on the hill above the herd to warm ourselves (I took off my boots and held my feet to the fire. The fire burnt through my sock before I felt heat.)
- Garry's brother in the morning on a wild-eyed Snip (Jim slopped onto the big rough gelding, reins uneven and hanging, slouching in the saddle. Snip always looked like he was a step away from exploding, but he never did with Jim, leaving us all wondering how he got away with it. Jim didn't talk until noon. He had worked out the soreness by then.)
- Garry sitting beside his horse in the grass on the side of a hill saying, "I hate cows," as he watched them all run back to the field we had just gathered (After rounding up a twelve-section field to the gate, calves turned back, then cows. We rode until our horses had nothing left to give.)

I used Chiquita exclusively for cutting out of the herd and she was fantastic. No doubt born with a gift for the work, the hours we had logged checking and handling cattle for our rancher neighbour had taught her well. Natural ability had developed into a finely honed talent. We were partners. I spotted the cow by the brand, then the calf. Chiquita picked up the signal and it was a done deal.

Together, methodically, precisely, we cut the pair from the herd. Work became a game as I challenged my horse and myself to be the best we could be.

Garry rode with a bullwhip. When he spotted an animal he wanted to cut out, he cracked it with his whip. The whip saved his horse steps and his horses knew it. They would wait for the whip to help. I believed my horses worked better because they cut without the whip, with one exception—Bubbles.

Bubbles, one of the government-owned mares, was a gem. We used her only for cutting. She had been severely cinch-sored[39] before we came to the Community Pasture and she carried a reminder of that time in her life, a massive permanent scar on her girth. Though healed, the sore would open again if Garry cinched a saddle down on her, so he snugged up the back cinch and rode with the front cinch hanging.

35. Garry on Bubbles at the herd. He had just cut a cow out and was turning away in this photo.
This was the only photo I could find of Bubbles. We were too busy to carry cameras to the corral. . .

Bubbles had an uncanny instinct about cattle. I could watch her for hours. She not only knew from the rider's body language which cow he had targeted, she also sensed where the animal was going to go before it moved. She knew the cow. She knew the capabilities of Garry's whip. She knew she could handle anything that cow threw at her . . . and the cow knew it. Bubbles made cutting cattle out of a herd look easy. Every time I looked at the ugly scar on her girth, I felt sorry for what she had put up with from another rider, but when I watched her cut cows with two inches of slack in the front cinch, I knew she was happy.

---

[39] A cinch-sore is a sore in the girth area caused by the cinch of the saddle.

I helped with roundup through September and October of 1964. I healed up and shaped up after the birth of my first child. By November, I was pregnant with my second.

Garry's employment as pasture manager ended October 31 until the following spring. Again, we needed employment for the winter months. This time Dad offered the solution. Mom had gone back to teaching and, with the road to the ranch closed in winter, could only be home weekends. Dad needed help at the ranch so Garry, Shayne and I moved in for the winter. We turned our horses out in a twelve-section field of government pasture adjacent to the Diamond Dot to paw for prairie wool. They would graze the high ridges where much of the snow blew off, quenching their thirst with every bite.

I did not ride much during the winter months. With a toddler and another baby on the way, I was housebound most of the time. In February, though, Dad stayed with Shayne so Garry and I could check the horses for any problems, especially one getting too thin. Like the winter before, I welcomed a chance to get out of the house in spite of the cold. I saddled Harold's big, strong gelding, Arrow, and Garry rode Cheevo. The horses wintered in a field a mile east, but they could be anywhere in twelve sections.

Heavy snow lay on the flat. With no trail through it, our horses broke into a sweat immediately. To rise out of the valley to higher ground where, we hoped, we could see the horses, we must cross low, brushy terrain, the brush buried in snow. We floundered through. At one deceptively heavy spot, I pushed Arrow belly deep and he panicked. Instead of walking a step at a time, he lunged, snapping me forward and back. Fearing injury (mostly to me), I led him through the next one. No better. He almost jumped on top of me, waist deep in snow, in his frantic attempts to get through. I wondered if we were going to be able to go on when we spotted the herd. Their long winter coats glistened with frost, but their eyes were bright and alert. I was content. My horses were healthy.

In the spring, when the snow had melted and meadowlarks were singing again, I was very much pregnant. I yearned to be in the saddle and thought I could ride a little, but I didn't have a horse. Both Cheetah and Chiquita were expecting foals in May. Harold had the answer. Neenah, smooth-gaited and quiet, was the ideal horse for my condition. I did not have to worry about spooking or any kind of mischief with Neenah. At seven or eight months pregnant, I was not foolish enough to do too much, but I could plod along and get out of the house.

One day Garry saddled to round up the horses running in a small field near the house and bring them to the corral. It would be a short ride and his sister would watch Shayne so I rode with him on Neenah. I knew better than to run over the hills and holes, so I tagged way back as he chased the herd in. As we approached the corral, a car pulled up into the driveway and two people got out, my doctor and his wife! I thought I might be in for a lecture but, after the initial surprise, he said, "I suppose it's all right to ride since you are used to riding. . ." His wife looked shocked. I was eight months pregnant.

Cindy was born the end of July 1965. My life with horses was now a life with *babies* and horses. Cheetah and Chiquita were raising babies of their own: Cheetah a pretty, little brown filly we named Concho, and Chiquita, a bay colt, Reno. Skeeter, a buckskin Quarter Horse stallion owned by Perrin Ranching Company, had sired both foals.

36. Cheetah with Concho, Chiquita with Reno in 1965.

For the next few years, my life settled into a routine around Garry's work and our children. We spent one more winter with Dad, but after that, we wintered at the pasture headquarters. Without a paycheck for five months, it was tough for financially. One winter, when Shayne and Cindy were two and three, Garry left after Christmas to work in Saskatoon and his brother, Bob, stayed with me. I got up at five o'clock every morning to feed the livestock—chickens, several cows and a few horses—before Bob caught the school bus. Morning chores included chopping a hole in the ice of the dugout so the cows could drink but when it turned forty degrees below zero, the water hole froze over before the cows finished eating and wandered down to the dugout. I had to find a time in the middle of the day when the kids were sleeping to re-open it. In the middle of the cold snap, the milk cow calved (in the barn, of course). I thought she would never quit drinking—eight pails I hauled to her from the pump! After that, I added milking to my chore list. Evening chores were a little easier because Bob could help. Garry came home in February.

In the spring, summer and fall, I fit riding into my schedule wherever I could, often when Garry was in for dinner, but my responsibilities to my family vastly limited my hours in the saddle. Except in September and October. Every fall I hired a babysitter for roundup and rode from dawn to dusk (or longer) rounding up and sorting cattle. In the summer months, we showed our horses at a few local horse shows, using the same horses we rode on the ranch. Cheetah did not have a foal in 1966, and I barrel raced and flat raced[40] her at the shows that year, but thereafter she raised me some fine babies.

It was at this time that an ordinary brown gelding with extraordinary talents came into my life. His name was Brownie.

---

[40] A flat race is a horse race.

A Life With Horses

Brownie, Racing and Rodeo

His hooves pound the beat, your heart sings the song.
~ Jerry Shulman

B rownie escaped my notice at first. A plain-coloured gelding
with an equally plain name, he blended into the prairie like
a red-white-face in a herd of Herefords. No white marked his face or
legs; no red or golden highlights brushed his dark brown coat; no
outstanding attributes caught my attention. At 15.2 hands, long-
backed and gangly, he moved like a colt who had not found his legs
yet, but his lazy, listless, laid-back personality plain-wrapped a
secret. He bucked, and when he bucked, he propped his front legs so
hard the rider's teeth rattled. He usually waited until his rider was at
a disadvantage too, like the time he bucked Garry off when he leaned
forward in the saddle to rope a calf! One of five government-owned
horses on the Beechy Community Pasture, Garry and I considered
Brownie only marginally valuable as a ranch gelding.

Brownie possessed hidden talents, however, and we gradually
found him out. Not as uncoordinated as he looked, he demonstrated
flashes of athletic ability on routine ranch rides. He responded to the

bridle, stopped, turned and generally performed any job we asked of him . . . without expending excess energy! Most surprisingly, he could run, and for a distance. Unlike Cheetah, he had staying power. Unlike Cheetah also, he needed to be *persuaded* to run.

My babies were born in the summers of 1964 and 1965 and horse showing came to a standstill. The next year, though, both Cheetah and I were ready to go back. Garry wanted to show as well so, for lack of a better horse, we pulled Brownie out of the herd and hauled him with Cheetah.

Brownie reined well enough to be moderately successful at all events. It was more about the fun than the competition anyway. Not specialized (one horse for all classes), we entered the same horse in pleasure class to flat racing. Brownie and Cheetah earned their share of ribbons, but neither was a pleasure horse. With Cheetah's wired-for-run disposition and Brownie's rough gaits, ribbons were rare in that class. Speed events were another matter. I already knew Cheetah could run, but I was slower to discover Brownie's speed. When we finally entered him in a flat race, another secret was out.

A racetrack circled almost every fairground for pony chuckwagon races, so horse shows hosted at least one flat race, usually the last event of the day. (Showing western pleasure after a flat race on the same horse would have been madness!)

I had had a taste of racing on Cheetah and I was addicted. When I retired her to raise babies, I knew who was going to take her place—Brownie. He could not only run but could run more distance. At every horse show, I entered him in the flat race and he won most of them, but the most thrilling win was the jackpot[41] race at the Beechy Fair.

The fair added a special race to the list of events that year, a half-mile race open to any horse that had not run on a recognized track. There was a ten-dollar entry fee and the jackpot would be split sixty/forty. High stakes! Count me in!

Before this race, I didn't think about conditioning my horses. They kept good muscle tone and cardiovascular strength from steady work on the ranch. This time, though, I wanted the best chance possible, so I put Brownie on a training program. I knew the race would attract some attention and I meant to win it. For about six weeks, I legged Brownie up for the big event, trotting and loping him

---

[41] A "jackpot" is a competition where competitors each contribute a set amount of money to compete. Total of all money is the purse for the race.

over the hills while Garry ate dinner and watched the kids. When the day arrived, I believed he was ready. I know I was.

Nine horses entered: Brownie, a Thoroughbred (definitely to be reckoned with), a full sister to Brownie who was fast but who I did not think would win against Brownie, an Appaloosa, and five others I do not remember. Rumours circulated that the Appaloosa had previously raced on a track, but no one could say for sure. Garry's brother, Bobby, rode the sister to Brownie.

The track was the one on which I had had the near-wreck with Cheetah in the relay race, the start line in the middle of the first long stretch, the final turn by the barns. A cable enclosed the entire outside of the oval and all the inside except the backstretch. We drew for position and I drew number three. Bobby drew up fourth. The fast Thoroughbred drew the rail. Bad news.

Brownie did not start as fast as Cheetah did. He was not built for quick speed, so I knew there was no use expecting him to jump off the starting line fast enough to beat the Thoroughbred to the first turn since she was already on the rail. I hoped I could get by her and others, if necessary, on the backstretch.

The beginning of the race unfolded just as I had thought it would. When the starter yelled "Go", the Thoroughbred left us all behind, and then had the advantage of the rail around the first turn. Brownie and I drew in behind her so we would not waste energy running a wider turn. When we cruised out of the turn into the backstretch, I pushed and drove Brownie, but he could not catch the mare and pass before the final turn. I could see Bobby in my peripheral vision; the main pack ran a few lengths behind.

The Thoroughbred mare had hugged the rail for the entire race. She had run steady and strong and exhibited no signs of weakening. I was not at all sure Brownie could overtake her. I didn't know how much reserve he had, but time was running out. I needed a burst of speed from Brownie—now! I always carried a bat when I raced him and when we pounded out of the final turn I reached back and cracked him across the hip.

He did not disappoint. With the first whack, he lengthened his stride, forelegs pulling ground under him. As much as I had ridden Brownie, I had no idea he had saved his best. The conditioning also helped I'm sure, but I was just learning he was that kind of racehorse. He had a "kick" at the end. He surged forward, easily passed the mare, and won the race. Only after the race did I find out one horse had veered off the track on the backstretch, dropped both front feet into a culvert ditch and somersaulted! Neither horse nor rider was seriously hurt. I collected fifty-four dollars for the win.

Mom, as excited as I, had watched the race, of course. Later in the day, she overheard the owner of the Thoroughbred asking about the horse that had outrun his.

"I can show you the horse," she said.

Mom took him to the barn where Brownie, cooled out and placid, stood tied in his stall. His head was down in the manager, eyes droopy, his long awkward body relaxed. He didn't look like he could run a lick.

"I thought that was the horse," the man said. His shoulders slumped a little. He could scarcely believe what he knew to be the truth.

I could have won many match races with Brownie.

For a few years, Garry and I showed whenever we could get away for a weekend. Most shows were a few miles from home and one-day affairs. We hauled in our truck with stock racks on the box. To load, we simply dropped the end gate and the horses jumped up into the box. Brownie loved to see over the front and would ride long miles that way, only fussing when he knew we were almost home.

A few shows were overnighters. Then we took a tent and a cooler with food, which rode in the box of the truck with our horses ahead of their front feet. Friends arrived at the show the same way. Not many owned a trailer.

Verna, one of the women who rode for us in the fall, and her husband, Allan, competed at almost every show we did. We camped together and sometimes shared a tent, as we did at Central Butte the night a summer storm interrupted our sleep. A tremendous crash of thunder, followed by a downpour, woke us. Sheet lightning lit up the interior of the tent; wind whipped the canvas and drove rain into the walls; the roof sagged under the fury of the storm. I looked up. There stood Allan, legs spread and planted in the center of the tent, arms stretched wide against the canvas ceiling and the force of the gale! The men did keep a roof over our heads, but with no floor in the tent, we were a bit soggy. I cannot remember if our horses were under cover. Often we tied them to our trucks or in outside stalls at a show.

Eastend, Saskatchewan, hosted a good horse show. One year a group of riders from Beechy made plans to attend. I remember this because it was a *big* event. For the first time, we hauled many miles to a show (If I could have seen into the future!). Most of the riders were farmers and most farmers had cattle, which they hauled in their grain trucks with stock racks. One man donated the use of his truck to haul our horses. By alternating head, tail, head, tail, etc., we loaded eight horses in his truck. Cheetah and Brownie were in the load.

Two cars brought the riders to the show. I traveled with three or four other women in a station wagon and that's where we slept that night. The men were not so lucky. They rolled their sleeping bags out under the stars and shivered all night when the temperature dropped to below freezing.

We had a fabulous, fun weekend, but I remember only one event of the horse show, the flat race! It was a popular event there. Cyprus Hills cowboys liked a horse race and waited for this one. This time I could not ride Cheetah because the rules of the race stated the rider must be sixteen years or under. I wanted my mare in the race, so I asked a young Beechy cowboy to ride her. He was more than capable of racing bareback, but rules nixed that so he found a flat saddle somewhere and fitted it on Cheetah, a first for both of them. Forced to watch as another rider piloted my mare to a win, I felt like Mom on top of the car at the Beechy race. When he rode back to me, he said her "turbo start" almost unseated him in the English saddle!

Harold and I had competed at Saskatchewan Cutting Horse Association shows a few years earlier. Now Garry and I tried our luck in that circuit. We did not have cutting horses, but the shows offered a variety of events. I left pleasure classes behind for barrel racing, pole bending, goat tying,[42] rescue race,[43] and the pony express race.[44] SCHA was a stepping-stone to a more specialized venue for my barrel horses.

The barrel racing bug had really bit me. I rode Brownie now (Cheetah had retired to raise foals.) and the plain brown gelding won consistently at horse shows. I was ready to step up to tougher

---

[42] Goat Tying is an event for women whereby a goat is staked in the arena and the competitor rides to the goat, dismounts, wrestles the goat to the ground in some way and ties three legs together so the animal stays on the ground.

[43] Rescue Race is a race with two people per team, one riding and one standing at another spot. The rider runs to the person on foot, who mounts behind the rider and both race to a finish.

[44] Pony Express Race is a race with two people, both on horses. One rider carries a bag of mail to a predetermined point, returns to the second rider, passes the bag, and the second rider rides the same route.

competition, the rodeo circuit. I entered rodeos approved[45] by the Canadian Cowboys Association.

Rodeo had always been in my life. I "attended" my first rodeo at a few months old, when Mom and Dad rode to the Clearwater Lake rodeo (twenty miles) with me! During my childhood, Dad competed at a few rodeos every year. As a teenager, I entered the rodeo arena myself—barrel racing, not riding broncs as my mother had! Barrel racing was not a recognized rodeo event then, but sometimes the show included it, no doubt for spectator appeal. By the time I ran Brownie, barrel racing had taken its rightful place with the other rodeo events. The purse was usually lower, but barrel racers could win enough to pay the next entry fee. The next few years were a round of raising family, Community Pasture work and barrel racing on a few weekends. Every chance I could, I packed the kids up, jumped Brownie in the back of the pickup, and hauled to a rodeo.

Brownie showed surprising talent given his questionable conformation. He developed his own style of turning a barrel. He did not use his hindquarters to drive forward but instead slowed forward motion with his front end and swung his hindquarters around. Cheetah did not want to set and turn at a barrel; Brownie could not wait to get there. Cheetah had running on her mind; Brownie did not want to exert much effort. I let him pick his way of turning and he took the shortest route, skimming the barrel with no room for mistakes. Because he looked for the turn long before he reached the barrel, I had to keep him running until he was in position or he set for the turn too early, like he did in a CCA barrel race in Austin, Manitoba.

The huge arena allowed a full barrel pattern, unlike some of the smaller arenas. The distance between the first and second barrels in an indoor arena was often just thirty or forty feet. In Austin, it was sixty. Brownie wanted to turn before he reached the second barrel and it was all I could do to drive him past the barrel enough to make a turn. That's when it happened.

When Brownie arrived at the second barrel, he was more than ready. He dropped his shoulder[46] and slammed his front feet in the ground. The force of the abrupt, rough, awkward turn popped me

---

[45] An approved competition is eligible for association championships.

[46] A horse "drops his shoulder" when he fails to keep his shoulder upright, which results in leading into a turn with the shoulder and a loss of correctness.

over the saddle horn onto his neck. The rubber bands I always stretched around my boots and stirrups to secure my feet when I barrel raced did their job well—my feet stayed in the stirrups! Around the barrel and driving for the third one a hundred and twenty feet away, I rode in front of the saddle with my feet still in the stirrups, not liking the ride much. When I braced one hand on Brownie's neck to push myself back over the horn and into the saddle, he dropped his head. I jerked my hand back before I pitched over. I had lost control. Brownie ran a huge arc in the arena and back to the gate with me still on his neck. Not one of my finer moments.

A bronc rider from my hometown met me at the gate.

"Are you the trick riding act?" John asked. Very funny.

37. Brownie and I in Meadow Lake Stampede in 1970. *Rick White*

I hauled Brownie to rodeos for several years including the fall I was pregnant with my third child at the end of the 1970 season. He won barrel racing money from 1968 to 1972,

In February 1971, Garry received unexpected news. The Department of Agriculture offered him a pasture manager position at the Crooked River Community Pasture in northern Saskatchewan, year around employment we needed. He accepted the job. Our daughter, Lana, arrived March 20. In early April, we moved. The

Department arranged for transportation for the small herd of cattle we now owned and several horses. We traded Chiquita's foal, Reno, now a dependable ranch gelding, to the Department of Agriculture for Brownie, so we could take him with us. Reno stayed with the Beechy Community Pasture.

To people who did not rodeo, the life I lived on the road seemed a little mad, but long drives with small children, breakdowns, sleeping in a tent and cooking on a Coleman was "normal". Only these road trips stand out in my memory:

Kinistino, Saskatchewan: Our family and Bob, Garry's brother, camped out on the rodeo grounds as we had many times before. The first day of the rodeo over, we retired for the night in the partitioned tent, Bob sleeping in the front section, Garry, Shayne, Cindy, Lana and I sleeping on the canvas floor at the back. We had spread a bale of straw under the floor and we were quite comfortable, if a bit crowded with three children between Garry and me. Sometime in the night, I heard wind and rain but dry, warm, and exhausted from the day's activities, saw no reason to stir.

"I'm moving to the truck," Bobby announced from the front of the tent. I didn't know what time it was, but it was very dark. Blasts of wind now drove the rain into the walls of the tent. I went back to sleep.

Various noises outside the tent gradually woke us at dawn. I started to wonder about my horse, tied to the trailer.

"Can you check Brownie?" I asked Garry.

Garry crawled forward and looked through the flap where Bobby had been sleeping.

"Oh, oh. . ." he said.

The front of the tent was under water, the cooler floating, food soggy. The only reason we had stayed dry was the straw underneath our bed.

Garry unzipped the front flap and looked outside.

"We have to get out of here," he said. Brownie, still standing by the trailer, echoed Garry's statement. I looked at my watch. Five o'clock.

All around us, tents had blown down, competitors taking refuge in their trucks. Some had tried to leave, but their outfits were stuck in the mud. The rodeo grounds, now a bog hole, did not resemble the grounds of the day before. Signs had been twisted by the wind. A huge tent had collapsed. A couple of horses ran loose. Everywhere, cowboys (one in his underwear) scrambled to load horses and go home. Many had had tents fall down on their heads in the night.

I bundled the kids into the truck, loaded Brownie and helped Garry pack up. Cold rain soaked us as we worked. This rodeo was over.

Austin, Manitoba: When Lana was a few months old, I entered the rodeo in Austin, knowing I would be traveling with the kids but without Garry. I broke the drive into two part days and, since I would be living in a tent at the rodeo, planned to get a hotel for the night on the road. A flat tire a few miles from home delayed me, but otherwise the drive went smoothly the first day. I was breastfeeding the baby, so would stop to care for her, and then drive again. Brownie, in the back of the truck with hay, tent and cooler in front of him, rode like the experienced traveler he was.

When I stopped for the night, I chose a little town with a hotel cheap enough I could afford. I asked the hotel manager if he knew anyone who could board Brownie, and he gave me directions to a farm. Lana was fussing and Cindy and Shayne were doing their best to quiet her as I drove to the property and parked in front of a friendly-looking farmhouse.

"Just a little longer," I promised the kids, sliding out from under the steering wheel and closing the door behind me.

Not sure what I would do if no one was home or if Brownie could not stay there, I climbed worn cement steps and knocked. A woman promptly opened the door, acknowledged me, then looked over my shoulder and stared. A white pickup with stock racks had parked in her yard. Two small children leaned out of the passenger window, from which could be heard the screaming of a baby. Behind the children, a white, shaggy head popped up (my Samoyed dog, Tanya). In the back, a brown gelding swung his head side to side (Brownie wanted to be unloaded!). I explained why I had come and she didn't hesitate. She boarded Brownie for the night.

By the time I'd fed everyone and put them to bed in the hotel room (with bar sounds below), it was eleven o'clock. I collapsed into bed myself, only to be wakened a short time later by scratching. I turned the light on. Shayne had chicken pox.

There's probably a reason I don't remember much about the rodeo.

Swift Current, Saskatchewan: Brownie, Lana and I traveled with another barrel racer to Swift Current rodeo. Marg owned a small camper and graciously shared it with the baby and me. Lana, three months old, slept in a basket. When I warmed up Brownie, I asked a passing cowboy to "Please hand my baby to me." after I had mounted, and walked and jogged him with her in my arms. If she was not asleep when the time came for my run, I passed her off to someone for those few seconds.

Marg was single and cowboys depended on her for coffee and conversation. One night we woke to a loud knock on the door.

"Marg, get up and make us a coffee!"

I waited. Maybe bunking with Marg was not such a good idea.

"I can't," she said. "The baby's on the stove."

38. Brownie and I at Hallonquist Rodeo (Saskatchewan). *Rick White*

39. Brownie and I Undecorating, Lloydminister, SK. *Rick White*

Brownie's best year was 1970 with earnings of over seven hundred dollars at eighteen rodeos, most of them approved. Now, almost forty years later, it doesn't seem like much, but cheap gas and ten-dollar entry fees puts that total in perspective.

When Brownie made a clean run, he usually took home a paycheck, but he tipped too many barrels with his close turns. I thought a lot of the gawky but more-graceful-than-he-looked gelding and respected him for what he could do, but I needed to retire him. I needed another barrel horse. Fortunately, I had planned ahead.

A Life With Horses

The Call of the Quarter Horse

The horse moved like a dancer, which is not surprising. A horse is a
beautiful animal, but it is perhaps most remarkable because it
moves as if it always hears music.
~ Mark Helprin, A Winter's Tale

Cheetah and Chiquita were grade horses,[47] not purebred or,
more accurately, not *pure breed.* Dad's registered Quarter
Horse, Copper Red Boy, had sired both, but their dam was of mixed
breeds. Red was the only purebred horse of any breed on the
Diamond Dot or with Garry and me. Our grade horses served us
well, tough horses able to do the work they needed to, but Quarter
Horses were seeping into Canada and we were interested . . . for
good reason! The Quarter Horse was bred to do what we were
doing—working cattle, barrel racing, flat racing. I had to have one.

Garry and I had purchased our first Quarter Horse locally in
1966. We bought Jay Bee's Jet, a black two-year-old stallion, from a
friend. His sire was Chub Hawk, who belonged to another friend, his

---

[47] Grade horses are not registered with any recognized breed association.

dam a mare by Old Red Bird. The next spring we bought a second registered Quarter Horse, Kit Mae, a nine-year-old mare. Kitten foaled out a sorrel filly by Skip Skooter shortly after we bought her that I named Skeena Skip and we bred her back to Jet. So began my relationship with the Quarter Horse and the American Quarter Horse Association.

There was never any question about who would train Jet. Like Dad, Garry did not show a keen interest in starting colts. I did. The young stallion was quiet, cooperative and willing. After a few rides, I used him to check and round up cattle and by the end of the year, I could even plop Shayne and Cindy on his back. In the spring, I turned him out with his band of mares, brought him in two months later and continued where I had left off.

40. Jay Bee's Jet.

41. Shayne and Cindy on Jet.

42. Beggar High.

In 1967, Garry and I looked beyond our immediate community for more Quarter Horses. We secured a bank loan (Can't believe we did that!), drove to Simms, Montana for Doug and Nancy Dear's sale and returned with a weanling stallion, Beggar High. The little sorrel, sired by Classy Bar out of a Leo bred mare,

looked athletic and intelligent. Not tall, but muscled and compact, it didn't surprise me to learn a steer wrestling horse lurked in his pedigree. He would be the next cross on our mares.

In October of 1968, Garry and I added to our registered herd again. We returned to Dears' production sale for broodmares. There were several in the sale, but I returned many times to a gorgeous two-year-old chestnut mare. I wanted her. Pretty, pretty head. Huge expressive eye. Long underline of a racehorse. Muscled hindquarters. Balanced and built to run. She moved with the grace and power of a cougar, exuding presence and a promise of talent.

43. Ma Dear (Duchess), three years old, in 1969.

I guessed the value of the mare to be well beyond our budget, but still I hoped, somehow, we would be able to buy her. A nagging inner voice chided me. *If you miss this mare, you will regret it.*

Nervously, I waited for the mare to come into the sale ring even though I did not intend to bid. Garry and I had discussed it, and concluded she would be too expensive. A young woman led her in. I watched from the bench as the bidding started. Again, I felt I had been offered an opportunity to own a special horse.

When the bidding stalled, I could stand it no longer. I elbowed Garry and he shot his hand up. Bids sputtered back and forth for a few minutes. I held my breath. Garry could not stay in much longer. Then the hammer fell and I ran into the ring.

The mare belonged to Dears' daughter, Barb. As she passed the shank to me, tears rolled down her cheeks. She loved the mare.

"Why are you selling her?" I asked.

"I got out-voted. What are your plans for her?"

"She's going to be my barrel horse."

We did not buy a broodmare at that sale, but we made a once-in-a-lifetime purchase—Ma Dear, 1966 daughter of Pasamonte Paul out of a Classy Bar mare. Her sire had run TAAA[48] at six distances; her dam had raced successfully; Quarter Horses with performance records enriched her pedigree.

Garry and I considered ourselves extremely lucky to own Ma Dear. Although we had stretched our horse budget to the limit to buy her, I knew she was worth far more. I bought her for a barrel horse and did not look beyond. I did not foresee how she would influence my breeding program and my life. I called her Duchess, a grand name for a grand horse. She would live up to it.

Life on the Community Pasture at Crooked River was similar to the one we had left except for one thing—bush! We were flatlanders. Handling cattle in trees was a new experience. Spruce and fir undergrown with shrubbery hid cattle from view and was not horse-friendly. Fields were smaller, but roundups were slower and a whole lot more frustrating.

Sorting the animals was different too. We pushed cattle through chutes and read tags to identify each animal. In the spring, someone (often me) recorded every tag number; in the fall, we sorted herds through chutes again to separate. Gone were the days on horseback cutting cattle out of a herd.

When the patrons delivered their cattle in the spring, we tagged and recorded every one and separated the animals, breeding and dry. At the end of each day, we drove the herds to their respective pastures. It was a family affair. Shayne and Cindy both rode well, so we devised a system to get the job done without hiring extra help for either babysitting or riding—one adult and one child rode and the

---

[48] TAAA is a rating of speed by the American Quarter Horse Association (i.e. A, AA, AAA, TAAA).

other adult drove the truck behind the herd with the other child and baby Lana. If Garry and Shayne rode, I drove and Cindy tended the baby in the truck beside me. Cindy and Shayne, not quite six and seven, "hired on" as riders.

For the summer of 1971, I hired a babysitter for Lana and rode for Garry to supplement our income. All summer I checked cattle in the fields. In the fall, I rounded up and helped sort. I especially loved riding the fields, solitary work but "alone time" with my horses. I familiarized myself with every meadow, patch of brush and forest in the new pastures and enjoyed new scenery. I checked for dead animals, writing down tag number and brand, and for pinkeye and foot rot. I did not treat animals in the field, leaving that job for those who could rope (!!), but sometimes I would take a cow home if she needed medical attention. I also wrote down the ear tag numbers of the bulls so we could account for every one.

That was the other change at this pasture. It was a bull station. One hundred bulls or more wintered at the headquarters, the reason Garry was employed year around. We shipped the bulls out to other Community Pastures in June, retaining thirty bulls for Crooked River.

Working with the bulls was at best frustrating, and at worst dangerous. Most were horned Herefords, a few polled.[49] *All* had a mind of their own. They fought among themselves, wrecking fences and, in summer, when they contracted foot rot and pinkeye, were more difficult to treat than a cow or calf. Garry administered drugs and topical medications in the field. He and a hired rider with their biggest, strongest horses, roped the bull, one the head and the other the heels, to treat him. Horses learned to face up[50] with a bull at the end of the rope!

We culled truly nasty bulls, but we did not always exercise enough caution handling them. I remember Shayne and Cindy helping us gather[51] the bull field before they got on the school bus.

Garry and I had sold Jet in 1969. We used Beggar now for our breeding program. When we moved, we owned a nice little herd of horses, several registered. Kitten was a baby-making machine. She

---

[49] A polled animal has no horns.

[50] A horse "faces up" when he stands facing the animal with the rope tight after the rider has roped the animal.

[51] To gather a field of cattle is to round up the cattle.

produced two foals by Jet and three by Beggar in rapid succession. In 1971, we added Lynn's Queen, and bred her to Beggar. Garry's brother, Bob, also kept a mare called Jay Bee's Searra with us and gave us every other foal from her in exchange for breeding and care.

Garry and I used "Coteau" in every name for our registered Quarter Horses. Coteau Kitkat, a 1969 sorrel filly out of Kit Mae by Jay Bee's Jet was the first. We kept some of our young stock and the little band of registered Quarter Horses grew.

I did not breed Chiquita as she was valuable as a ranch horse. In 1973, I sold her to a local farmer with a few cows. He told me later, "This mare knows more than I do about handling cattle." Didn't surprise me. I wondered if he had stayed on her. . .

Cheetah, however, I continued to breed, even though her foals were grade. She raised good babies. Her 1965 filly, Concho, may have been the best. I started Concho and used her for pasture work for several years. Like her dam, she was little but tough. It was Concho I rode the day the cattle ran back at the gate (Garry's "I hate cows!" understatement), the only time I felt her try to quit. I knew if Concho could not go on that day that none of the horses could. Energetic, but not as high-strung as Cheetah, the little brown mare turned into the perfect horse for Shayne. He rode her first in the corral when he was six years old, but soon they accompanied Garry and I checking cattle on roundups.

44. Concho and Shayne in 1972.

Another one of Cheetah's fillies, a black mare sired by Jet, we gave to Cindy. She rode Ebony for roundups and general riding, but when she developed an interest in barrel racing, we sold Ebony in favour of a horse more suited to the event.

45. Shayne, Cindy and Lana with Samoyed puppies (1973).

Cheetah, my friend and my confidante, should have been with me for many years but, in 1973, at eighteen years old, my tough little mare could not win her last race. She had suffered a knee injury, probably from a kick, and it had not healed. The swollen knee hurt her with every step. I winced watching her. The time had come for me to help.

To my parents, loving your horse also meant recognizing his pain and ending his suffering. They impressed this upon me with all the other rules about caring for my horse. I knew two ways (and reasons) for ending a horse's life. If the horse broke a leg or in some other way was not "fixable", the owner shot him; if the horse became unsound or aged to the point of not being able to winter out on the prairie, the owner shipped him to the plant.[52] All my life, my parents and other ranchers sent horses to the plant when they were too old or crippled to fend for themselves. I grew up accepting this fate for horses I had known. Conditioned to the practice, I did not consider another solution when I knew I must not let Cheetah suffer any longer.

Usually, a truck picked up the horses destined for the plant in Edmonton, but I could not bear the thought of Cheetah jostling with

---

[52] The plant is abattoir for horses.

others in a big truck. Garry and I were driving to Edmonton and we hauled her to the abattoir ourselves.

I don't know what I was thinking. When Garry unloaded Cheetah, I realized what I had done. I wanted to change my mind, to load her back in the trailer and take her home, but I didn't know how to say so. Today, that is exactly what I would have done.

I did not lead her to her death, but I must accept ownership of her fate. I watched. Willingly, with complete trust, Cheetah followed Garry up the ramp and through the big doors into the abattoir. When her brown rump disappeared into nothingness, I wailed. That final picture of Cheetah blueprinted in my mind, I vowed never to send a horse to slaughter again and I have not.

Garry and I had a strong interest in Quarter Horse racing and agreed it was time for a new stallion, one bred to run. With my interest in barrel racing, focusing on horses with speed and athletic ability made a lot of sense. We committed to a trip to a huge sale of running Quarter Horses in Oklahoma City in October 1973. Many yearling stallions of running bloodlines were consigned, and we intended to purchase one. Again, the bank approved a loan.

We arrived in Oklahoma City in the middle of the night before the sale, which started at eight o'clock in the morning. We dashed to the barns at six but could not possibly view all the horses before the first one sold. At first, it didn't seem to matter, the prices so far out of our league we could only watch. Sometimes bids jumped by ten thousand dollars.

Five hundred horses went through the sale, far too many for the number of buyers. Predictably, bidding slowed and prices dropped as buyers left and, at one o'clock the next morning, we bought a brown yearling stallion, Question Mach. Later still, I could not resist a second purchase. We did not need two stallions, but we could haul another so why not? I had spotted a son of Top Moon out of a Bar Depth mare. He was black, fine boned, and long-hipped with a pretty head and an eye that missed nothing. Although immature, he looked like he could run. We bought Seco Top Moon for nine hundred dollars.

In 1975, we sold Beggar High and in 1976, we let Question Mach go after breeding a couple of mares to him. We had chosen Seco to keep. He would be the next cross on our mares, some daughters of Beggar.

46. Seco Top Moon.

We registered Seco in my name. He suited my personality and reminded me of Rocky and Cheetah, clean limbed with the same flat bone, not big, but big-hearted. Seco measured a mere 14.1 hands, but looked taller under saddle. I started riding him when he was two. He did not buck and as long as I gave him something to do, he was happy. Though some would say he was hot,[53] I preferred to think supercharged. His energy was concentrated, not out of control. Like a rubber band stretched to the limit, he waited to be released for action. I would have a mare later with that same controlled energy.

Seco and Duchess were my personal horses. They would play a huge role in my life and in my breeding program in the years ahead. Most of the horses I own and ride today carry the genes of Seco and Duchess.

The long-ago dream was becoming a reality. Garry and I had a pasture full of Quarter Horses. We continued to breed, improving our stock and selling some. By 1974, we owned a stallion, broodmares, young stock and Duchess. For Duchess, it was a banner year.

---

[53] A "hot" horse has too much energy.

47. Seco Top Moon in a class at Tisdale Saskatchewan. I think this was a reining class. Seco always attracted a lot of attention at shows because he was black, pretty and talented. He is bitted up here, but I showed him first in a very light bosal (hackamore). Several people were surprised that I could. Although he *looked* like he was a handful, he was easy to control.

Duchess 10

Quietly she stands, head low, tail swishing,
Water dripping from her lips.
All is right in her world.
Her eyes half-closed, dreamy, wistful,
Bespeak love and trust,
Recall perhaps another time.
The roar of the crowd, the national anthem,
The thrill of the race, a triangle of barrels.
Her babies or mine,
Family, friend.
Her kind eyes soften as she nuzzles the filly at her side.
Clear water, sunshine, green grass, freedom,
Companions—horses and I.
She asks no more.
~ Sharon Gates

Duchess was bred to run. I wanted to see her on the track. Quarter Horse racing was new to Canada, the closest in Alberta, but she was eligible for three-year-old races the year after we bought her. Garry and I made phone calls and booked her with a trainer in Okotoks. Then I started riding her.

Riding Duchess felt exactly like she looked, like riding in a Cadillac. (After Brownie, I appreciated that.) Always just a breath away was power. Smooth, *controlled,* power. Where Cheetah was always a little out of control and Brownie was "in a minute", Duchess was "on demand". Everything came naturally and easily to Duchess. She stopped, backed up, turned, and changed leads effortlessly. I owned a good one.

In the spring, we sent Duchess for race training. Glowing reports from the trainer confirmed my faith in her. In fact, the owner of the facility he worked out of asked if I would sell her. For a brief *(very brief)* time, I considered his offer (I could buy two good Quarter Horses for the price), but I could not part with Duchess. I might never own another one like her.

We could not afford to drive to Alberta to see Duchess until the last race of the year in August. She had raced four times prior to the Quarter Horse race in High River with one win (an exhibition race in Victoria), and a second, third and fourth on her race record.

I barely recognized my lean, fit, pumped-to-run mare. Her already large eyes opened even wider at the prospect of a race. By now, she knew what to expect.

"She is ready today," the trainer said, very quietly. He was not spreading this news around it seemed.

The race was a 400-yard sprint. Rare Bud, her biggest competition, had just won a race in the States. Duchess drew number one position, Rare Bud number two.

I had raced on dirt tracks at little open shows, between grain swaths in fields and across the prairie. This was different. I *watched* my mare run. From the stands, I *watched* her load into the gate. I *watched* the others load. I *watched* the gates open. I trembled with anticipation.

It was worth the wait. From the gates to the finish, my Duchess led the field and set a new track record: 21.40 seconds. The local newspaper reported the win the next day:

Big Payoff Highlights Canada's First Quarter Horse Race

An $88.20 payoff to two lucky $2 ticket holders highlighted pari-mutuel results of Canada's first all Quarter Horse race meet held in High River Fair Grounds. The big payoff came in the third race, a 400-yard sprint for three-year-olds, when Ma Dear upset the field. $2 tickets on the long shot returned $88.20 to win and $24.20 to place. Rare Bud ran second and paid $4.20 to place.

48. Duchess wins in Okotoks, Alberta (August 1969).

Neither Garry nor I held a ticket on Duchess. . .

I had told Duchess' former owner I bought the mare for a barrel horse, but Duchess' barrel racing career would have to wait for a few years yet.

When I brought her home from the track, I reacquainted her with a western saddle and snaffle bit and rode her as often as possible until winter. Without skipping a beat, she settled into life at the ranch. I had not lost sight of my ultimate goal, but barrel racing was on the back burner. Duchess must fulfill one more commitment. In the spring of 1970, I bred her to War Fly. I planned to sell the foal to recoup some of the money we had invested in her. I had waited patiently through her brief racing career as a three-year-old and through basic training as a four-year-old. I could wait through a year of motherhood.

Duchess birthed a beautiful chestnut filly, Coteau Coquette, two weeks after Lana was born and two *days* before we moved to Crooked River. I left her and the new baby in care of my mother until we could safely move them to our new home.

Duchess and Coquette joined the other broodmares for the summer, but I started riding Duchess again as soon as I could wean the filly. Coquette was as pretty as her dam and I would have liked to keep her, but I knew I must sell. My brother, Harold, bought Duchess' first foal for a steer wrestling horse.

At last, I could begin training Duchess for barrels . . . in the garden! There had been no garden plot at our new home, so Garry had cultivated a large area back of the house for the following year. That is where I introduced Duchess to the cloverleaf.

She was remarkably easy to pattern on barrels, always willing, always happy, incredibly smooth-gaited with none of the front-end roughness of Brownie, more mellow than Cheetah but with the same speed. Her effortless turns at high speed amazed me. She ran hard to each barrel, rated[54] for the turn, and wrapped her body around the barrel. Powerful hindquarter muscle maintained forward motion so that she floated around. She ran the entire pattern low-headed, one ear forward and one back to me on the turns, both ears forward between barrels.

In the summer of 1973, I entered her in a few local rodeos—Kinistino, Shellbrook, Sandy Lake and Spiritwood, all within a hundred and fifty miles of home. There was money up for the event and the experience was invaluable. I couldn't resist entering another event, the flat race, at some rodeos, but I had to race Duchess with a saddle. Racing her bareback would have been easy after the first stride, but she shot off the starting line with such power I could not keep my position over her neck. At one race, a rider squeezed in on my left (no draws for position at these races and he wanted to run closer to the rail). "Move over or I'll take your leg off when we start," he warned me. I pressed my right leg on Duchess so she would not move.

"I'll take my chances," I said. I was not going to be intimidated. Besides, I had complete confidence in my mare's speed. He hooked his leg tight behind mine.

Duchess exploded off the starting line. No chance of losing a leg. No chance of losing the race either. Like the race in High River, she led the field.

Duchess took to rodeo life. She understood why she was there and loved to compete. That was the key to her success, that she loved barrel racing. She liked to work for me too, but she had one quirk I did not heed—she resented a rider pushing her too hard. She had bucked a jockey off for exactly that. I learned the hard way. I could bat her for speed, but if I overdid it, she retaliated.

At Yorkton, Saskatchewan, the rodeo arena was carved out of

---

[54] A horse "rates" by transferring weight to his hindquarters to prepare to turn.

the infield (the area inside the oval racetrack). Massive chain link gates closed the track off for the rodeo but included a portion of the track in the arena. The barrel pattern was set up at an angle with the third barrel hugging one of the gates. In the first go[55] of the barrel race, Duchess had slowed down before that barrel, costing precious time. I had a chance to use the arena before the second go and I knew what to correct. I loped her through the pattern until we left the second barrel, then batted her all the way to the third to encourage her to run every stride to the barrel. She ran hard, of course, but just before she turned, she had had enough. She dropped her head, rounded her back into a running buck (This time she did prop her front legs!), and spiked me to the ground. According to those who watched, I skidded on the right side of my face to a grinding halt against the bottom of the big chain link gate. I did not get up. I had lost consciousness.

When I opened my eyes, a circle of only-mildly-concerned cowboys looked down at me. (Later, in a feeble attempt at humour, I quipped, "I thought I'd died and gone to heaven.") One helped me to my feet and another caught Duchess, who ran out the other gate and around the track.

Sliding on the right side of my face had peeled skin and ground arena dirt into the abrasions. My neck and back ached from the chug-chug-chug down my spine when I slammed into the fence and my eye turned black, of course. I took the blame for my injuries, though. I got it. Bat Duchess once or twice. No more.

Mae and her two daughters had traveled with me to Yorkton and they were watching me school Duchess from the stands. As I lay unconscious in the arena, Mae jumped up and hollered for help.

"They sure took their time coming," she said.

If Mae thought cowboys complacent in the face of injury, she may have thought we were all *crazy* after the first night in the tent.

Although many contestants owned campers, I did not. We put up our tent on the grassy area back of the chutes, spread straw under the floor for a "mattress", and rolled out sleeping bags. Outside the door, we set a folding table and, on top of it, a Coleman stove for cooking. Around us, other barrel racers, mostly in campers, parked. After the usual visiting, we all went to bed.

Sometime in the night, Mae woke me. "What's that?" she asked.

---

[55] "Go" is a short form for go-around, one barrel racing run at a rodeo with two or more runs.

From the outside, an animal pulled at the straw sticking out of the bottom of the tent. I thought it was a dog. I assured Mae all was well and went back to sleep.

The next morning, Mae mixed pancakes for our five children while I attended to Duchess, tied to the trailer. I looked around. The stock contractor had turned all of the rodeo stock in the infield. We had been sleeping in the midst of horses, steers and *bulls*! Mae was cooking breakfast at our tent with the kids playing around her. I wasn't sure how she would handle this, but I was about to find out.

"Mae, look behind you," said Doreen (another barrel racer) from the door of her camper.

There, a few yards from our cook table, stood a massive Brahma bull, quietly eying her. Mae turned around.

"Oh, I'm used to it now," she answered, flipping flapjacks with unsteady hands.

We had set up our tent on the path to the water trough. All morning a steady procession of bucking horses, steers and bulls paraded past our camp!

Duchess was in the money almost every time at the rodeos in northern Saskatchewan. I was ready to take the next step to tougher competition, the CCA circuit, when she over-reached[56] in her paddock at home and lopped off the bulb of one heel. The injury healed slowly, left an ugly scar, and forced me to cut barrel racing season short.

In the early months of 1974, I started Duchess on a conditioning program in preparation for the barrel racing circuit. Now sound and healthy, I legged her up in the snow for a month or so. I could not school her on barrels, but I believed she knew her job. I was ready to go on the road again. In March, I loaded up for Moose Jaw, two hundred and sixty miles away, for the first Saskatchewan Girls Barrel Racing Association-approved show in conjunction with the spring horse show. Dad went with me to help with Lana, then three years old.

Duchess scored her first approved show win at that show, albeit through the back door. The rider leading the first go, who by all means should have won the aggregate, had a mishap in her second go, leaving Duchess with the win. I was happy enough with her but

---

[56] When a horse over-reaches, the hind foot strides too far forward and hits the back of the front foot.

not ready to say she was a superstar yet.

When I came home from Moose Jaw, spring work at the Community Pasture kept Garry and I tied up until June, when I entered two shows on the same weekend. Duchess won both of them. Next weekend we hauled to Radville and Prince Albert rodeos—first and second! I collected $166 for the win at Prince Albert. In the two weekends, my old books show a total of $459.25 in prize money. That doesn't seem like much now, but the year was 1974. My mare was hot. The end of June I hauled to the Meadow Lake rodeo. The purse[57] was good, so I hoped to add to my earnings. Duchess ran true to form and won the first go. In the finals,[58] we ran reverse seeded[59] order, so I ran last. Duchess watched each horse go through the gate and when it was our turn, she coiled like a spring and ran completely by the first barrel in spite of my efforts to turn her. No prize money that time.

Still, I knew I had a good one. She was fast, quick and smooth, a deadly combination. She did not look as fast as she was because of her long stride. The cowboys watched her (Quite a compliment!) because they could not believe she clocked the time she did. She had a secret though. She did not waste a motion. She ran with flowing, effortless grace, every stride with purpose. Without the automatic timer, many would not have believed the time she posted. The barrel race itself sometimes lasted a mere fifteen seconds, depending on the dimensions of the barrel pattern, but every second was maximum effort and speed. Every millisecond counted. I relied on a straight controlled run from start to finish. Duchess did that.

As she competed at more rodeos, Duchess knew exactly what to expect. She felt the excitement of a race even though I promoted as much relaxation as possible into her warm-up. She stood at the in-gate with every muscle taut, her great heart pounding under my left leg. When we entered the arena, her eyes widened, her nostrils flared, but still she waited for my signal to run. She rarely charged through my hands,[60] so I could keep her straight at the start of the

---

[57] Purse is the total prize money for the event. The purse usually includes a given amount (added money) plus part or all of the entry fees.

[58] The Finals of a competition is the deciding performance of top competitors determined by previous competition at that show.

[59] "Reverse seeded" is a term for the order of go for a performance—reverse order of riders' standing i.e. 10th rider goes first and first rider goes last.

[60] A horse runs "through the hands" when he ignores direction from the rider through the reins (bit).

barrel race. I counted on gaining a little time running in a straight line with very little angle to the first barrel. Many horses need to start at a wide angle to the barrel because the turn is extremely tight, but Duchess did not. She gained time rounding the first this way. The consistency of her turn at the second barrel, the most complete turn of the pattern, and her incredible speed from the third barrel and across the finish line took me to the pay window almost every time.

I had not intended to make a run for the championship in 1974. Most barrel horses cannot handle the pressure of continuous hauling the first year on the circuit. Duchess, however, thrived on competition. I decided to go for gold.

With three children, the youngest three, campaigning wasn't easy. We had a horse trailer now (better for Duchess than hauling in the back of the truck) but no living quarters or camper and no money for hotel, even if I won. Garry could not always go with me, so I traveled alone much of the time. I was on the road almost every weekend and weekdays in the summer. Duchess continued to win and our earnings climbed. She almost never hit a barrel and was usually in the money.[61]

In between rodeos, Cindy rode Duchess and barrel raced her. Cindy had started riding her when she was seven, just a peanut on her back. Duchess adjusted her speed and moves for the little rider. She *loped* around the barrel pattern. She was smooth-gaited anyway, but she carefully repositioned her body if necessary to be under Cindy's weight. Even loping, Duchess and Cindy usually won the class.

Duchess and I led the CCA at the end of the year and secured the championship, a saddle, belt buckle and trophy. It was a prestigious win. We also qualified for the Canadian Finals Rodeo in seventh place and competed in the first year of CFR in Edmonton, Alberta. I was so happy to be there I didn't care if we won money! Unfortunately, Duchess came up with knee lameness and I did not own a back-up barrel racing horse. I almost scratched,[62] but a vet advised me that running her would not injure the knee any more, so I bandaged and ran all six goes. She finished fifth.

Duchess and I had one more competition before winter, the SGBRA Finals held in conjunction with Agribition in Regina in late November.

---

[61] The horse and rider are "in the money" if they win money at the rodeo.

[62] When a competitor scratches, she cancels her entry.

49. 1974 Canadian Cowboys Association Champions.

50. The Canadian Cowboys Association Awards Banquet. Duchess won this saddle, a silver and gold belt buckle and a trophy (November 1974).

51. Duchess and I at the Canadian National Finals Rodeo in Edmonton Alberta. Note wrap on right knee. *Ken Marcinkoski*

Duchess led the standings going in the SGBRA finals but, unlike the Canadian Finals, total money won during the year *including* the finals in Regina determined year-end championship. At the CFR, competitors qualify with total earnings but are equal at the finals (called "sudden death" because the winner of the finals becomes the champion). If I did not compete at the finals in Regina, another barrel racer could overtake my lead in the standings and win the championship.

By now, I was more than mildly concerned about Duchess' subtle lameness. Never happy riding a horse that hurts, especially when the event is as demanding as barrel racing is, I again considered forfeiting the competition, but rules allow girls to substitute horses. I called the Carlsons in Meadow Lake. They owned two grey geldings, neither one of which I had ridden. Teenage girls barrel raced the horses and I had long ago recognized the talent of both. I asked if they would lend me one of the geldings for the finals.

The owner told me the horses were running out, had winter hair and no shoes, but he would be happy to lend Dixie to me. I picked him up, rode him in the snow at home for a few days, loaded both him and Duchess, and headed for Regina. I had one chance to use the arena and walk the horses around barrels prior the competition.

The finals consisted of four runs. We ran in the order of the year-end standings. Since I was leading, I ran first every time. Still hoping Duchess was strong enough, I rode her for the first go, but she was not herself. I had to switch horses.

The girl in second spot for year-end standings won the first go and added to her earnings. She was a hometown girl, completely familiar with and at ease in the arena, as was her horse. She could quite possibly win every go if I could not ride Duchess. If she did that and I did not make any money, she would win the championship, which included the use of a horse trailer for a year and a saddle. If I could keep making money (even if she did, too), I could maintain my lead.

Dixie did his best. He placed fourth for the second go. The third go, with the fastest running time of the show, he tipped the first barrel. It was my fault. I ran him to it the same way I ran Duchess and he did not handle the turn. The hometown girl kept winning and she was closing the gap between us in the year-end standings. I knew exactly what I had to do the last day. I had to win the go.

I phoned my husband the night before the final run.

"I may have lost the championship," I said. "Dixie has to win tomorrow and Jamie has to be third. If she is second, she is year-end leader and champion."

Dixie and I ran first and posted a fast time. Jamie ran second and did not run faster but was only hundredths of a second behind. As I waited through the remaining eight riders, I prayed for a time splitting our running times. One girl did that but tipped a barrel. I had to settle for the reserve championship. I believe the difference in our earnings at the end of 1974 was twelve dollars.

Duchess needed a rest. X-rays revealed bone chips and calcium deposits in her right knee. I should not have used her for the fall championship runs. I turned her out to run the hills and one year later, x-rayed again. The calcium deposits had absorbed. Duchess was sound.

Garry and I took a giant step of our own in 1976. We bought a piece of land adjacent to Crooked River Community Pasture and made plans to develop it and move. We bought a house trailer, built a barn and moved the livestock. The move was complicated by an accident. Just before we moved the end of July, Garry and I competed in the Nipawin Horse Show and entered the Gretna Green Race. The race involved one rider (me) racing to pick up another (Garry) and running back, first team back over the starting line wins. We had run the race several times on Cheetah, who was both fast and small enough for Garry to mount easily and quickly. We decided to use Duchess, practicing riding double[63] around the barns before the race. She offered no objection to the extra rider.

I lined up with the other riders. A hundred yards or so down the track, our "passengers" waited in another line. When the whistle blew, Duchess and I dashed to Garry, but he took more time than he should have jumping on. Two riders had already left before he was in position. Straddling Duchess behind me, he wrapped his arms around my waist as I leaned over her neck and asked for more speed. We were gaining on the lead horses when Duchess took exception to Garry over her loins, started to buck, and eliminated the problem. Out of the corner of my right eye, I saw Garry land on his feet, his ankle turn and the knees of another horse hit him square in the back. The horse sent him sprawling and ran over him. I regained control of Duchess immediately but too late to help Garry. He broke ribs and an ankle and underwent abdominal surgery in Saskatoon that evening. A few days later, with the help of friends and neighbours, I moved our belongings from the Community Pasture to our new property. Garry was laid up for two months.

I hauled Duchess a bit in 1976 prior to Garry's accident and she felt as good as ever, but I believed the stress of a full year on the circuit would be too much for her knee. I had bought a big palomino gelding, Major's Aquarius, for a replacement barrel racing horse and in 1977, I bred Duchess to Seco.

---

[63] Riding double is the phrase for two riders riding one horse, one rider in the saddle and one behind the saddle.

Duchess was, without doubt, the best mare I had owned and obviously should leave a legacy. My decision to breed her was, in my mind, a turning point in her life, but if I considered her career as broodmare the last chapter, I was wrong. She had much more to do. Duchess would found a dynasty of Wildwood Quarter Horses.

52. Duchess and a few of The Dynasty she founded (1999).

53. Duchess, Mahogany, Tamarac and Tamarac's first six fillies (1999).

A Life With Horses

Horse Training, Horsemanship and Horses

*If you have seen nothing but the beauty of their markings and
limbs, their true beauty is hidden from you.*
~ *Author Unknown*

My horse training knowledge, thus far, had evolved from
practical experience—a growing horse business and work
on the Community Pasture—but I wanted more. I read books and
articles in magazines; I listened to horsemen and horsewomen I
admired; I watched how others handled horses. I soaked up horse
training information wherever I could find it and started to see what
worked and what did not. I tried different methods, retained what I
liked and discarded the rest until I developed a program that worked
for me.

With new foals arriving every year, it didn't take long to realize I
needed a plan to stay on top of my game. If I offered horses for sale,
I needed to be sure they were *ready* for sale, so I established a

routine and stuck to it. I halter trained the foal in the summer of his first year using the method I had been taught at home, the important difference being he was not a long yearling! I roped the foal to halter, wrapped the shank around a stout post and took up slack[64] until I could tie to the post. The baby fought, of course, but I stayed with the foal and eventually, after jerking backwards and leaping forward many times, he stood with lead shank loose. (A strong halter was important because if it broke, the training went the other direction.) At that point, I untied and asked him to lead, only a step at first, and rewarded by loosening the shank and petting. When he accepted my handling, I touched his face and smoothed my hands over his neck, back, rump, belly and legs. Then I picked up the feet one at a time until he would stand relaxed for a few seconds (*only a few seconds*) with his foot in my hand.

Now, I work with foals earlier and have revised my program to an even gentler method. I first teach the foal to be "encased" by my hands like this: Standing on the left side of the foal, I place my left arm under and around his neck with very light contact and my right arm behind his rump. I maintain only soft contact, trapping the baby lightly between my arms. If I use force, the foal will jump out. When he is accustomed to this "box", very minimal pressure with my left arm (if he wants to go forward) or fingers pushing on his rump (if he wants to go back) will keep him between my arms so well I can push him anywhere I want. At a month old, I halter and lead, usually with a rope around the rump (which takes the place of my arm). I can usually control the situation by myself by controlling the head with my left hand and the bum rope with my right, even leading the mother at the same time. Of course, my mares are used to the method too. . .

I did not handle the foals after the summer halter lesson until weaning, when I offered a refresher course. In their yearling year, besides hoof trimming and worming, I taught them to lead off another horse, the "ponying" I referred to earlier. Leading from another horse was an important part of training. Work in pastures and around the corral required leading horses from another and it was maddening to be in the middle of the job dragging a horse that

---

[64] "Take up the slack" is a phrase for gathering up rope between the horse and the post by pulling as it loosened.

should have been leading. Half hitching[65] the lead shank around the horn wasn't safe (tied solid or "hard and fast"), but dallying (not tied solid) helped. Still, it could be quite a fight. That's the reason ponying was part of the colt's training as a yearling.

If we had not sold the colts by the time they turned two years old, I rode them. I did not start them at the beginning of their two-year-old year, as is the custom now. Usually, the riding began in late summer or early fall. When I could ride the colts without bucking or running off, they sold better. If they didn't sell, I always had work for them on the ranch.

I was impressed with our Quarter Horses. They were intelligent, quiet, athletic and very trainable. The combination of strength and athleticism would have been dangerous if they had been nasty, but the Quarter Horses I raised and trained must have been gentle, because the colts I started under saddle in these years did not hurt me. Though my memory is probably faulty, I do not remember one throwing me, though I do recall a ride that scared me.

I had started riding Coteau Cameo, one of Kitten's fillies by Beggar. I wanted to keep her. The little sorrel mare was pretty and had a fire in her that appealed to me. She was coming three[66] but small. Training had started late and now winter had arrived in Crooked River. Because I was constantly dealing with excess energy, I hoped riding in a flat covered by two feet of snow would help.

It was very cold. Skidoo suits were just becoming popular (Wish I had had one of those when I was riding to school!) and Garry had one, so I put it on. It rustled when I walked and Cameo's eyes lit up as I approached her, but I got on anyway. As soon as my seat swished into the saddle, she bolted, charging through the gate into the field of snow. The skidoo suit crackled with every jump. I could not stop the noise, of course, and the more she jumped, the worse it was. The leather reins slipped through the heavy mitts I wore and my butt slid around in the saddle. I circled the flat and, with one tense step after another and a lot of "easy" and "whoa", made my way back to the barn in a cloud of steam, mine and Cameo's.

"I don't need this skidoo suit anymore," I told Garry as I unzipped.

---

[65] A half hitch is a knot or hitch made by looping a rope around an object, then back around itself, bringing the end of the rope through the loop. Usually used with a second half hitch.

[66] "Coming three" is a phrase describing a horse not yet three years old, but who soon will be.

I owe my horses of these years a debt of gratitude. The art of horsemanship is an ongoing process and I made many mistakes. The horses themselves taught me how to be better. I learned consistency is everything. If I repeated a lesson the same way, my horse learned the lesson quicker. I learned there are more stubborn riders than stubborn horses. I learned about timing. I learned to be patient. Most of all I learned there is always more to learn.

Training my horses was a lot of trial and error. A background of horses and many hours in the saddle helped, but there was more. I had opened a door a crack, caught a glimpse of what was on the other side and wanted it. In these years I felt the first stirrings of a deeper connection than I thought possible with the animal I had always loved. This thread would not be broken.

Garry and I steadily built our herd of Quarter Horses. We crossed Seco Top Moon with Kit Mae, Lynn's Queen, Jay Bee's Searra and Cameo. Quarter Horses were extremely popular. We had no difficulty selling the babies, allowing us to reinvest in new ones. We bred for speed with athletic ability and, to that end, in 1975, bought Miss Cameo Jet (by Rovin' Jet by Jet Deck), two daughters of Lightning War and Jodella (Depth Charge breeding). I spotted Jodella at a Quarter Horse show . . . in a Western Pleasure class! She looked like she should be on a racetrack, not in a show ring, and I bought her on the spot. She was bay, about 15.2 hands, three years old and definitely a barrel racing prospect.

I knew Jodella could run, but I tested her speed. Meadow Lake Rodeo always hosted a Quarter Horse flat race. I had run the race on Major's Aquarius, the big palomino gelding I had picked up for a barrel horse. Now I entered Jodella. (My excuse for entering flat races with my barrel horses was "to see if they can run".) I knew the race would be tough for it was a popular event among the riders there and they ran good, fast horses.

Keeping with Quarter Horse standards, officials sectioned off two hundred yards of a half-mile oval track, the longest possible straight stretch. Entered in the race were two grey geldings I knew well. One was Dixie, the barrel horse I had borrowed for the SGBRA finals. Both horses were very fast. I had the utmost respect for them. It was going to be a horse race!

Nine horses showed up at the start line. An official had drawn names out of a hat for positions—grey in number seven position, Jodella in eight, grey in nine.

To win the race, I knew Jodella had to be the quickest off the starting line, so I brought my barrel racing bat. With a standing start at a line across the track, horses fidgeted, but Jodella and the greys were straight. When the starter said, "go", I batted. Jodella left the line first, but I was not at all sure she could stay there. I could see a grey nose on either side. I leaned over her neck and focused on the finish line. For all of the two hundred yards, nothing changed. All three horses maintained positions with Jodella in the lead. It was a thrilling victory.

Shayne and Cindy had watched the race from a perch on the fence surrounding the track. When I rode back to them, I was more excited about the win than the seventy-five dollar prize.

"Did you see Jodella? Did you see her win?"

"Yes," Cindy said, "but why did you run all the way around the track?"

She was right. I ran the entire oval pulling Jodella back to a walk.

I would not have bet on a rerun of the race. The grey geldings were indeed very fast. Their riders were young and probably not prepared for what I asked of Jodella at the start line. Another day, the outcome could have been different.

54. Jodella. Note deep heart girth and long underline.

I continued training Jodella for barrels and hauled her to a few rodeos, but she was not the barrel horse Duchess was. She had tremendous speed, but I struggled to control that speed running at the level required to compete in approved rodeos. Cindy had always liked Jodella—they had a connection—so we sold Ebony and gave Jodella to her. Cindy rode many happy hours on "Jo", although she lives with "washboard shins" from barrel racing days on her.

55. Jodella and I running barrels at home.

In 1976, Garry and I leaped into the world of racing Quarter Horses. We had bought racing-bred Quarter Horses (Duchess and Seco) but racing was too new to Canada and it was difficult, if not impossible, to earn a racing record for our horses. We needed an already-proven stallion.

We loved Duchess, so I researched AQHA for all sons of her sire, Pasamonte Paul, that were rated on the track. There were not many and some were not for sale. Eventually, we settled on Pas Paul Pas. I talked to his owner on the phone and I liked what I heard. Paul was a bit of a "Cinderella story". His owner had begged and borrowed money to buy him and race him. Garry flew to Oklahoma to see the bay stallion and made the purchase. Hard to believe now, but I stayed home.

56. Pas Paul Pas. 350 yards 18.62 (1968). *Ralph Morgan*

57. Pas Paul Pas. *Ralph Morgan*

Pas Paul Pas, Superior Race Horse, TAAA at six distances, had set track records in Texas and won numerous bush races. He was everything we wanted—bay, about 15 hands, with a quiet eye and fantastic disposition. He was so kind, in fact, I did something with him I should not have done with any stallion.

We pastured our broodmares in a small field a hundred yards from the barn. Every other day I checked them with Pas Paul Pas to keep track of reproduction cycles and breed the mares when it was time. At first, I led Paul to the mares, but sometimes it meant walking to the back of the field. Some things don't change. I still hated to walk, leading a horse, so I *rode* him to the mares in the field bareback, got off, checked the mares, bred a mare if one was ready, and rode back to the barn. I could do that because he was so easy to handle. However, I have since realized the folly of my ways. I do not recommend the method and would never handle a stallion like this now, even with a disposition as gentle and kind as that of Pas Paul Pas.

We bred our mares and waited for results. In the summer of 1976, Paul moved with Seco and the rest of our horses to our new property. The next spring the first Pas Paul Pas babies arrived, beautiful Quarter Horses bred to run but with the athletic ability and brains to be any kind of horse we might need—ranch horses, rope horses, barrel racing horses. However, as our horse business thrived, our marriage did not. In the summer of 1977, Garry and I separated. By mutual agreement, I stayed with Shayne, Cindy, and Lana on the property we had so recently purchased. With us resided my dogs (I bred Samoyeds.), two stallions, several mares, foals and young stock.

Part 3

Horses and Training in Saskatchewan

The horse will leap over trenches, will jump out of them, will do anything else, provided one grants him praise and respite after his accomplishment. ~ Xenophon

Building a Business with Horses

"He's not going to look back if you don't," he said, "they're the most
forgiving creatures God ever made."
~ Nicholas Evans, "The Horse Whisperer"

On my own with three children, several horses and no money,
I thought long and hard about my options. I must earn a
living, but I had not worked outside my home except on the
Community Pastures. I *had* worked with horses. I had bred, raised
and trained horses. I had spent hours pouring over horse books and
magazines, brainstormed with other horse people and researched. I
knew the horse business. Training horses would be hard work, but I
was young and strong. Best of all, I would be at home for my
children.

So, on my small property in the unlikely location of Crooked
River, Saskatchewan, Wildwood Training (later changed to
Wildwood Reining Horses) was born. I had pastures, a big barn and

a patch of summerfallowed ground to ride on, all I needed for my business. I would breed, train, show and sell horses.

When Garry and I separated, we offered most of our Quarter Horses for sale, holding back three apiece. Garry took Pas Paul Pas, Tacoma Maid, and a young Seco Top Moon mare. I kept Seco, Duchess and a young Pas Paul Pas mare, Spirit. Cindy's mare, Jodella, also stayed with me. We had to sell our cattle too, but I kept a young Charolais range cow with a late calf for my milk cow. Our milk cow had died and I couldn't imagine not having our own milk. Over the first winter after Garry moved out, I kept her in the barn because if I turned her out I would not get her back in. I tied a back leg to the stall post when I milked her so I wouldn't get my head kicked off. My neighbour told me I had "more nerve than Dick Tracy", but I needed the milk, cream and butter she could provide.

Over the next two years I cared for, advertised, and eventually sold, the mares, foals and yearlings jointly owned by Garry and me.

I wanted to build up my herd again with my three mares and Seco. I hoped Duchess, already bred, would foal out a black filly, a perfect beginning for my new business and new life. She didn't let me down. Wildwood Majesty, a tiny ebony filly with a star and white socks, arrived in the spring of 1978, the first of many quality Quarter Horses to carry a "Wildwood" name.

I needed income from as many aspects of the horse business as possible. Seco contributed with breeding fees to outside mares and my mares produced sale prospects. I rode for the rest, but since I did not have an indoor arena and winters in Crooked River are long and cold, I could not guarantee my work to my clients from December to March. Though I rode my own horses in winter, ground conditions were doubtful at best and impossible at worst. For at least four months a year, I could not accept horses for training. The rest of the year, I worked to capacity, taking as many training horses as I could ride in the daylight.

I was in business. True, the facility lacked some of the amenities that would have made training horses easier and safer, like a round pen to start colts or an enclosed area to ride in, but I had a barn with a dirt alley and big stalls with dirt floors. That's where I often mounted a horse for the first time—in the stall. I progressed to the alley (with both barn doors closed) but could not accomplish much real training in the barn. After two or three days, the trainee "graduated" to open spaces.

58. My house trailer at Crooked River, Saskatchewan.

59. Barn on Crooked River property (photo taken at house trailer).

A dirt trail ran between the barn and house yards and the unfenced plot of ground I called my arena. Behind a row of young willow south of the arena, was my hay field. A wagon wheel-fenced lawn edged by lilacs on one side and a long flowerbed on the other defined the house yard, the barn area about a hundred yards east. A grove of tall poplar marking the junction of four properties sheltered

129

my house trailer, tucked in the northwest corner of my acreage. Quarter section grain fields butted up to the corner from the north, west, and the northwest, separated by thin to non-existent rows of brushy poplar. On various horses, in a variety of circumstances, I toured all three properties. In 1980, I built a small round pen that saved my neighbours' fields.

60. Aerial view of my yard in Crooked River.

I charged two hundred dollars per month, which included board for the horse, and I accepted every kind, even ones who had not even had a halter on. There was no shortage of horses to train, but most were in training only thirty days. It amazed me what a horse learned in the first month of training. A client brought me a colt that had not been ridden and twenty rides later, I could walk, jog, trot and lope the horse, move him off my legs and back him up. I sent him home bathed, clipped, conditioned and ride-able.

Although most horses were dependable and *safe for me* at the end of the month, I could not guarantee the horse would be safe for the owner to ride. I rode five times a week (sometimes more often) and I knew it was unlikely the owner would. I gave the horse something to do when I was on him whereas the owner might simply walk down the road or across a field. My "thirty day wonders" were going to be "seven day wrecks" if they did not stay on a training program. I understood this completely and in no way blamed the customer—it was why I had a job—but I encouraged them to leave the horse in training longer. Few did.

Horses of all descriptions and breeds came and went in the next few years. Many were of mixed parentage and sometimes unknown age, but I trained many purebred horses too. Arabians were popular in the area, and I started several. I liked the Arabians though many thought them flighty and high-strung. Arabians seldom bucked, but one trait I found frustrating—the way the Arabian used his body when spooked. Unlike Quarter Horses, who spin around on their hindquarters, the Arabians I rode turned on the front. I found the move maddeningly difficult to sit well. The breed is capable of splendid use of hindquarter muscle but often need to learn.

A Morgan breeder sent me several of her registered horses for training. She did not ride much herself, and wisely wanted her horses trained. Ash, an agreeable chestnut gelding, was the first. He was the kind of horse I might have forgotten—easy to train, no problems. I think I only had him a month. I have more reason to remember the next two she dropped off at Wildwood.

Hope, a two-year-old palomino mare, arrived loose in a stock trailer. She had never been haltered. We backed the trailer up to the barn door, unloaded her into the barn alley, and guided her into a box stall.

In the next two or three days, Hope learned to lead. Then I took her to the round pen and worked her there. I round penned[67] her, saddled her and lunged her before I got on. She bolted.

In the round pen, she had nowhere to run except around the outside. At least that's what I thought. I tried to guide her head toward the middle of the pen so she would not think of jumping over the top rail, but she didn't respond to the bit. No surprise with only limited groundwork. She ran and bucked for a few seconds, then turned, dived straight across the pen, and put her head between her knees. I flipped over her neck and smacked the rails with my back.

Determined and ready to get on again, I jumped up. The first step changed my mind. She had hurt me. I would not be effective and she would learn the wrong lesson if she bucked me off again. Contrary to everything I believed, I put her back in the stall.

I was sore for a few days, but when I saddled Hope next time neither one of us had forgotten the first lesson. I knew what to expect and she knew what worked for her. I had to have a plan.

---

[67] "Round penned" is a term used to describe working a horse in the confines of a round pen.

I lunged her and stepped on. My seat barely touched leather when she bolted again, but this time I *asked* her to go. If I could keep her in forward motion, she would not be able to buck hard. It worked. She was not having half as much fun after twenty laps of the round pen! Hope was not safe for most people to ride when her owner picked her up, but for thirty days, I had the upper hand.

Bourbon, a black Morgan stallion from the same breeder, was not a problem to ride, but he would not lope quietly in a circle. He circled all right, but at a run. The grain field by the yard was summerfallow, and I had patterned a large circle there in the deep footing. The heavy ground was an advantage because the horse had to work harder but could be a disadvantage if open space gave him a sense of freedom he did not have in an enclosed area. Of course, my arena was not fenced anyway. The circle in the field was a good training tool and that's where I took Bourbon.

I had a solution for horses that would not lope a circle and I tried it on the young stallion. He was good in the bridle, but I had been coping with his overabundance of energy long enough. I trotted the circle a few times, then asked him to lope. Instantly he accelerated and this time I did not try to restrain him. I used only enough inside rein to keep him circling. I planned to allow him the freedom to run at his chosen speed until he slowed down of his own volition.

In my mind, (thinking like the horse and appealing to the lazy side of the animal), Bourbon would quickly see the futility of expending massive energy running in circles, but I had already taught him I would restrain him when he pulled at the bit to run. He *welcomed* the freedom. We raced around the circle. I tugged and released the inside rein to keep him in the circle, and rode it out. He ran faster. I resisted the temptation to draw back on the reins, but I was getting tired . . . and worried! I didn't want to hurt him. Finally, I felt a slight decrease of speed, exactly what I was looking for. I asked him to step it up. He did but slowed again. I asked for one more circle, and allowed him to walk. The next day, when we loped, he was off again. I did not touch the reins. He ran hard for one circle, and then loped like a pleasure horse. He never did it again.

I usually had at least one Quarter Horse in training. One of these, Crimson Pixie, was an exception to the "thirty-day rule". Her owner booked her for a several months of training so I could show her.

Showing halter and pleasure did not excite me like barrel racing, but Pixie was bred for those classes and her owner wanted her shown, so that's what I did—I trained and showed what the customer wanted. I gained valuable experience in those disciplines from Pixie.

Though Pixie was a beautiful mare, she had a mind of her own. When she did not want to perform, she refused, flat out refused! She detested leaving the yard. I insisted. When we returned to the arena, Pixie thought jogging around the rail was wonderful!

61. Crimson Pixie and I at Connaught Fair, Saskatchewan.

Luckily, I figured the mare out. I used the basic training program I always used but never lost sight of the goal, a pleasure horse with impeccable behaviour on the rail of the show pen. I chose the location for battles—anywhere but the rail! Before a class at a show, I worked her in the middle of the pen while other riders lazily walked and jogged on the rail. I could see the frowns on their faces.

"What is she doing?"

"She doesn't need *that* for a pleasure class!"

"That mare is loping much too fast for pleasure!"

I continued to work my program in the middle of the show pen. When I joined the others on the rail, I was as good to Pixie as I knew how to be. She loved the rail! I kept it that way. If she ever learned differently, I would not be able to show her.

I had not forgotten my barrel racing background. Although I could not go on the road, I could "chase cans" once in a while at home and most often I rode a Quarter Horse. If the client expressed interest in barrel racing and the horse was trained enough to start on barrels, I jumped at the chance.

One year I bought a barrel racing prospect. It was a planned venture, a conscious decision to buy a young horse to train and sell, but finding the right horse for the right price was harder than I thought it would be. I learned I was fussy. Usually, after arranging a viewing, I knew I would not buy when I first laid eyes on the horse. Finally, I found and purchased a good one. His name was Kaliberry Chance.

Chance didn't knock me over with good looks but, on further inspection, I could not fault him. His pretty head and kind eye attracted me first. At three years old, the good-legged, sorrel gelding's real value surfaced as training progressed. I started him in the fall, rode him a little in the snow, and trained him on barrels the next summer. He wanted to please and liked to run barrels. In the fall of his four-year-old year, I advertised him as "ready to run" and told a friend of mine, "The first person that tries him will buy him." Such a statement was unusual for me, but it was true. A girl saw the ad, drove to my yard, rode him and hauled him home. Chance sold for $3000, good return on my $800 investment, I thought, but if I had totaled feed and training, I would have been lucky to break even. Chance contributed in another way. He boosted my confidence in my ability to select a good prospect.

In the next few years, there would be a few barrel racing prospects in my barn. My own Wildwood Willow, sorrel daughter of Duchess, was one of the best. If I had thought I could ever compete again, I would have kept Willow. I trained her on barrels but sold her because I could not go on the road. She became a top barrel racing horse. Barrel racing was not out of my blood yet, nor would it ever be.

I rode in rain, snow, wind and heat. In the summer, every kind of nasty bug imaginable bit my horse and me as we walked, jogged, and loped circles in the oval in my hay field. Horse flies, black flies and sand flies bit hard, driving the horses crazy, and the horses struck and reared at the nose flies, but the mosquitoes were the worst. They blackened my horse's neck leaving a bloody trail when I wiped them away, and chewed a line of angry bumps on my forehead under the peak of my cap. I felt sorry for the horses. I sprayed before I left the barn, but it didn't help much. A battalion of biting bugs forced me to work at faster gaits and I couldn't walk the horses to cool them down without a full-fledged attack. I built smudges for the horses in the pasture, but the ones I rode were at the mercy of the bugs.

62. Wildwood Willow (daughter of Duchess) in 1983.

The roots of Wildwood Reining Horses are deep in that patch of dirt in northern Saskatchewan. In the winter, I rode my own horses; from March to November, I rode clients' horses. From each, I learned. I showed at open and Quarter Horse shows in all classes. From each show, each class, I learned.

Sometimes I brought Seco or Jodella to barrel race, but my barrel racing career was over. I still had an opportunity to work cattle, though. I lived only a mile from the Community Pasture and I eagerly accepted any employment there. Roundups and pasture work provided excellent training for the colts and put a few dollars in my pockets too.

Though I no longer milked a cow, I still grew a huge garden, canned, baked all my bread and raised a beef each year to ease the cost of living. My business, if not booming, was at least making a living for my children and me. Though independent and working a job I truly loved, I was looking for a new challenge. I had ranched, barrel raced, and started colts. My horses and I were ready to advance to another discipline.

A Life With Horses

Reining In My Life

*It takes a little courage to ride beyond the status quo, but with each
stride, the view along that road becomes more and more exquisite.*
~ Leslie Desmond, Horse Handling and Riding Through the Feel

I developed a keen interest in reining in 1979. I had watched
the event some years earlier but did not like the way trainers
manhandled horses through maneuvers. The reining I saw now was
prettier, the horse more willing. He *wanted* to spin; he *wanted* to
stop. He reined because he *wanted to, not because he had to.*

"If reining can be done like that, count me in," I said. In
February 1980, a single phone call pivoted my life with horses in a
new direction.

I knew Vern and Molly Sapergia from Saskatchewan Cutting
Horse Association days. They operated a horse training facility south
of Moose Jaw and showed clients' horses in shows all over
Saskatchewan. Vern was making a name for himself in the reining
world. In fact, his performances had opened my eyes to the changes
in the reining event. Vern's horses performed the difficult maneuvers
with finesse. Fluid softness replaced jarring roughness. I wanted my

horses to rein like that, so I boldly asked if he could teach me.

"I want to learn to rein," I said to Vern, "but I don't have money for lessons. If you and Molly have work for me, I can pay that way." They agreed.

Mom and Dad stayed with my children and horses at home and, in March, I loaded Seco and hauled three hundred miles to the Sapergia ranch. For two weeks, I absorbed reining. I observed. I listened. I rode. On Vern's trained reiners, I felt the exhilaration of a horse spinning, the smoothness of a lead change executed with finesse, and the power of a deep-in-the-ground sliding stop. I was hooked!

From six o'clock in the morning until late at night, I was part of their world. When we weren't riding, we were feeding, cleaning stalls or breeding mares. I asked questions nonstop and practiced what I learned on Seco. For the first week, I was on "information overload", but slowly it all began to make sense. I took the fundamentals of reining home with me and something else—a renewed friendship. I had competed with Vern and Molly in the sixties. Though much had changed, a common thread still connected us—horses. Similar interests had led us back to the same path. We all loved the reining horse.

When I returned from Sapergia's, I couldn't wait to try out my newfound knowledge. Unfortunately, other than Seco, who was not reining material, I did not have a horse in the barn with enough training to rein. The horses coming to me had not been started and most stayed only a month, not long enough to begin reining training. That's when fate stepped in and helped me in the name of a little grey Arabian gelding called Dark Mo.

In the previous year, I had started Mo for friends of mine, Bob and Janet. He was a wonderful little horse—quiet, friendly and willing. I rode him a month, then turned him out to pasture. A mere two days later, I found him standing on three legs. He would not put any weight on a front leg and hopped to the barn. X-rays revealed a hairline fracture of the pastern. We were devastated—prognosis for fractures in horses is not good—but he cooperated so well (mostly by not standing on the leg) that the break healed. In the spring of 1980, after my two-week crash course in reining, Mo came back to me sound . . . and he wanted to be a reining horse!

I approached Mo's owners and they agreed to continue training with the goal the hackamore reining class in the Saskatchewan

Stakes and Futurities in October. I was ecstatic. I had a reiner!

Mo absolutely loved to be ridden. What I lacked in experience, he made up for in natural talent. At 14.2 hands and compact, his conformation suited reining. I did not have good ground for sliding stops, but he stopped anyway, the true mark of a reining horse. He changed leads effortlessly. (Good thing because I didn't have much of a lead change program!) Far away from any help, I muddled through on my own with an occasional call to Vern. In September, about a month before the show, I hauled to Sapergia's for more instruction. Mo's spins were not good and I was stuck. Two days later, we headed home with better understanding.

I could not float under the radar at the Saskatchewan Stakes and Futurities. In a world of Quarter Horses, Mo was the only Arabian and he looked every bit the part. Other competitors teased me about my choice of breed, which didn't bother me, but I was very, very nervous about competing. Just as Mo stood out as a minority breed, I stood out as a newcomer in a field of experienced reiners. I was positive I should not have entered.

Mo exhibited none of my stress. Relaxed and happy, his confidence bolstered mine. I learned a truth from him: *A horse will do what he has been trained to do if given the chance to do it.*

The competition was decided by two goes. As I exited the arena after the first, strength drained from my legs, from stress and emotion, not physical effort. I leaned against Mo's grey, sweaty neck for support when I got off. Mo and I had been far from perfect.

That was not good. Too many mistakes.

Due to a malfunction of some kind, no one announced the scores until four or five competitors had completed their patterns. Several people congratulated me, but I thought they were just being kind. Although on pattern, Mo and I had made errors.

Later, when I watched the video, I finally figured it out. Perfect reining patterns are rare. Mo placed second in that go-around and third in the aggregate at the show. In a yellowed newspaper clipping I still have are these words:

> Another great little hackamore horse was Dark Mo. He was at Moose Jaw representing the Arabian breed and he literally stole the heart of every reiner there as he slid and spun, rolled back and circled the arena with class and confidence.

I could not have been prouder of Mo if he had been mine.

63. Dark Mo at play. I took this photo in my yard. I often turned Mo out to graze there in the day.

After training and showing Mo, I focused even more on reining. I still started many horses for my clients, and every one I checked out for reining ability. I knew not many of my customers would be willing to leave a horse in training with me long enough to finish for reining as Mo's owners had. If I wanted to rein, I would have to look to my own horses for a prospect. I set my sights on Wildwood Mahogany.

Mahogany was born the same year I competed with Mo. Sired by Seco out of Duchess, the pretty bay mare with three socks and a star, strip and snip, was refined and dainty. Not a carbon copy of either her sire or her dam, but a combination of the two, she showed the conformation of a racehorse, slightly long-backed like Duchess, with a swan-like neck that reminded me of Seco's, only better. To this day, I have not seen a better neck and throatlatch on any of my horses. Mahogany would be my next reining horse.

While Mahogany grew up, my reining education must continue, for it was far from complete. I showed Mo in reining classes at Arabian and open shows and he was a dream! He impressed everyone, especially me, with his talent. Most importantly, he instilled in me the necessary confidence and experience I needed to enter the reining pen.

64. Mo and I in a Trail Class.

65. I showed Mo in a variety of classes. Here we are in Saddle Seat in an Arabian show in Melfort, Saskatchewan. He did not place in this class, but he won the Arabian Reining later at this show.

Mo came to my barn just prior to another male figure entering my life. Henry and I had known each other since I moved to Crooked River, but our paths had not crossed for some time. In late 1980, a chance meeting at a community dance and a renewed friendship blossomed into a loving relationship that would last several years.

66. Henry and I in my yard.

Henry, a former RCMP, now farmed a few miles from me. He did not own even one horse and had very little interest in riding, but he supported my lifestyle . . . and came to my assistance! He never complained even if the problem was horse-related.

"How do you manage to have flat tires in my yard or mechanical problems just down the road?" Sometimes breakdowns happened farther away than that.

Connaught Fair: I knew I would have to make two trips to the grounds with the trailer. The evening before the show, I hauled two horses. On the return trip, around a long sweeping turn, I glanced in the rear view mirror and saw fluid on the highway that appeared to be leaking out of my truck. Even my limited knowledge of all things mechanical told me I should not drive any farther. I stopped and got out.

A liquid substance (which turned out to be transmission fluid) pooled under my truck and ribboned the highway as far back around the corner as I could see.

I have to call Henry.

Depending on the kindness of strangers to get word to Henry, I waited for a motorist to stop, and asked him to phone. Henry towed my truck to his shop and worked all night to get me back on the road with the second load of horses early the next morning!

Swan River Fair: On another "horse show run", the drive shaft fell out of my truck on the way to Swan River, Manitoba. The breakdown occurred a few hundred feet from a garage a few miles from my home, so I phoned the mechanic there and asked him to tow the truck, jumped my horses in a girlfriend's trailer and left. I phoned Henry later to tell him what had happened and to ask him to "please pick up my truck and trailer" and meet me in Hudson Bay, sixty miles from home, on the day I returned. Of course, he did.

Henry may not have had the passion for horses I had, but he respected my business. He once told me he previously viewed horse owners as frivolous and silly about their animals.

"I can see you're not like that," he said. "Horses are a real business."

Hmmm... Right about Wildwood (It *is* a business.) but about my relationship with my horses. . .?

67. Cindy on Mo, Shayne on Concho, a friend on Duchess. I sometimes took my children and others on trail rides. This is one of those rides.

In November 1982, one of my clients agreed to send her three-year-old mare, Bobby, and me to a Guy Gauthier clinic in Beechy. The mare was talented and I believed she would rein. Guy had stunned his competition in the U.S. and Canada in his limited career. I was fortunate to have a chance to learn from him, but winter was upon me when I returned, so I had little opportunity to apply his expertise. Mahogany was two years old and started. I rode her a little in the snow-covered fields, and waited for spring.

Mahogany was bred to run, not rein, but she was what I had and I planned to show her in the 1983 Saskatchewan Stakes and Futurities. I rode her all summer. It was the first time for a long time I had one of my own horses in training. Because I needed to ride paying horses, mine were on the back burner. This time, though, I kept Mahogany on a reining program.

Unfortunately, Mahogany did not finish the year. I aborted my plan for the futurity in September when she developed an unexplainable condition similar to tying up.[68] I was sure I had stressed her with training although Vern couldn't believe it. I quit riding her. Reining would wait. In later years, we competed at many shows.

68. Wildwood Mahogany (Duchess x Seco Top Moon) in 1982.

---

[68] Tying up is a medical condition characterized by profuse sweating, rapid pulse, stiffness of gait, and tense muscles, associated with exercise after a period of rest,

A customer with good Quarter Horses had brought me a two-year-old mare that year. He was willing to take April all the way to reining futurities and wanted me to ride her. I started her in the fall and planned for the next year.

April's conformation *screamed* "reining horse"—clean-limbed, balanced, muscled and very athletic. She had eye appeal too—blood bay with coppery highlights and a "Look at me!" presence. No one would miss April in the pen. She was hot, a character trait not particularly good for reining, but we were convinced she would perform when it counted.

I liked April and admired her tenacity. Sometimes, though, that same character trait embarrassed me as it did in the horse show in Swan River.

I hauled her to a few shows in the summer for experience. I did not enter her in reining, but I thought pleasure classes would be good for her. The Swan River class was large and the ring small. I had made three or four rounds on the rail when I knew I should not be there. April's muscles knotted under my legs. Horses crowded her and she jittered and bounced. Not only was I not going to win anything, I was going to disrupt the class. I needed to leave.

I signaled the judge to request permission to leave the pen and he motioned me into the middle. Not exactly what I had in mind. I hoped I could disappear out the gate!

I did not show April in the fall. I thought she could do better with someone else and I advised my client to send her to Vern to finish and show at the Saskatchewan Stakes and Futurities. They both protested, but I wanted the mare to have the best chance. I had had a frustrating problem with April's stops. One time she would slide thirty feet and the next time she would run right through the stop[69] when I said "whoa". I hoped Vern would have more luck. He didn't, but he discovered a trick to getting her shown. If he did not say "whoa" and eased himself out of the saddle a bit as if to get off, she buried her butt. (Reminds me of how Harold and I stopped our horses when we rode without bridles or saddles!) Apparently, April had learned a negative connotation to the word. At some point in her life, someone had punished her while saying "whoa". She panicked if she heard the word. She stopped best without a verbal command.

---

[69] "Run through the stop" is a phrase describing a horse who completely ignores the rider's requests to stop and continues to run.

April placed eighth in the futurity. I later heard she was a cracking good barrel horse. Guess reining was not her thing.

Mahogany, though not a superstar reiner, suffered through my learning pains with others. Later she raised one of the best reining mares I have ever owned. The pedigree of most of the broodmares, reining horses, working cow horses, and reining prospects I have today can be traced back to Mahogany. She is a crucial link in my breeding program.

69. Mahogany and I go English in Swan River, Manitoba (1982).

70. Mahogany and I winning Trail Class in Hudson's Bay, Saskatchewan.

I could not know what the future held as I rode my heart out in north central Saskatchewan in the 80's. I took one day at a time. I was healthy, my family was healthy and I was making a living doing what I loved. I doubt if I imagined for a moment a future without horses, especially reining horses. Though reining was on the back burner, the flame still burned. Reining was in my life to stay.

A Life With Horses

Rehabilitation and Rescue

I'm kind of sorry now so many were caught, 'cause I have a lot of respect and admiration for the mustang. The fact that he'd give us back the same medicine we'd hand him, with sometimes a little overdose, only made me feel that, in him, I had an opponent worthy of the game. Even though I'd get sore at them when they'd put it over on us and rub it in a little too hard, the satisfaction I'd get at catching some wise bunch didn't last very long when I'd remember they'd be shipped, put to work and maybe starved into being good by some hombre who was afraid of them and didn't savvy at all. For they really belong, not to man, but to that country of junipers and sage, of deep arroyos, mesas - and freedom.
~ Will James

I strived to keep my horses safe, to provide a safe environment, prevent sickness and disease and be ever watchful over their general health. I built sturdy pens, vaccinated and wormed, but in spite of my efforts, my horses required medical attention sometimes. I managed minor cuts and sicknesses at home, but I knew when to call a vet, often for sutures. Ebony's "vet visit" is one of the most memorable.

One bitterly cold morning in January, a telltale trail of blood in the snow led me to the black mare. One of several horses wintering in the small area around the bull barn at the Crooked River Community Pasture, Ebony had evidently wedged her foot between two obstacles and gouged a deep groove along the coronet band when she pulled it out. Blood oozed from the cut. I brought her into the barn, prepared to treat the injury, but when I couldn't stop the bleeding, I called Bob, my veterinarian. He arrived twenty minutes later. Ebony stood motionless in the stall, blood pooling in the straw at her feet. The thermometer *in the barn* read twenty-five below Fahrenheit.

"I can't suture this," Bob said. "It's too close to the hoof. I'm going to pressure bandage."

Starting at the fetlock and working down to the hoof, Bob unwound several layers over the coronet. Blood oozed through the wrap. Ebony's head dropped and her eyes dimmed.

"She's going into shock!" Bob said. "I'll have to give her a blood transfusion. Does she have a sibling?"

"Yes," I said. "I'll catch Medina."

Bob's hands numbed as he worked, but he transfused Ebony with blood from her full sister in an icy "operating room" and saved my mare. He remembers that call as one of his worst . . . and most expensive. While he spent two hours with Ebony, a trunk full of drugs froze in his car!

Bob saved another horse of mine. He had gelded Spade, a black son of Cheetah, with no complications, but the next day I called him back. Spade was bleeding profusely. As he worked to stop the hemorrhaging, Spade, anesthetized and flat on the ground, quit breathing. Bob literally jumped up and down on him, until we heard first a shallow breath, then a big sigh. Spade was going to live.

In Kitten's case, Bob referred the patient to the Western College of Veterinary Medicine in Saskatoon. Barbed wire injuries are always bad, but Kitten's lacerated leg was one of the worst I have ever seen. She and her two-week-old filly pastured with other broodmares in a small field near the house, a field I used for the mares when they foaled so I could check them every day. On this evening, I found Kitten with a shredded hind leg. She must have hooked the leg over one or more strands of barbed wire at the hock and pulled or jumped forward. Muscle and skin hung from the front of the hock down to her pastern; fluids and blood ran down her leg onto the ground. She needed immediate attention; she needed a vet.

Quickly, Garry and I loaded Kitten and her filly into the trailer, phoned Bob, and Garry headed for the clinic seventeen miles away. I stayed with the kids, thinking Garry would be back after the vet sutured her leg, but he phoned to say Bob had stopped the bleeding with a pressure bandage and was sending him on to the Veterinarian College in Saskatoon. He would drive into the night to get Kitten the help she needed.

I talked to the veterinarians at the College the next day. The prognosis was not good. Kitten had severed the main tendon and it had snapped up so they could not retrieve and repair it. As a broodmare, she could walk all right that way, but they feared arthritis would set into the hock joint. If that happened, they could not save her. They were feeding her filly in anticipation of what they considered inevitable.

Kitten fooled them. She came home with bandages on both legs (because of the extra stress on her good leg) and raised her foal. I changed bandages every day. A month after she was home, I had to call Bob again. Kitten had opened up the wound, probably by lying down or getting up, and had lost so much blood she needed a transfusion. The gutsy little mare beat the odds again. By the end of the year, only a jagged scar remained, though she walked with a slight shuffle. She conceived during her healing time, raised another foal the following year and several others in the ensuing years with no sign of arthritis.

Healing hurt horses was a responsibility that came with my chosen career. I strongly believed rehabilitating difficult ones was also my responsibility. If I took a horse for training, I should not send him home because he objected to a training program. I knew it would be hard to stay in business if I quit too easily, so I persevered with every horse, even nasty ones. Two American Saddlebreds finally convinced me I not only risked serious injury to myself but also to my clients by training horses that would never be dependable.

My barn was full when the woman approached me to start her two geldings. I told her I could not take them, but she insisted, so I agreed to ride one if Roberta, a girl who kept her own training horses at my facility, would ride the other.

The pair arrived on a large, rickety, open-topped trailer. Bert and I watched as the owners unloaded them with a system of ropes, one person on each side of the trailer each with a long rope attached to the halter. The horses crashed down the ramp front feet flying and eyes wild. Bert and I looked at each other. *This can't be good.* One horse was five, the other seven.

Hoping for the best, we stalled the geldings one on each side of a hip-roofed outside shelter and pen and looked at their feet, ragged, cracked and broken.

"Have they ever been trimmed?" I asked.

"No."

I advised the owner that I would have to get a farrier to trim both horses and she agreed to the extra expense and left. Bert and I contemplated what we had gotten ourselves into.

The farrier and Bert's friend, Cal, arrived that evening to trim the pair. When Bert entered the pen to catch the gelding she was going to ride, he turned, kicked, and left an imprint of his hoof on her thigh.

"He can't do that!" Cal said, and stepped in to help while Bert limped to safety. When the big sorrel wheeled again, he whacked him on the butt with the lead rope, whereby he crashed through the side of the pen and left the yard. After Bert and I saddled up two broke horses and retrieved the bad boy, the two men roped him, tied him down and trimmed his feet. Bert had seen enough. She did not want to ride him.

The next day I introduced the seven-year-old to the round pen. He bucked with the saddle, pinned his ears,[70] and showed other signs of nastiness, but I felt I could not quit on this one. I lunged him saddled and bridled, at all times asking for a relationship with me by encouraging his participation in the exercise (that is, looking at me when I pulled his head toward me). As he gradually tired from trotting and loping around the outside of the round pen, I imagined a glimmer of understanding in his eye and allowed him to slow down, whereby he turned and charged me with his front feet! I escaped by rolling under the rails, but I knew then he was dangerous. I phoned the owner to pick up both horses. I explained that I could not guarantee the horses would be safe to ride after a month of training (Actually, I was positive they would not be!) and recommended she auction them and buy one quiet one. I knew they would sell for meat, but they were not worth rehabilitating. She picked up the horses and

---

[70] "Pinned his ears" is a phrase used to describe a horse laying his ears back in anger or defiance.

paid the farrier bill and board, but she wasn't happy.

I learned a lesson from these horses: *I should not accept mature horses of unknown parentage and handling for training.* I certainly should not try to rehabilitate them in thirty days. Older horses are set in their ways or carry "baggage" from previous attempts to train. They may not be safe to ride for many years and I would not be doing owners a favour by returning a horse that could hurt them. Someone had used the gelding that charged me for a practice bucking horse, a fact I was not aware of when I agreed to ride him. I made the right decision sending him home, even though the owner was annoyed. I redeemed myself a few years later when her daughter brought a horse to me that was trainable. The fate of the Saddlebreds is unknown.

Rarely did I ride a horse that I could not train into a dependable mount. Most problems were small, more about the horse asserting independence than meanness. I remember an Appaloosa gelding that refused to move forward. Since forward motion is about as basic as it gets, I had to correct him or no one would ever be able to ride him. When his owner came to watch, I demonstrated my solution for the problem.

"When he balks," I said, "slap him over his rump with the reins like this until he goes." I slapped him with my reins.

The gelding kicked but did not move forward.

"If he still doesn't go forward, slap him again."

He kicked higher. I slapped.

"And again."

I slapped with the reins again. Both hind legs lashed out. I slapped. He kicked. I slapped. He kicked. I slapped. Finally, he walked ahead and I didn't hit him.

"See. That's how it works."

"Fine for you to say," the man said, "but I wouldn't be on the horse by now!"

I guess horses like the Appaloosa were the reason I had a job. I'm happy to say he had learned the lesson by the time he went home to his owner, one of many who needed a confident rider and a training program.

It was not in my nature to give up even when risking injury, but twice more I sent horses home. Even if they had not hurt me, I would have been endangering the owners, who in a month would be riding them. With less experience than I, they had every chance of getting in a wreck. Both had bucked me off, both were tricky about it and, in both cases, I felt bucking would show up for a long, long time. I passed my opinion on to the owners and they may have believed me, but they had to find out for themselves.

"I have too much invested in this horse to auction him," one said of the recently gelded five-year-old.

I could advise only. Both horses hurt a rider later.

It was inevitable. I was going to see an abused horse and want to save it. A tiny newborn filly was the first, but I was only Marion's partner for this rescue.

I met Marion in the early seventies when she worked part time at the Community Pasture. She had married and moved away for a few years but had returned to the area and we had become fast friends. A tough, talented woman with very much the same attitude as I (There's no such word as "can't"!), Marion shifted into overdrive and I joined her when we found a foal in need of our help.

Marion and I had attended a local horse sale. Before we left the auction barn, we wandered around the pens. Most were empty, but in one, a wee, sorrel filly a few days old stood forlorn and dejected, no mare at her side. We could not understand why she was alone. Where was the mother? We sought management to ask questions.

Hard as it is to believe, the auction had sold the mare and foal separately . . . and the new owner of the filly could not be found. No one knew where he was; no one knew how to reach him; no one knew when he would be back.

When we found out the man who had purchased the filly was probably in the bar, we went into action. We asked how much the foal had sold for and, of course, the man had paid but a few dollars. Marion offered a little more money if they would let us take her and, against all rules, they did. She had bought herself a responsibility.

I played only a small part in this rescue. I helped bring the baby home. We lifted her into the back seat of Marion's car and I rode with her to Marion's barn. She rested her head on my lap under the blanket and looked up at me with wide questioning eyes. She must have been frightened, but stress had exhausted her.

Marion named the little filly Cherry Ridge. She sewed a tiny blanket to keep her warm and spent long hours with her in a stall. Her love and care was not enough. Little Cherry succumbed to pneumonia.

An Arabian mare was the object of my next rescue mission. I knew the breeder and had started the mare for him a few years before. I liked her. With a new owner now, she was pregnant, underfed, and had been trapped under a fence. I went to see her and offered to take her home on the spot. The owner didn't argue. Perhaps she wanted what was best for the mare.

The mare thrived under my care, and the foal she carried grew inside of her. I turned her loose in the yard every day to graze wherever she wished. She blossomed. Her coat was shiny, her eyes bright. I loved to see her happy and healthy. It was time to find her a home.

Barb, a woman who lived nearby, had fallen in love with her. She was thrilled at the prospect of caring for her and the expected foal. I knew she would be pampered the rest of her life. It was a win/win solution.

As the mare's foaling date approached, Barb became concerned. She felt something was not right even though the mare was healthy and active. She brought her to the Western Veterinary College in Saskatoon for a check-up and the news was devastating—the foal and reproductive organs were scrambled. The best vet care in the world could not save either mare or foal. Barb's pretty, grey Arabian mare did not come home with her.

Again, the rescue had a tragic ending. My experiences saving horses have not been successful. Would I do it again? Absolutely.

A Life With Horses

Wildwood in Saskatchewan

The horse you get off is not the same as the horse you got on. It is your job as a rider to ensure that, as often as possible, the change is for the better. ~ Author Unknown

The years blurred together. My children were growing up. Horses came; horses went. I raised a few; I sold a few.

I thought I would not ever sell Majesty, but I needed money and could get a good price for a pretty, black Quarter Horse mare. I let her go. Now I wish I had kept her, but I take comfort in knowing she had a great home, a successful show career and lived to a well-earned retirement. Like so many of Duchess' fillies, she was an outstanding performance mare and for that reason, her owner did not ever breed her. She leaves no legacy.

I raised a few foals every year, all sired by Seco, with one exception. The owner of Last Sip, an AQHA sorrel stallion, had always loved Duchess and wanted a foal crossed with her stallion. In 1981, I leased Duchess to her, a two-year contract whereby she bred Duchess to Last Sip each year. She would keep the first foal and I the second. The outside breeding afforded me the opportunity to introduce a new blood line to my herd with no cash outlay (always a consideration). Duchess produced a sorrel colt splashed with white for Last Sip's owner and a sorrel filly, Wildwood Willow, for me. Willow, a trained barrel racing horse, is another mare I should not have sold but, as with Majesty, I needed the money.

71. Wildwood Willow running barrels in the arena at home.

I kept two of Jodella's foals. The bay mare, when bred to Seco, produced blacks, and that may have been the attraction. Lana needed a horse to call her own, so I gave Indigo, a leggy mare with a quiet disposition, to her. Shadow, a colt I later gelded, arrived a year later and I held him back for myself. Although both horses took their sire's colour, their conformation was Jodella's. They stood at about

15.2 hands, solid black with no white markings. Together they made a striking pair, much as Pride and Rocky had so many years earlier.

72. Wildwood Indigo and Lana in the field.

73. Indigo and Lana in Costume Class in Tisdale, Saskatchewan. The Spanish costume is red—stunning on Indigo!

74. Indigo and Lana Trail Class in Tisdale, Saskatchewan. Lana showed Indigo in all classes in local shows.

75. Wildwood Shadow and Marion in Bjorkdale, Saskatchewan (1987). Shadow was only three years old in this photo. I trained him in the snow the winter before.

76. Indigo, Lana, Shadow and I in the house yard. *Crawford Studios*

77. Wildwood Shadow and I in Western Pleasure class at Bjorkdale, Saskatchewan (August 1987).

Spirit, the Pas Paul Pas mare, produced every year and I sold all of her foals. I did not have time to train my own horses. Even some of those I kept back I later sold if a buyer came along. Horses were my business and I could not afford to pass up a sale.

Training horses for others was my main source of income. A few were repeat customers, bringing me one or two horses a year. Sometimes a client left his horse with me long enough to show in Quarter Horse or open shows, but mostly I started colts and sent them home in a month.

By luck alone no doubt, I was not hurt much in these years. The possibility of serious injury lurked within the next green horse, defective equipment, unsafe ground or my carelessness. One time my foot caught in the stirrup when I got off at a gate. Another time my foot tangled in a lunge line. Both times, my awkwardness in winter clothes caused the mishap; both times, "whoa" saved me.

I never allowed myself to be afraid. Horses sense fear and I would lose an advantage. A bay two-year-old Quarter Horse mare tested my nerve more than any other horse.

Gypsy had been handled very little. She had run with the herd all of her short life, except for halter training. I knew her sire, our stallion, Pas Paul Pas. I knew her dam. I had ridden a brother. Gypsy was different. As soon as I saw her, I knew I had my hands full. I understood horses with attitude, lack of trust, or lack of training, but I suspected Gypsy did not think rationally. That scared me. I hoped my program would instill confidence in both of us.

She was difficult to catch, so I kept her in a stall for a few days, but she needed more exercise. I turned her in a very small outside enclosure and left her halter on, but when I went in to catch her, she would have no part of it. I called Henry to help (I had to ride her.) and he said he would come right away. I went back to the barn to try one more time while I waited for him.

When Henry arrived, he found me sitting on the ground outside Gypsy's pen rubbing my head and not making much sense. I had cornered the mare to catch her and this time she had stood long enough for me to approach, but as I reached out to attach the shank to her halter, she turned into me, knocked me to the ground with her shoulder and ran over me. A horse has just four feet, but I think every foot hit my head twice. Several swellings rose on my head immediately.

"Why didn't you wait for me?" Henry asked. "I said I would be right here." He didn't understand. . .

The episode did little to alleviate the fear I already felt for this mare. A horse will usually turn away from, not into, a person; a horse will usually avoid running over someone. Gypsy did both. I was lucky she had not killed me.

When I finally mustered up enough courage to get on Gypsy (after more ground work than I had ever done on a horse), I felt like I was one step away from a wreck. I dreaded every ride and my day was better when it was over. I saw and felt nothing to change my initial feeling. I still believed she did not think. I could not predict what she might do, where she would do it or why. With all the patience and understanding I could give her, she did not change. She never trusted me.

After three weeks training, I discovered Gypsy was full of worms and I had to lay her off until she recovered. Let me think about this. . . I was riding her when she was sick? I didn't look forward to riding her when she was well! Fortunately, the owner took the matter into her hands. She did not like her any better than I did and sold her at an auction with appropriate warnings. The man bought her because she could run, but he got into trouble right away. She bucked him off, ran away and, yes, she was fast, *very fast.* He couldn't catch her. The last I heard of Gypsy she was running wild.

I was bucked off, spooked off, reared off, rolled off and fallen on but suffered few serious injuries. Some unplanned dismounts were pure accidents, others due to carelessness. Many times, it was a matter of the horse learning. My experience with Chiquita taught me I was not a bronc rider, so I concentrated on developing a program for starting horses under saddle that discouraged bucking. Discouraged—yes. Eliminated—no. The inevitable happened, usually because I was not paying attention.

Meadow Lark—three-year-old Quarter Horse mare with some fancy moves. I was getting along nicely with this mare, but I never let my guard down. Except once. It was blistering hot. I had finished my ride for the day on Meadow Lark and she was dripping sweat. Bert was working a horse in the round pen and I walked by, reins loose and now thinking of other things, like what we would do later in the day.

"Hey, Bert," I said, waving my hand in her general direction. "You know what we. . ."

Meadow Lark cut my suggestion as to what we should do that evening off in mid-sentence. She bogged her head, sucked out from under me and ran, leaving me sitting beside the round pen looking up at Bert who (making no effort to hide her amusement) continued to work her horse. I was not hurt and laughed at my carelessness. When

I returned from trudging through thick brush in the heat to catch Meadow Lark, the humour of the situation had escaped me.

Breeze—three-year-old Quarter Horse gelding, quiet and well-mannered. The day was spring-like, but with a frosty feel to the air. Cindy and I were riding in the ditch along the highway, a welcome change from snow banks. The snow was almost gone, melted into ice-capped puddles in the ditches. Cindy was riding Seco.

"Watch Seco," I cautioned. "He likes to try to bolt for the fun of it when a car passes."

A truck whizzed by. Seco was fine. Breeze bucked me off. I slid on my belly through one of the icy puddles, breaking the crust with my chin. I envisioned the scene from the driver's perspective and laughed. He slowed, looked back, and then sped away. Can't say I blame him. There I sat in a frigid pool of water with pieces of ice hanging off me, laughing! I must have looked like I lost my mind.

78. Seco and Cindy in Children's Day Parade, Bjorkdale, Saskatchewan (August 1980).

Echo—three-year-old Quarter Horse gelding, athletic, quick and strong. Echo should have bucked me off several times but never did. He *did* hurt me, however.

Echo came with several quirks. He was hard to bridle, difficult to mount and he bucked. I had started him as two-year-old and some annoying problems had surfaced, all of which required perseverance to overcome. He fought bridling. Once he jerked away and tore my pinky on the headstall, sending me to the hospital for stitches. He dreaded mounting. If I didn't get on in one smooth move, he became so agitated I might not be able to. Contending with the slightly eccentric personality of this horse spawned a phrase I still use in reference to training—"Get it done and get out of there."

Echo was so athletic I knew I didn't have a chance if he bucked, so I worked with him from the ground first, especially when he returned to my program at three. With only a month of riding the year before and limited riding by his owner, I needed an advantage. Echo had hauled three hundred miles to my barn.

No better time than right now. . .

I led him to the round pen. Bert's friend, Cal, had loaned us a system of ropes to use on broncy horses in a round pen. Echo was a candidate. The ropes worked from a block and tackle at the withers, with a loop (protected with rubber) on a front foot and a long line to the handler. The idea was to lunge the horse, say "whoa", and pull the front foot up, then release the foot when (*and only when!)* the horse looked at the handler.

Echo had always been nervous about his legs, but Bert and I managed to attach everything in the proper place and I sent him to the outside of the round pen. He scatted a little but, having been saddled and lunged, accepted the strange gear. Then I said "whoa" and pulled. The next ten seconds were a blur of dust, ropes and horseflesh, long enough for Echo to wind himself up in a twisted, tangle of rope and fall in a heap. He lay on the ground, wild-eyed but motionless, trussed like a Christmas turkey.

For a moment, Bert and I didn't know what to do. Given Echo's sensitivity around his legs, we weren't sure we wanted to squat down beside him to sort out the mess of ropes, but we had no choice. To his credit, Echo, eyes rolling, didn't move a muscle as we worked the rope away from his body and legs. He rose to his feet slowly, as if in shock that he could. I never put the ropes on him again. He did not need another lesson. If he raced around the pen and I *whispered* "whoa", he slammed on the brakes and snapped his head around to ask me to save him!

All the round pen work and riding when he was out of shape sored Echo in the cinch area. I could not lay him off, so I slid a disposable diaper under the cinch to protect him and kept riding. I usually lunged him in the round pen first, and one day, before I stepped up into the stirrup, I walked around to his off side to check that the diaper was still in place. He anticipated my touching the sore and, when I reached for the cinch, jumped forward and cow kicked[71] me on the outside of my right knee, dropping me to the ground. I rolled under the bottom rail, sick with pain. For a few minutes, I moaned and groaned, then hobbled to the house. Painkillers and

---

[71] A cow-kick is cowboy slang for a forward, sideways kick from a horse's hind leg. (Can also be used as a verb.)

lying down seemed to be a good idea but, after a few minutes, I got up again. I suspected I would be laid up and there were tasks to finish while I could still move. My leg was already stiff, but I dragged it back to the barn, finished the ride on Echo and made a feeble attempt at working a barely started, but gentle, two-year-old.

I was right about the being laid up. The knee, badly injured, swelled to twice its normal size and tormented me if I tried to walk on it. Cindy rode my training horses for three days, excluding Echo and a broncy three-year-old mare of my own, and then I had to go back to work. The leg did not bend at the knee, but I could stand on it with everything aligned so I could mount. I could not turn my right ankle to pick up the stirrup, so reached down to place my foot in the stirrup after I was in the saddle. I couldn't apply much leg pressure on the right side of my horses either. A month later, the knee had not improved, so I went to the doctor. He told me to lie on a table and then, to evaluate the degree of injury, manually bent my knee. I yelped in pain! He could not do more without sedation and because he could not positively diagnose the extent of the damage, he recommended a cast from hip to heel. I burst into tears. Seven horses in the barn to ride, three kids to provide for, no insurance. In the cast, I would not be able to do anything with the horses. I left his office, drove home, and continued to work as I had been doing, however painful. I walked a lot like Kitten with her severed ligament— dragging a stiff leg. I remember carrying a pail of grain to one of the horses, tripping on a clump of grass and falling to the ground immobilized with excruciating pain. For the rest of the summer I cared for and rode the horses like that. (The knee eventually healed. The following winter, my kids stretched the ligaments by standing behind me and pulling my leg up as much as I could tolerate. I regained full flexion.)

Echo had three weeks off. Then I hired a young cowboy to help me get him started again. We lunged him in the round pen before riding. I advised him to get on quickly, which he did, except he mounted cowboy style (from the side) with the reins loose. Echo bucked him off in two jumps. He got on again (from the shoulder and with a shorter rein) and this time he stayed there.

I had not yet discovered the tremendous talent masked by Echo's attitude. Sired by our stallion, Pas Paul Pas and out of a top-notch barrel horse with speed to burn, Echo's purpose in life was to be a barrel horse. Because I suspected he needed more to think about, I started him on barrels and I knew right away. Strong, fast and lightning quick, Echo was born to run barrels. Because he loved the event, he didn't think about what "might" happen, which almost certainly saved me serious injury when equipment failed. I used a running martingale then, and one day, running the pattern at full throttle, Echo dropped low on the third barrel (as he should), stuck his front leg over the martingale and ripped the bridle off his head. I had a moment of panic (A dynamite horse running at full speed with no bridle is intimidating.), but he focused only on finishing the pattern. He had plenty of issues and they all flashed through my mind, but he kept me safe. Echo sold at four, a finished barrel racing horse.

79. Echo in training for barrels in 1980. This photo is taken in the arena in my yard. Note halter on Echo under bridle for ease of bridling.

Business, family and a relationship consumed more hours than are in a day but, with organization and by combining one with another, I hoped I fulfilled my responsibilities to each. While Shayne, Cindy and Lana were in school, I rode and cared for the horses and when the bus dropped them off, they helped with barn and house chores. Then there were the extra curricular activities— hockey, figure skating, piano lessons, swimming, Cadets, etc.—that I "bussed" them to.

Although Henry's two children did not live with him, he was very much involved in their lives. All day he worked on his farm as I did on mine, and spent quality time with them when he could . . . and with me! Sometimes in the summer, we took Sunday afternoon off to take all the kids to the lake or barbecued in one of our yards. Once in a while, we camped overnight at a lake. In this way, we could enjoy each other without leaving our children out. We all liked the water.

Henry's daughter, Andrea, loved horses and wanted to ride, so I started her on Duchess. Later, I trained a mare for her. She is an accomplished equestrian today. Since Henry's interest in horses and riding was minimal, we rarely rode together, but on one occasion, we combined our interests in a unique race. I rode; Henry canoed.

The race was called the "Louis Riel Race". Teams of six people each—two runners, a rider, two canoeists, and a biker—met in the outskirts of the small hamlet of McKague. The first runner sprinted to the horses and passed to the rider, who ran through bush to the riverbank and handed off to the canoe. These two people paddled down river to a biker, who peddled to the last runner. This runner carried wood, matches, a pot and water in a backpack. When he reached the finish line (the starting line), he kindled a fire, hung the pot, and boiled water. After racing the course, time stood still waiting for that water to bubble!

The first year I ran this race, I used Jodella, who was not in shape but finished her leg of the race all right. The team finished second. The next year I rode Willow, only three years old. I had not viewed the course, so trusted directions and flags to point me to the river. When the runner passed the baton to me, Willow and I thundered down the road a hundred yards or so to a marked turn along a barbed wire fence. We galloped between fence and forest for maybe a half-mile before the trail headed into trees and bush and the real race started. I remembered a rather short, uneventful run to the river on Jodella, so was completely unprepared for a tree hanging over the path in front of me. I estimated the jump to be about three feet. I had never jumped Willow, but I was in the race to win. With *almost* no hesitation on my part and none on Willow's, she cleared the log. That year our team—Henry in the canoe, four others and me on Willow—won the Louis Riel Race in McKague, Saskatchewan.

80. The "hand-off" from the runner to me and Willow in the Louis Riel Race at McKague, Saskatchewan in 1986.

81. Champions Louis Riel Race. McKague, Saskatchewan (1986).

My horse racing days seemed to be behind me, more by circumstance than by design (The horse shows I competed in didn't host races.), but I had not quite given it up. As head boss for the local horseshow, I lobbied for a flat race, a two hundred yard straightaway, and I planned to run Seco.

I knew Seco had speed to spare, but I had never flat raced him as I had Cheetah, Brownie, Duchess, Major and Jodella. Therefore, he had not lined up with a group of horses, had not been asked to give all from the first stride. He felt the excitement, though, as we lined up at the starting line. Tense with anticipation, muscles bunched under my legs, he waited for a signal . . . and froze to the ground when the flagman dropped his hand! A second later, he ran, but on such a short race, could not make up the distance. As I walked him back to the trailer, I overheard someone ask the man who had won the race (on, ironically, one of Cheetah's colts), "Where did that black end up?"

"Dead last," the smug winner replied.

I wheeled around.

"Would you like to run that race again, only this time for money?" I asked.

"You bet.'

By agreement, and because both horses were pumped and ready, we walked them up to the line together for an even and fair start. This time Seco was ready to run.

The race was over as soon as it began. Seco ripped away from his opponent with the first stride and gained every stride for two hundred yards. We finished several lengths in front and I pocketed twenty-five dollars. I relished the win for reasons other than the money.

I credit this time in my career with teaching me much of what I know today about horses, their habits, mentality, and way of thinking. I lived with horses all day every day. I fed, groomed, rode and nursed horses, and not only my own! Every new horse brought to my barn for training or breeding furthered my education.

Most of the horses I accepted for training stayed only a short time. I started the colt and sent him home to his owner. I relied on my training program and my intuition to complete the task in the most effortless way. I learned from every one.

I also attended clinics and judging seminars in the area if I could afford to, talked to other trainers and read books. Sometimes a horse show committee asked me to judge a show. As with coaching, I was reluctant at first. I lacked confidence in my abilities as a judge; I did not feel qualified. Friends finally convinced me I had many years of knowledge to offer and I accepted a few judging positions. I eventually enjoyed judging performance horses, though not comfortable placing halter classes,

"I am being paid for my *opinion*," I reminded myself, and I judged the class according to which horse I would like to buy or ride. I believe judges should judge a halter class with an eye as to how good the horse will perform under saddle, so that is what I did.

The more I learned about training horses, the more I discovered I *didn't* know. If I got cocky and thought I knew everything, I stopped learning. I remind myself of this often and still know it to be true.

I coached more and accepted invitations to teach clinics. Sometimes the clinic lasted only one day but, more often, a weekend. One of the most memorable clinics is one in Spiritwood.

Marion had been asked to teach the 4H clinic, but when the organizer told her multiple clubs would be attending she wisely suggested a second clinician—me. Thus it was that Marion and I headed for Spiritwood, a small town in northern Saskatchewan, to instruct a weekend clinic.

We planned our program as we drove. We would ask some questions, divide the kids into groups, each take a group and go from there. We prepared for a mixed group of horses and riders. We did not foresee the chaos that awaited us.

The leaders had assembled horses and riders in an indoor arena. We looked around and counted. Forty kids ringed the indoor rink with horses of all descriptions—ponies, farm chunks, wild-eyed broncs and the odd good looking, pleasant animal. It wasn't going to be easy.

We like to think we made a difference that weekend. We hope several children were spared injury because we demonstrated a safer way to handle horses, and that one or two found out how much a horse is capable of learning. What I do know is Marion and I worked as hard as we ever had for ten hours a day. We taught safety first, fearing someone was going to get hurt. We dealt with bad tempered horses, stubborn horses and many simply not trained. We rode almost every one, explaining what we were doing as we rode.

The horse I remember above all others is a squatty grulla with a neck the same length as his head and just as stiff. The rider could not complete a circle on him. Every time, the horse grabbed the bit in his teeth and piloted his young rider back to the group standing at the end of the arena. We were getting nowhere. A bad habit was getting worse. I took over.

The first step was getting any forward motion, which meant using the reins over his fat butt. Then I tried to lope the circle. Naturally, he did the same with me so back to the "over and under" technique when he ditched the circle in favour of his friends. It was a bit of an ugly scene. I was winning, but "the program" might look drastic to the bystanders. (The rider didn't seem to mind!) I explained as I rode.

"I'm not hitting him on the top part of the circle because he's being good," I explained, "but when he leaves the circle, I convince him to go back (with the reins over his rump). That way he will learn if he goes where I want, he is not corrected."

I *hoped* he would learn. I did win that battle and after a few rounds, we loped circles. Did I think he had learned his lesson? Yes, he learned *Sharon* got the job done, but I would have bet the farm he would still make the decisions with his owner.

At the end of the first day, Marion and I, bone tired, collapsed in our hotel room too exhausted to eat. There was a knock on the door. The organizers of the clinic wanted to know if we wanted to go out for drinks that evening. We looked at each other. We never missed a chance to go out, especially since, for one night, we had no family responsibilities.

"No thank you," we said together. "We're just too tired."

The next morning we were back in the arena for more of the same. At the end of the clinic, everyone was safe. Mission accomplished.

Coaching my own children was sometimes just as challenging as clinic students but for different reasons. The horses were better, but we were much too close for coaching to be effective. Marion and I often said we should teach each other's children. I didn't have the same gift for keeping them on their mounts, either. Shayne and Cindy still talk about when Mom decided they should each start and train a colt. The horses of choice were two-year-old daughters of Seco named Sheba and Shasta. With no round pen or arena, riders (including my children) rode in the open. I helped Shayne and Cindy saddle and work their colts from the ground, and then it was time to ride.

Shasta bucked Shayne off twice in quick succession, one time running to a fence and throwing him there.

"I'm not doing this," he told me.

Cindy didn't have any better luck. As I watched from the porch, Sheba bucked her off five times before she left the horse: in front of the saddle, behind the saddle, crosswise, forward and backward. As she picked herself up from the ground, I hesitated. She knew the rule: Get back on the horse. I wondered if I should stop her this time. Sheba was not a bronc, but that day she looked like one.

The mare was still standing where she had unloaded Cindy. Still pondering over what would be the best course of action for horse and rider, I watched Cindy catch her, put the reins over her neck, and mount.

Good enough. "You can get off," I told Cindy. "I'll ride her."

Although Shayne and Cindy continued to ride, I aborted the "Start Your Own Horse" project. Shasta had a few issues, maybe in part due to the bad beginning. Sheba abandoned bucking almost right away. I rode her for a few months and sold her.

It was with Jodella that Cindy bonded. She called her "Jo' and remembers her with great fondness. Jodella was not particularly easy to ride but was kind in nature. She and Cindy showed a little, especially barrel racing.

Cindy did not like to lend her horse out to anyone, but she may have been slyly glad she did one Sunday. Two male friends of mine visited, and with them was one of Cindy's teachers, a young athletic man who taught physical education as well as other classes. He and Cindy had not been getting along.

I was working Jodella on barrels when the men arrived and they asked to see her perform. After I ran the barrel pattern, Cindy's teacher asked if he could ride her.

I hesitated. My arena was not fenced. In fact, the pasture at the top of the property had not been fenced either. Jodella was not hard to manage unless she was running, though, so I saw no harm in Dan riding her.

"Just don't squeeze with your legs," was all the advice I gave him. I knew he was athletic and if he gripped with his legs, Jodella would run.

I guess he forgot. Jodella bolted out of the arena, across the road and disappeared over the hill with Dan clinging to her back and hollering. While Cindy didn't look as concerned as she should have been, I imagined the worst. I ran after them, dreading a nasty scene on the other side of the hill, and met Dan leading Jodella. He would not say what happened.

Although Shayne liked all animals and was comfortable on a horse, he did not want to ride or show. Cindy (and later Lana) showed with me and became accomplished horsewomen. Cindy worked with me the summer before she went to university. Her "trainers" were a two-year-old Thoroughbred mare to condition for the track and a Quarter Horse mare I believed to be quiet and safe that bucked her off the first time she rode her. What do I know?

82. Cindy on Ginnaleo (the training horse that bucked her off) in 1982.

Cindy may have felt lucky she was not hurt that summer. A visit home from university was a refresher course in what could happen if horse training was your job.

She was bringing a new boyfriend home to meet me. I expected them for dinner but was continuing the education of the newest trainee at the barn. A client had brought me a two-year-old palomino filly right off the range. No one had handled the young mare, so we had ran her out of the trailer into the barn and into a stall. I had roped her in the stall and fashioned a "war bridle"[72] with the rope to teach

---

[72] A "war bridle" is a halter fashioned from a rope, used to sharpen a horse's response by putting pressure simultaneously on the nose, chin and poll. Should be used by experienced handlers only.

her to lead. She had learned much in the first lesson, but with Cindy coming for the weekend, I was anxious to continue the training.

I had closed both doors so I could use the dirt alley. The mare was understandably sore from the rope over her nose and poll, so I was cautious when I asked her to lead. Pull a little, give right away when she took a step, etc.

The door opened a crack.

"They're here," Lana said.

"Great. I'll be right up."

I had lost my attention and the filly's for a second. When I reached for the rope to slip it over her head, she reared up and brought a front foot down on my skull.

I knew the mare's indiscretion was my fault. I was not hurt badly, but she had opened a three-inch gash on my scalp. Dark red blood trickled down my face as I walked to the house. Cindy and the new boyfriend met me at the door.

"I'd like you to meet my mom," Cindy said. Then they took me to the hospital for stitches.

I still supplemented my income with periodic work at the Community Pasture only a mile away. The manager always needed extra hands for roundups and, since I knew the pasture and was experienced help, he hired me. The paycheck was a bonus. I appreciated the opportunity to ride off my own property and cattle work provided great education for the horses. Rides at the Community Pasture were fun-filled days with cowboys and horse people, with a couple of exceptions. Weather for fall roundups could be cold and miserable, even wintry, and those days riding was only a job. The worst rides, though, were the ones for "bushed"[73] cows. If cattle were missing, we could be sure they were in the bush so, every fall, the manager, his wife, myself and one other rider attempted to chase, scare, or trick the errant animals out of the trees. It was frustrating work, guaranteed to try the patience of men, women and horses. Many times, after we pushed a cow to the edge of the bush, she turned and almost knocked us down diving back in. If we managed to wean the animal away from the bush, one of the men roped her and tied her to a tree. (Later someone drove back with a trailer to pick her up.) I rode Seco most of the time. He never refused to run after a cow, even with brush slapping him in the face.

---

[73] "Bushed" cattle will not leave the trees or bush.

I look back on these years as my "strong" years. Healthy, emotionally content, and happy with my lifestyle, I could not imagine doing anything else. True, my standard of living may not have been what some would have considered adequate, but I was with my horses.

Somewhere in the back of my mind, I must have had a breeding plan. Duchess would be with me forever, of course. I had also kept Mahogany back.

Still, I sold Seco. In 1984, he was twelve years old. As he aged, he would be harder to sell. I knew who wanted him and I made the call. Two days later, he was gone and I held a cheque for four thousand dollars. I had trained him and spent hours and hours on his back. No one understood him as I did. I hope he was all right. I don't know because I never went to see him.

83. Seco Top Moon.

By 1987, though my days were still filled with horses, there had been many changes in my life. Shayne and Cindy had graduated and moved on to lives of their own. Lana, in high school now, would soon move out, too. My parents were both gone, Dad in 1982 and Mom in 1986. Time for a change. I could train horses in B.C.

Part 4

Horses and Training
in B.C.

I've spent most of my life riding horses. The rest I've just wasted.
~ Author Unknown

A Life With Horses

Wildwood in B.C.

A horse has no future. It cannot greet the sun and say today will be better. It can only reflect upon days of past experiences. It is our job to create a positive past. ~ *Karen West*

I chose Armstrong for my new home for several reasons—horses grazed in almost every back yard, the Interior Provincial Exhibition grounds hosted breed shows, open shows and a rodeo, and an indoor facility was in the planning stages. Armstrong would sometime be the heart of a thriving horse industry in the Okanagan, the perfect location for my business. Besides, Mae (from Yorkton rodeo days) now lived there with her husband, Bob. During the summer of 1987, I planned my move. Mae located a small acreage I could rent with an indoor arena, and boarded Lana so she could start grade eleven in Armstrong in the fall. I packed.

Relocating with a daughter, six horses (sold the rest) and two dogs took some organization. I advertised the Saskatchewan property for sale, but it did not sell. I went ahead with my plans anyway. I owned the car my mother had willed me, an old Dodge truck and a two-horse trailer with living quarters, all of which I wanted to move with me. Henry offered advice.

"Trade that Dodge off," he said. "No one but you could have kept it on the road this long. You're pressing your luck." He could attest to the truck's health and well-being since he had been under the hood a few times! My Dodge truck had served me well, but Henry was right. I sold it and bought a 1978 GMC three-quarter-ton from a friend. It was orange.

"It's got some years on it, but it will get you to B.C.," Gordon said.

Henry helped me move. In early October, we loaded Shadow and Indigo in the horse trailer, a Samoyed dog in each vehicle and headed for Armstrong.

I was thankful for the company. . . and the help. Flat tires (two on the truck and two on the trailer) plagued us. I took a photo of Henry changing every one. In the first, he clowned, making a face at the lens; in the last, he scowled. Only once, exhausted and facing night driving in the mountains with truckers tailgating the horse trailer, did *my* strength crack. On the side of the highway, Henry patiently waited with me until I could go on. About midnight, we drove into Bob and Mae's yard and unloaded Shadow and Indigo. The next day we hooked up a borrowed four-horse stock trailer to the GMC and hurried back to Saskatchewan.

Now late October, I prayed for good weather for the second trip. I would be traveling alone this time with four horses out of Saskatchewan, across the windy plains of Alberta, over Roger's Pass to the Okanagan Valley.

I fashioned short racks for the truck so I could pack as much as possible in the back of the truck. In the front of the box, crosswise, I set the freezer (full of frozen food) with the electrical cord hanging through the rack so I could plug it in at night. Then I leveled the load with some of my belongings (I would move the rest in the spring.) and tarped it. In the trailer, I loaded bagged oats and potatoes, forks, shovels and four horses—old Duchess, her daughters, Mahogany and Hickory, and Mahogany's six-month-old filly, Tamarac. Early on the morning of October 25, 1987, I gently nestled my hoya plant in a laundry basket, set it on the passenger seat of the cab, slid behind the wheel, and opened the book that is my life to the first page of a new chapter. As I drove out of the yard that had been my home for ten years, I looked only ahead, to an uncertain but exciting future.

On the road, my confidence dimmed. Weighted behind by the load and the trailer, the front end of the truck felt airy and light to my hands on the wheel. The "squirrelly" feeling was disconcerting.

"I think the freezer should have been on the hood," I told friends later.

Worried, I phoned Marion for moral support. I did not want to phone Henry, who didn't think I should be making the journey alone anyway. He would have accompanied me again, but I would have had to send him back on the bus. Besides, we had agreed to the separation and had to cut ties.

Friend that she is, Marion dropped everything, met me on the highway in her little car, and drove behind me to Drumheller, Alberta. She brought CB radios (No cell phones then!) so we could keep in touch on the road. The load took some getting used to, but gradually I relaxed. An alternator problem delayed us for two or three hours in Kindersley, Saskatchewan, but we used the downtime to replace the tarp on the load while the truck, trailer and horses were in the garage. The wind had already whipped the original one loose and shredded it.

I said goodbye (and thank you) to Marion the next morning and continued uneventfully for the rest of the day until Golden B.C., where I detected a noise in my truck. I wanted it checked before driving Roger's Pass. Since the mechanics had left for the day, I got a motel room and called Mae. I turned Duchess, Mahogany and Hickory out in a small pasture by the highway owned by a woman the gas station attendant put me in touch with, and left Tamarac in the trailer overnight. The next morning a mechanic looked at my truck (The problem was a loose bolt on the U-joint. Good thing I stopped!) and I continued to Armstrong. I met Bob and Mae on the highway. They had worried after my call of the previous night and had driven to meet me.

I took only a few days to unpack, and then advertised my business. Within a few days of my arrival in B.C., I hosted demonstrations and booked clinics to promote Wildwood. A few people left horses with me to train right away, but until Wildwood was established, I would work other jobs, riding and coaching in the evening.

I'll just keep doing what I do and let people come to me. They have to see for themselves.

In the spring, my rented property sold and I moved again. The forced move turned out to be a blessing because a friend of Mae's rented a wonderful little acreage to me just a few kilometers from Armstrong on Grandview Flats Road. A doublewide trailer, small barn, crude arena, and pasture adequately fulfilled my needs. During the years I lived there, I added a freestanding box stall and a large turnout pen, digging railway ties in the hillside by hand, prying rocks loose with a crowbar and clawing them out until my knuckles bled. Those railway ties are still standing.

84. Arena on Grandview Flats, Armstrong B.C. (1988).

85. The house on Grandview Flats (1988).

I spent many happy hours riding in that rocky, oddly-shaped arena. All day, I rode and coached. I started colts, fixed problem horses and advanced training on a few. Several riders booked weekly lessons and I taught regular group lessons away from home.

86. Working a young horse in the arena.

Wildwood was still primarily a horse training business, but teaching was a natural extension of training and showing. Coaching riders was now a significant portion of my business. In Saskatchewan, I had enrolled in the National Coaching Certification Program, took Level I theory and passed the evaluation for Level I technical. Reluctant because I felt insecure, the courses pushed me in the right direction. In B.C., I enrolled in and passed Level II and III NCCP theory.

Putting my program into words made me think twice about everything I told my students. Sometimes lessons reinforced what I knew and sometimes I needed to find a different way. Students learned differently, and I learned to recognize strengths and how much pressure each one could handle. The horses were not equal either. I taught the rider and I taught the rider to teach the horse.

"You are the horse trainer," I said at the beginning of the first lesson. "As soon as you step on your horse, you are the one who is training."

I found it challenging at first to "feel" from the ground, but eventually I "rode" with my riders and directed small changes in hands, legs or seat without stepping on the horse. In the end, I learned as much as my students did. I addressed issues I had not seen before, developed new ways to handle old ones and, sometimes, a new way to say what I meant.

Although I encouraged individuality, my students mirrored me, a huge responsibility!

"I'm not telling you this is the only way," I said. "I'm telling you this is what works for me."

Always rewarding, coaching was at its best if the student won over me. As Vern told me when I posted a higher reining score than he did on Mo in the first reining competition of my reining career, "It's the biggest compliment of all when my student performs better than I do."

*****

Duchess was twenty-one years old when I moved to B.C. I would have loved to raise more foals, but she could not conceive. This was hardly the end of her usefulness, though. She was a superb lesson horse, especially with children—extremely smooth gaited and ever-conscious of the child on her back. She positioned herself under her young rider, and if the child lost balance, she "caught" him, slowing to a halt at the same time. She loved children and was proud of her role.

Lana and I both showed in open shows in 1988. Indigo and Shadow showed in all classes, even English. For one show, I loaned Shadow to an English rider and the judge *loved* him, placing him first in six out of seven classes. I also showed Hickory, the full sister to Mahogany.

I sold Mahogany in 1988 to a woman in Armstrong. I could not afford to breed and, as usual, needed money. I also sold her full sister, Hickory, and Indigo sold later for a barrel racing horse. Shadow turned into a fine all around gelding. He won everything from pleasure to reining. He was an excellent example of training on a program because his abilities far exceeded expectations. I attribute his talents to a great disposition. I called him a "perfect gentleman". As a lesson horse, I remember Shadow most for changing leads even if everything the rider asked was wrong! He was a great confidence builder. Vern Sapergia once asked me if I thought Shadow could change leads every two strides down the pen.

"I'll try," I said, and we did. Shadow taught me how to *love* lead changes.

87. Wildwood Hickory and I in Western Riding, Armstrong B.C. (September 1988).

88. Wildwood Shadow and I in English tack, Armstrong, B.C. (1988).

In July of 1989, a wonderful opportunity came my way. An Italian businessman, on Vern's recommendation, offered me a job training and showing reining horses in Italy. The timing was perfect since Lana had graduated and soon would be on her own. I accepted the job.

Vern, already working in Italy, had visited his family in Canada and was returning to Europe with his daughter, Shawna, who would holiday with her father for a few weeks. Because I was alone and had not been to Italy (Heck. I had not been on a jet!) Vern asked me to travel with them. With plans and connections in place and a friend house sitting my rented acreage in Armstrong and feeding my few horses, I boarded the plane.

I had not met Gianni Gentile, the man who hired me, but he and Vern's employer were friends. They had arranged for me to spend a few days with Vern in Bari riding two reining mares Gianni had purchased before proceeding to Gianni's farm southeast of Bologna.

An uneventful, but long, flight landed us in Rome where we transferred to a small plane (I would have still been in Rome if Vern had not known what to do!). In Bari, a man picked us all up and drove us to Vern's apartment.

From the time I stepped off the plane, "culture shock" engulfed me. No signs in English, no one spoke English and so many people. . . Then there was the traffic! I'll never complain about busy highways in Canada again. Many times, on a two-lane road, four vehicles drove—fast! Scooters, bikes and pedestrians wedged in between cars. Not everyone stopped at stop signs. Almost no one signaled a turn. Downtown, narrow streets hampered travel even more. I noticed most cars did not have side view mirrors. . . In this foreign, slightly frightening world, horses anchored me.

Vern rode and showed several trained reining horses and was training three-year-olds for the Italian Reining Futurity. We started riding early, partly because of the oppressive heat, and broke for a few hours in the afternoon. A cutting horse trainer and his family lived with Vern and worked out of the same barn and we all had great fun in and out of the arena. Sometimes, after dinner, we wandered around town in our hats, boots and spurs, causing quite a stir. Italians were not used to seeing cowboys on their streets!

After a few days in Bari, a farrier drove me to my place of employment seven hundred kilometers up the Italian Riviera and inland to the Gentile farm near the small mountain village of Corniolo. Finally, I met Gianni, his wife, Ombretta, a son and daughter, and several horses. I would be living in a rustic stone house above the stable. They used the house as a summer home, but also owned a house in Corniolo, ten kilometers away. The house was entirely mine to use, except when the family came for the day. They called the farm Tropoggio.

Gianni had picked me up at the main highway. He spoke fluent English, so we visited as we drove up the mountain to my new home. He pointed out several Argentine horses in his field.

"They need vaccinations."

"I can do that," I said, and so I impressed him first with, not my riding, but my ability to give a vaccination!

The months at Tropoggio were very therapeutic for me. Alone most of the time, my workload light compared to what I had left in Armstrong, I took care of myself better than I ever had. My only responsibilities were looking after myself and working horses. Men fed and cared for the horses.

I did not have a vehicle for some time, but when Gianni finally left one for me, I drove to Santa Sofia, mostly to develop film. The villagers spotted me immediately as different (I heard, "Seniorita Americano" several times.) and I felt extremely self-conscious. I was much more comfortable riding in the quiet arena by the Bidente River or up the mountain high above Tropoggio.

I started a two-year-old, haltered a weanling, trained and showed two reining mares and coached. Sugar was my favourite, if only because she had suffered abuse from a rider at one time. Ragged

89. Italy: Looking down on Tropoggio.

90. Sugar and I high above Tropoggio in the mountains.

91. Rome. Coliseum in background.

scars extending from shoulder to hip marred her right side, evidently from sharp spurs. It took most of the summer for the pretty, sorrel mare to trust me enough to change leads in the middle of the pen without taking the bit in her teeth and running off, but by the time I left, she had regained enough confidence to show successfully. I rode Sugar in the mountains every week. Mesmerized, she cocked her head and stared up the mountain as we rode. She had come from the U.S. and probably had never been out of an arena or seen a mountain.

The girl from the Coteau Hills of Saskatchewan would have never seen *any* of Europe if she had not been given this opportunity, but sightseeing beyond Corniolo was hard to fit in with my job. However, when Vern and Shawna visited, Gianni and Ombretta drove us to Florence. Also, Gianni gave me a quick tour of Rome before I got on the plane to return to Canada.

My business at home had come to a screeching halt in my absence. I returned to Armstrong in November and life gradually returned to what it was before I worked in Italy—caring for my horses, training and coaching. In the spring, Lana moved out and I lived alone with my horses and dog. With less parental responsibility, I could pursue other interests, like trail riding.

92. My home over the stables in Italy (1989). The stone house had a fireplace, marble sink, running water but no phone, television, or radio. I lived quite comfortably here for almost four months. I had access to a vegetable garden and picked figs outside my bedroom window.

93. The arena I worked in every day in Italy. Sugar and I, Vern Sapergia on Anna, Shawna Sapergia with Foxy. (1989)

I had great interest in riding B.C. trails, the perfect way to experience the mountains and, at the same time, give horses downtime from arena work, I searched for trail riding information (maps, books, etc.) to no avail, so I started close to home. Larch Hills (Salmon Arm) was popular. I had already ridden there with friends, with Lana, and on my own. Actually a cross-country ski area, the trails offered diverse riding conditions, scenery and solitude. Wildlife inhabited the area too—deer, moose and bear. I hauled my trailer with living quarters to Larch Hills several times in the next few years, parking by the chalet and crude horse pens, riding during the day and relaxing with my horses in the evening. Once, when I turned the truck and trailer around in the confined lot, I backed into a boggy hole. I looked at the trailer sunk in mud, said, "Oh, well. . .", and saddled my mare and rode. Two days later, when I needed to go home, I rode down the mountain to a phone. I had someone in mind to help me out of my predicament. Luckily, he was home and pulled me out.

94. A moment with my horse in Larch Hills. *Penny Ogasawara*

I liked Larch Hills, but soon I wanted to explore new territory—different, higher, wilder—and I constantly searched for new trails. In the years ahead, I would find many.

In 1990, I bought a pair of two-year-olds for reining. I squeezed in several rides on trails between many hours in the arena and these two turned out to be two of the quietest, "most broke" three-year-olds I ever owned. The mares learned to be real horses (hobbled, tied to trees, carrying saddlebags and ropes), but the outings were not without a cost to me. I usually managed only two days away from home at a stretch and my absence meant extra hours to catch up later. I remember pulling into my yard after a short holiday in the mountains to find a truck and trailer in my yard, notes on the pad by the telephone from the girl doing chores, and the telephone ringing! Yes, it was difficult to fit a trip to the mountains into my schedule but worth the effort. I would expand my knowledge of B.C. trails in the next few years. Some experiences would be magical. Some would be frightening. All would be memorable.

95. Docs Double Copy (Dee) on a trail ride in Larch Hills.

*****

Reining was my focus now. I studied reining. I bred and bought for reining. I trained reining. The bug had latched on to me for life in Italy. I was determined to promote reining in B.C.

"If there can be that much enthusiasm for the sport in Italy, surely B.C. can get in the game," I said and, with that, B.C. Reining Association was born.

The association did not fly with the first effort. Whether I failed to capture interest or whether the timing was not quite right, I am not sure, but my first attempt failed. By 1991, however, with the assistance of a few other dedicated horse people with like interests, BCRA was active. For the next several years, I hauled to arenas in the area Saturday mornings to teach reining at group sessions to club members. It was great fun to watch the progress of horses and riders. With the help of handouts and volunteer leaders, the association promoted reining. Before long, we added a newsletter, to which I contributed content. Regrettably, writing (and sometimes editing) for the newsletter added to my already-crowded schedule, so I could not contribute as much as I would have liked.

The reining association hosted demonstrations, riding sessions and a three-year-old futurity held in conjunction with the 1991 fall

Quarter Horse show in Armstrong. Now British Columbia reiners had a venue for their futurity horses in their home province. I would surely be entering mine. Unfortunately, the futurity started one year too late for my homebred Wildwood Tamarac.

Tamarac

In the steady gaze of the horse shines a silent eloquence that speaks of love, loyalty, strength and courage. It is the window that reveals to us how willing is his spirit, how generous his heart. - L. McGuire

I wanted to rein so I bred my mare to a reining stallion and waited for my superstar. I was not disappointed. In the spring of 1987, I watched Mahogany foal out a sorrel filly by Solanos Peppy San in my barn in Saskatchewan. The baby shook herself free of placenta, directed her ears and eyes at me and whinnied, not a soft nicker but a full-throated whinny. While her exhausted mother lay in the straw heaving, she took in her surroundings, completely comfortable with her brand new world. I sat back and really looked at her. A bold white strip ran down her face. Wide-spaced, intelligent eyes and flaring nostrils reminiscent of her grandma Duchess gave her otherwise average head a classic look. She had not inherited Mahogany's beautiful neck, but otherwise she was everything I had hoped for—a filly with the conformation to rein. A few days later, when she ran, turned and slid to a stop, any doubts I may have had evaporated.

96. Wildwood Tamarac is born April 9, 1987.

"I have a reining horse." I boasted to my friends and described her athleticism. "She spins and stops already."

They tolerated my bragging, obviously believing me to be an over-indulgent mother, but no one could dampen my enthusiasm. I named my future reining star Wildwood Tamarac and waited for her to grow up.

97. Tamarac July 1987.

Tamarac's babyhood was uneventful other than an encounter with barbed wire. The first day I turned her and Mahogany in the pasture, she ran into the fence. She carried an eighteen-inch scar across her chest for the rest of her life.

In the fall, Tamarac moved to B.C. with her mother and grandmother. The following spring and summer, on the Grandview Flats property, she hung out with her family in the field and watched me ride. That winter, as a yearling, she "played reining horse" in the icy arena. As I watched from the house, she delighted in scaring me by running hard from one end to the other much as I do when I fence[74] a

---

[74] "Fence" (*verb*) is a term for a training exercise for reining horses. The rider runs the horse in a straight line to a fence and allows the fence to stop the horse.

horse. I almost covered my eyes as she ran as hard as she could in a straight line to the fence. Instead of turning (as I thought she would) and slipping, she planted both bare hind feet on the ice and slid straight into the boards, where she looked up at me as if to say, "What's the problem?" I had myself a reining horse!

Training Tamarac required only showing her what to do. I rode her first bareback with a halter, then around the arena, then to the neighbouring farm. I saddled her with no complications and training began. I had ridden her only a few times before I went to Italy; on my return, I wasted no time. If Tamarac were to compete in three-year-old futurities the next year, she would have to be on a regular training program. The Goldrush Futurity in Calgary and the Saskatchewan Stakes and Futurities, established three-year-old reining events, and a futurity in conjunction with the Quarter Horse show in Langley B.C. were my goals for Tamarac.

I took her talent and trainability for granted. "It may be a long time until you have one this good again, Sharon," Vern predicted. I know now he was right.

I had not trained a horse for reining futurities since Mahogany (whom I laid off after an unexplained affliction). Though, as a trainer, I needed to show futurity horses, I was not comfortable pushing a young horse that hard at such an early age. To reconcile my program with my doubts, I promised myself two things: (1) I would condition my horses to the best of my ability prior to high intensity training, and (2) I would recognize that not all horses possess the ability to be a reining horse, especially at three years old. To that end, I conditioned with gradual increase of difficulty, mountain riding and even some "hard surface" legging up and, if my prospect could not perform (either mentally or physically), I didn't push him to do something he was not capable of doing. I have adhered to these two rules to present day to minimize stress injuries in my reining prospects.

Tamarac was not a big three-year-old. She stood about 14.2 hands, with a huge hip. The *drive* for everything she did came from that hip . . . and strong hocks. Her correct conformation and wiry build made her fabulously flexible. A fellow competitor once commented, "She looks like a little gymnast," as he watched me school her.

I had trained Tamarac ten months prior to her first futurity in Langley. She could not slide on the ground in my arena, so I trusted she would know what to do when she felt firm-based footing. I should never have expected her to slide when she had not had the benefit of good sliding ground, but I didn't have a better plan.

My goal for the Langley show was only to expose my young mare to competition, experience for the other two fall futurities. Her runs were relaxed but average. I have a special memory of her at Langley, her first reining show. We walked to the middle of the pen for pattern five, stopped, and I lowered my hand to her neck. She stood quietly for a moment, then tipped her head to the left, tipped it to the right and dropped it in the centre. I had not lifted my hand, had not given any cue (unless it was telepathic), but many, many times I had flexed her to the left and right, then asked for vertical flexion in schooling sessions. She was working the program!

98. Tamarac in Goldrush Futurity in October 1990. *Sharon Latimer*

Next, I hauled to Calgary where, to my amazement, she placed eighth of thirty riders. She seemed thrilled to be able, at last, to slide. Three weeks later, in the Saskatchewan Stakes and Futurities in Moose Jaw, she stopped so hard in warm-up that her hindquarters slid out of control and she almost fell over backwards. Unhurt but frightened, confidence shaken, she was not at her best in the competition. Also at this show, a rider ran into us in the warm-up pen,[75] nearly knocking Tamarac to the ground.

---

[75] The warm-up pen is an arena for "warming up" horses for competition.

In the next two years, Tamarac did much to promote reining in B.C. BCRA was young and reining demonstrations were part of the promotion. I used Tamarac for many such demos, including one dressage show, where we executed reining maneuvers to music. In a full-skirted red dress to the strains of *Maleguena,* I circled, spun and slid Tamarac in the tiny dressage arena, but the spectators were silent.

They hate it!

Obviously, I was not accustomed to dressage shows. Unlike reining, the spectators were *supposed to be quiet.* When Tamarac slid to her last stop, the crowd cheered as loudly as any reining show.

Tamarac, my willing partner, my loyal friend, my reining star, was up for anything I wanted to do except one. She hated trail riding! Where other horses benefited from time out of the arena on the trails, she only tolerated it. She did not see any point to spending hours in the bush. We went out several times, but she made no secret of her reluctance. She poked along, swinging her head side to side, always trying to turn around and go home. One time she did.

I often rode my horses on the mountain behind the property I rented and usually took my camera. The sun was setting as I rode to the top. A beautiful sunset painted the western sky. I visualized a spectacular photo of Tamarac backlit by the sunset, so I stepped off and dug out my camera. Tamarac grabbed a few mouthfuls of grass while I adjusted settings for the photo. Carefully, I arranged the dropped reins and stepped away. Through the lens, the picture was as I had envisioned . . . until the object of my photo took advantage of her window of opportunity, wheeled and fled down the mountain. An hour later, with the broken bridle in my hands, I caught up with her at the first closed gate.

I have many wonderful memories of Tamarac in the show pen, which she loved. In her next-to-last performance in the Freestyle Reining at Calgary in 1992, she carried a Podoco foal, her first. The next spring she birthed a bay filly I named Destiny.

Tamarac produced six fillies before she foaled a colt. She had ten foals in total, all extraordinarily talented. Recently, a writer for a magazine asked me to name my favourite broodmare.

"Wildwood Tamarac," I said.

"Why?"

"Because I bred Tamarac to several different stallions and all her foals are performers. She's the magic in the magic cross.[76] And also because she is a granddaughter of Ma Dear (Duchess) and the link to future generations of reining horses."

Tamarac usually passed down a distinctive trait to her foals in addition to talent and athletic ability—a droopy lower lip! Someone once remarked Tamarac's lip sagged so much she looked tranquillized. That's how relaxed she stayed in the show pen.

99. Tamarac's first four fillies: Whisper, Destiny, Kokanee, and Promise. (1997)

Her final foal, Wildwood Courage (named for Tamarac's final year of life because she raised him fighting cancer) is in training for the Working Cow Horse event and promises to be a star.

I pulled her out of the broodmare band in 1996 for one last performance. With her current filly weaned only a month and pregnant with another, she captured the hearts of spectators, if not the judges, with a Freestyle reining to *The Rose*. After the final spin (with reins draped over her neck), we slowly walked to a be-garlanded Promise, her baby. Years later, a woman told me a man sitting beside her at that performance turned to her and said, "I think this is the first time I ever cried at a reining show." He wasn't the only one. As I approached my husband and Promise on my beautiful sorrel mare, a few giant tears splashed off of the swells of my saddle.

---

[76] "Magic cross" is a term for the best cross of stallion and mare.

Making a Commitment 18

O Master and Guardian, hear me,
For I call and need thy care.
Give me when I am strong enough to ride, a trainer kind and calm.
Find me a gentle hand to guide,
A firm and purposeful one to right me when I am wrong
O Maker, give me a rider
Who is at least as wise as I!
~ Florence Gates from "A Horse's Prayer"

As reining gained popularity in B.C., more shows included the event. In 1991 and 1992, BCRA hosted four reining classes in Armstrong in conjunction with an AQHA show. A new reining club at the coast, Pacific Reining Horse Association, did the same. Both associations planned to host reining shows approved by the National Reining Horse Association in the near future. I needed reining prospects to stay in the game.

The two-year-old mares I bought in 1990 had good, if not spectacular, breeding. I put them in training and planned for futurities the next year. I used Vern's "step by step" program, the one he had introduced to me ten years before in Moose Jaw. I had tweaked the program to suit my style, but it was essentially the same program. To keep me current, to introduce others to a solid training program I believed in, and to promote reining, I flew Vern out a few times a year for clinics. During this time, I helped Vern write a book about his method of training. He liked the handout sheets I had put together for BCRA riding sessions and asked if he could use the same format for his book. We spent many hours after clinic days pouring over notes and discussing how to say what he meant to say. Vern wanted to publish a clear, concise training manual simple enough for a rider to understand if he did not have access to lessons or clinics. Several of my students bought his book and told me they rode with it open on their saddle horn. I always recommended it.

The two young mares, Dee and Peppy, contributed to my bank of reining knowledge in a big way. They tolerated me through many hours of spinning and sliding, forgave my mistakes and rewarded me with glimpses of brilliance when I got it right. The true test of a training program is how well the horse performs with an amateur rider. Both mares sold to new homes in their four-year-old year and continued to educate non-professional reiners. All the hours in the arena and in the mountains had instilled a quiet confidence in them, invaluable to inexperienced riders.

It was time to buy more horses. This time, I purchased two mares from Alberta, one of which I sold almost immediately. The other, Docs Champagne Taste, would be my next futurity reining horse. My goal for Champagne was the NRHA Futurity in December 1992, the "big one" in the reining world, but competing in the Futurity would be expensive and include a long haul to Oklahoma City. I could not swing it alone. A friend of mine, Bette, stepped in. We worked out the details of the partnership and training began.

"Champagne taste on a beer budget," Bette said.

The little sorrel mare was talented and sweet, with a gorgeous head, small ears and the eyes of a deer. She was tiny for a two-year-old, with fine flat bone, a long hip and muscled hindquarters, the deciding factor for my purchase. Willing, strong and not fragile at all, Champagne carried herself like a champion.

Champagne's training progressed smoothly, even faster than I expected. I started riding her in May and, the next year, Bette and I began making payments into the NRHA Futurity. Early in her three-year-old year, she executed all reining maneuvers well enough to compete in the fall. She was our star.

100. Docs Champagne Taste

In October, Champagne and I reined in Langley and Calgary. In November, I hauled to Moose Jaw to meet a group for the long trip to Oklahoma.

The Futurity makes huge demands on a three-year-old and I had long ago committed to having my futurity horse in the best condition possible. Champagne was sound, healthy and very fit for the grueling week of competition. She was still not big, but every muscle was rock solid. She had been in training for many months. I had hauled her to different arenas, ridden in the mountains, and shown in two competitions. She was ready physically and mentally.

My first trip to the NRHA Futurity was a huge step. I could not improve if I did not challenge myself, and this was a challenge! I hoped for a decent performance and, although the runs were not perfect, many others were not either. Champagne stood up to the intense training very well, maybe too well. Vern had teased me many times.

"Your horses are in such good shape you have to ride them longer to show them."

He may not have considered that when he watched Champagne and I warm up for the second go in the Futurity.

"She is ready now," he said. "Just walk her until you go in."

I took his advice . . . and wished I had not as soon as I loped into the pen for a run-in pattern. Champagne felt too "bright", too fast and, though not out of control, too willing to add her ideas to mine. She needed a longer warm-up! Still, the little mare presented herself well and returned home sound of mind and body, which, after all, is most important.

101. Champagne and I in her first 3 year old Futurity, Langley B.C. (Fall 1992)

I went on to show, trail ride and round up cattle on Champagne in her four-year-old year. She had tremendous heart, courage, tenacity, and the soundness of limb to stand up to difficult rides and long days under saddle. That spring, my future husband borrowed her for a cattle drive in the bush.

"Are you sure she's going to make it?" asked one of the cowboys, sizing up her fragile-looking conformation.

"She will still be going when your horses aren't," he answered and, after several grueling hours pushing cattle up a mountain, she was.

Champagne is another important link in my reining experience and I am grateful for Bette's support. She is now in Bette's barn, where I am sure she has a home forever.

During these years, I became fascinated with Freestyle Reining, reining maneuvers performed to music. The music inspired me and costumes, though optional for the class, added to the drama. I had already performed several reining demonstrations to music. It was natural I would want to ride the class.

Dependable Tamarac was the first horse I used for Freestyle Reining (and multiple reining demonstrations) and she always performed well. Later, I freestyled Wild West Cody, a black gelding. He dressed up stunningly in a red Spanish dress to win reserve championship at Cardston South Country Slide In with *Maleguena,* the routine I used in Calgary on Tamarac. Another year, we performed to music from *Zorro.* I, with black cape and mask, and he, with his black hide, could have been mistaken for Zorro and his black stallion, except, of course, I did not leap off a balcony onto his back!

102. Freestyle: Wild West Cody and I, *Maleguena. Diane C Nicholson*

I performed Freestyle to a variety of music and most routines I considered successful. The flapper performance, however, was a dismal failure. Riding in high heels did not work! I wanted to be somewhere else right in the middle of something I had to finish.

With the computer, I got creative. I edited music and added narrative. A poem or reading at the beginning, especially when I walked into the arena, was very effective. I strived to touch the hearts of the spectators and most times, I did. One woman told me, after watching a routine that included a poem, "It made me want to go out and do something good."

Performances evoking emotion did not sway the judges, however. It was important *to me* to ride to the music, and for the music to tell a story, but I felt the effort escaped the notice of the judges. I understood if reining maneuvers were not up to standard, but I hated to be beat by a "crash and burn" program or a costumed-up performance that did not fit the music. However, I continued to ride the class and did it my way. Freestyle can be a wonderful training tool if the rider chooses the pattern carefully, so I considered that as well. For as long as I show, I will ride Freestyle.

Beginning in 1991 and for several years after, I actively served the B.C. Reining Association on the Board of Directors. I thought my involvement was necessary to promote my event and to provide a venue for reining. Another reason I volunteered may have been a tremendous feeling of accomplishment for goals attained by BCRA. One goal eluded BCRA, however. The Board of Directors launched a "United We Stand" campaign whereby all reining enthusiasts in B.C. would come together in one association. We failed. Several reining clubs sprang up in the province.

The board turned its attention to another goal. There were whispers of reining becoming an international event and our association definitely wanted to be a part of that! Reining Canada, the struggling national reining association, was already in place. BCRA offered support and worked with Reining Canada from that point on. Again, I became heavily involved, traveling to meetings, tracking reining earnings for Reining Canada and publishing a newsletter.

Interspersed with training and showing my reining horses and volunteering on reining associations, was coaching and starting colts, the bread and butter of my business. In my little hillside arena on Grandview Flats, I rode long hours on a variety of horses. Most were not started but not difficult. By that time, I had started so many colts under saddle I could get the job done with relative ease. Sometimes, a horse challenged me if he was older or had had a bad experience, but other than a few bumps and bruises, I had no serious wrecks for several years after I returned from Italy.

Every horse I rode, I checked out as a reining prospect. Every horse in the barn was on the reining program if he was with me for only a month. The first month of training was the same regardless of the discipline, but in the back of my mind, I thought, "reining". If the horse was with me for longer than a month, I introduced him to turn-arounds;[77] if he stayed six months, he would probably learn a little about all reining maneuvers. One winter I rode two Tennessee Walker stallions for their owner until his trainer arrived. I had to try lead changes, spins and stops. "These horses are in top shape," the trainer said after he took over. "What are you doing with them?"

"Reining training."

103. Spook and I.

104. Spook (Tennessee Walker) – demonstration Armstrong B.C.

---

[77] Turn-arounds are spins.

A Life With Horses

Smart Like a Fox 19

I never encountered a horse in whose soul there was no harmony to call on. ~ Vicki Hearne

Many horses have passed through my barn. I remember some for their talent or lack of, some for their intelligence or lack of, and some for their personality. One or two are just unforgettable. Fox was one of those.

I heard about Fox long before I met him. A friend of mine described the gelding to me with all of his inadequacies. He said Fox was a candidate for my program. He must have told the woman who owned him about me because she called, gave a complete history of her horse, and asked if I would be willing to take him for a couple of months.

"He has issues," she said. "You should know Fox will be a challenge." A combination of personality quirks and training wrecks made him difficult to work with, she told me. I agreed to take him and we arranged for his transportation to my facility.

The fourteen hundred pound grulla gelding of Morgan breeding came with a history all right. He was not cranky or mean but liked outsmarting his handlers. He was good at it. He broke halters if tied; he didn't like vets or farriers; he barely tolerated trainers. Once he backed out of a tie stall and kept backing up until he crashed through the side of the barn! Penny had raised him and, for ten years, had worked around his neurotic behaviour. Over the next few months, in her charming, witty style, Penny told me numerous tales of Fox's escapades. In the next few weeks, I would add some of my own.

Penny had cared for Fox through multiple serious injuries—his, not hers—and had even ridden him on his good days, but now he would not let anyone saddle him. She was convinced that he knew no one would ride him if he didn't have a saddle on!

Fox arrived at my barn two hours past the appointed time, skinned up around the face and legs from winching him into the trailer. Apparently, he didn't like to load either. I told Penny I would deal with the loading problem later after he was more used to me.

"No time like the present to get him started on my program," I said. I led Fox to the arena and asked the man who had hauled him to bring the saddle and bridle to the middle of the pen.

"You're going to saddle him?" he asked.

"Not yet."

Penny had given me the low-down. Fox knew all the tricks to avoid saddling—if I tied him, he would pull back and break the halter; if I hobbled him, he would lie down; if I did not tie or hobble him, he would leave the scene.

I knew what he had prepared for. I was going to try something he had *not* prepared for. I picked up the lunge line and whip, stood beside the tack in the centre of the arena and lunged him, an exercise he accepted.

Fox was out of shape and fat. After a few minutes of lunging, he showed signs of quitting. I pulled him into the centre and picked up the blanket to put on his back, prepared for the inevitable. True to script, Fox slithered sideways away from the tack and me. I calmly put the blanket on the ground again and went back to lunging. Again, he tired quickly and again I brought him to the center to saddle. Again, he left. Again, I lunged.

The third time I brought him to me, this time dripping with sweat, he allowed me to saddle him. Handlers had tied, hobbled and otherwise bullied him into standing for saddling. This, an object lesson, he understood. I mounted, rode for a few minutes and ended the day on a winning note.

I used the same method to saddle for the next few days. When I thought he respected me, I switched to saddling by the barn. When he moved there, I said "whoa". If he didn't stand, I kicked him hard in the belly, and repeated "whoa". He knew I meant to get the tack on his back and did not give me any more problems saddling. Getting the upper hand the first day made the difference.

The riding progressed fairly well for the next two weeks. Fox was "on the program" and, although I cannot say he was enthusiastic about lessons, he resigned himself to my schedule. It was time to tackle the loading issue.

At two o'clock on a very hot day in July, after his ride, Fox and I began what Penny later named "A Loading Marathon". I parked my trailer in the driveway of my yard, brought Fox to it and asked him to load. Of course, he did not. I didn't expect he would, but he not only refused to get in, he refused to be anywhere *near* the trailer! Every time I walked him to the trailer door, he threw his head in the air and backed up faster than I could train any horse to back up. I repeatedly asked (by tapping him with a shortened whip) until I could position him with his head at the door of the trailer and he stood there. Then I praised him. After multiple attempts, he walked in. I went to the house for a glass of lemonade.

Although Fox now stood in the trailer, the lesson was not over. I intended to load and unload him several times. Fox had planned the day a little differently.

After my lemonade break, I backed him out, walked him around, and asked him to step into the trailer again. He balked again and now I couldn't lead him even to the door.

I had been "loading" Fox about two hours and the Okanagan sun was taking a toll on me. The schooling had deteriorated to Fox running backward, towing me by the halter shank. I could feel heat exhaustion coming on, but I didn't want to quit. I needed help and I knew who to call. Don Williams had demonstrated the patience required to finish this loading lesson. He was to say later, "I should have known if Sharon needed help with a horse, it wasn't going to be easy."

Don arrived a half hour later, took one look at Fox and accusingly said, "He's got welts on him!" I didn't answer.

He took the shank and whip from me and, with all the confidence of a man demonstrating "how one is supposed to load a horse", asked Fox to step up into the trailer.

Cluck, cluck. . .

With the first "cluck", Fox shifted into reverse. Dragging Don by the halter shank, he plowed through my garden and down the steep bank to the barn in a haze of fine pulverized dust, oblivious to multiple cracks from the whip Don wielded. I waited. Man and horse emerged from the dirty cloud, Don grim-faced, Fox not in the least fazed by the recent activity. Rivulets of perspiration mapped muddy tracks down Don's grimy face.

"Do you see why he has welts now?"

It was going to be a long afternoon.

We did not try to force him into the trailer. Instead, we asked and asked and asked. If he stood facing into the trailer, we allowed him to rest. If he backed away, we aggravated him by tapping him with the whip. The "tapping" got progressively harder if he kept backing. Eventually, he learned to stand at the door of the trailer, so we asked him to step up, again correcting *only* if he backed up. *Four hours later*, Fox would load into the trailer but would not stay there. We didn't try to block his exit if he backed out; we wanted him to stand willingly in the trailer stall. Positive he could outlast us, Fox loaded and unloaded just as fast. The lesson became a battle of wills.

Sometimes you don't get everything you want. Almost dark now, Don and I had to compromise. He had worn us down. We had to find a place to quit.

"Fifty times," Don said, "and we'll call it a victory."

Sixty times, we loaded Fox and sixty times he backed out as soon as his chest touched the front. I hosed him off and turned him out. Don and I, filthy, caked with sweat and dirt, were so tired we could hardly speak or walk. I phoned Penny.

"Do you want me to ride Fox or teach him to load? I don't think I can do both."

"He better learn to load," she said.

Don and I were not sure that night, but we *had* won the battle. Two more hours of loading lessons the next day won the war. The next time Penny came to watch me ride Fox, I eagerly showed off his loading skills. Penny had brought her camera.

"You better get that thing ready," I said. "This isn't going to take long."

I lined Fox up about six feet behind the open trailer door and tossed the shank over his neck.

"Get in Fox." I said quietly.

Fox almost ran into the trailer . . . and stood there. Penny had disappeared around the side of the trailer. She was speechless.

"Did you think he had gone right through?"

"Wouldn't surprise me."

At that moment, the eight hours we spent teaching Fox to load was almost worth it. Victory was mine.

Fox had turned a corner, or so it seemed. He was comfortable to ride and did all I asked without a fuss. I enjoyed my time with him. He was not through with me. . .

My small arena had been cut into the side of a hill. Railway tie posts with rather dilapidated boards enclosed the area and rocks, many of them thrown out of the arena by myself, littered the slope to the pasture below. Though crude, the arena served me well. Here, I rode Fox almost every day.

The schooling session had progressed as any other to loping circles. As we loped, I laid the outside rein on his neck, then gave a small tug with the inside rein to remind him his nose should be toward the center of the circle. His head was down. He was not fighting me. The lope was cadenced and correct.

We had loped several circles without incident until, as we approached the point of the circle looking out over the fence above the steep rocky incline, Fox had a thought of his own. He picked up his head, focused on a distant figment of his imagination, and crashed through the fence, breaking several boards and one partly rotted railway tie. For the few seconds before impact, Fox and I were airborne.

I'm going to come up on you and spank your butt!

Then Fox fell and I rolled off . . . on the rocks.

"Anything a little Bute[78] would help?"

My veterinarian had been driving past my property and couldn't miss the gaping hole in the fence, the cloud of dust, Fox standing in the pasture below, and me stomping after him. He tried, unsuccessfully, not to laugh.

"I'm fine."

I caught Fox, led him back to the arena, and finished the ride. Any thought he had of exiting the arena through the gap he had made in the fence, was gone. The smart horse was smart enough to know he had made a mistake. He had not counted on the other side being so unpleasant. I earned the title of "Woman from Snowy River" from the vet.

---

[78] Bute is the short form for Butazone, an anti-inflammatory drug.

Fox went home a reconditioned horse, if not a completely changed one. Penny had new 'Fox stories' to add to the ones she already had. Some problems I could not fix. Penny would not be able to trust him tied and Fox would always test his handler, always try to do it his way.

Fox enjoys retirement with Penny now. One summer day, her daughter decided to take him for a ride and he tried an old trick—avoiding the saddle.

"Don't p*** me off!" she warned him and he stood. He must be getting old.

Trails, Trials and Triumph
20

Riding is a partnership. The horse lends you his strength, speed and
grace, which are greater than yours. For your part you give him
your guidance, intelligence and understanding, which are greater
than his. Together you can achieve a richness that alone neither can.
~ Lucy Rees

Partnerships can take many forms. I partnered with *people* both personally and professionally. Partnerships with the *horses* evolved from many hours in their company. Almost every day, I interacted with horses either collectively or individually. My children helped with feeding and cleaning stalls when they lived with me, but I always groomed, saddled, rode, cooled down and untacked every horse. I didn't mount a saddled horse, ride, then pass the reins to someone to unsaddle and cool out. Although trainers with a barn full of horses cannot train them all without help, I chose to keep only a number I could comfortably manage myself. My horses performed best with this kind of partnership with me.

With my last child out the door and Wildwood a one-woman operation from feeding in the morning to closing the barn door at night, my relationship with the horses became even closer. Several clients noticed that their horse followed my voice or looked to me when they rode in my arena. At that time, partnerships with horses were the only ones in my life. That was going to change.

Don Williams and I had crossed paths many times. I visited his facility, a few kilometers from mine, for horse functions. He attended clinics I arranged with Vern, assisted in the organization of BCRA and participated in BCRA riding sessions and, of course, helped me teach Fox to load. In the winter of 1993, friendship developed into a romantic relationship with a little help from horses.

Usually, I rode in my outdoor arena on Grandview Flats all winter but, in 1992-93, snow and ice rendered the ground unusable. Desperate for good footing, I asked Don if I could board training horses at his barn and use his indoor for a couple of months. He agreed.

The Williams property was beautiful. A majestic log house backed against the mountain overlooked a barn, arena, pastures and hay fields. Don and his ex-wife had run a small cutting horse operation there for a few years, but had listed the property for sale following the dissolution of their marriage. I felt lucky to be able to ride at such a wonderful facility. The thirteen-stall barn with a heated mezzanine above the attached open-sided arena, round pens and hot walker provided everything needed for a horse business. I worked out of the arena for two months. During that time, Don asked me out and we dated regularly after that. He took me out for dinner or to an archery shoot (a new hobby) once in a while, but we spent much of our time together in the company of horses. I was thrilled. Don shared my love of horses!

I devoted several hours of my day to Wildwood, but we found creative ways to combine my work with time together. Don helped me ride my string[79] or accompanied me to clinics, and sometimes we hauled to a ranch for roundups, but the best hours with Don and the horses were the ones on the trail. As often as we could, we loaded two riding horses and two pack horses in Don's big, noisy stock trailer and headed to the mountains for a couple of days. I often rode the horses I had in training, horses I didn't own, for these rides. I always phoned the owners for permission. No one ever refused. Small wonder. Trail riding was priceless experience for a young horse.

---

[79] "String" is the group of horses one rider is responsible for or rides.

Don knew of a trail to a cabin in the Monashees so he organized the itinerary for the first ride on the May long weekend. I was in charge of horses. I chose Champagne for myself, and Lenas Cool Lady Di, a three-year-old mare in reining training, for Don. Wild West Cody, Don's two-year-old, was ready for a light pack and a new experience. Bobby, a four-year-old Appaloosa with a bunch of issues, was *not* ready, but he was going anyway.

Bobby was a big, strong, good-looking gelding with multiple problems. He came to me for training two years after a wreck that had put his owner in the hospital—the saddle had turned on his back. The accident might have happened the day before he arrived. He had not forgotten! He freaked about anything or anyone moving on or around him. "He's an accident waiting to happen," Don said when he watched me ride him. Bobby needed to be packed.

We arrived at the staging area for our outdoor adventure in time to set up camp for the night, unloaded the horses and hobbled them in a meadow beside a swift-flowing creek to graze. When we tied them for the night, Bobby forced us to deal with one of his issues— halter pulling. He had already broken a halter before we left home when we tied him to the fence while loading the others.

We looped the shank around a tree and stepped away. Bobby was nothing if not predictable. He immediately flew back and leaned on the rope. *Once a halter puller, always a halter puller,* I thought. I had never guaranteed anyone I could fix this annoying and dangerous vice. That day, however, we discovered, quite by accident, a new approach to an old problem.

We had tied Bobby to a young, supple tree. When he pulled, the tree bent with him and smacked him in the face, startling him into jumping forward. He pulled again and the tree smacked him again. He repeated this useless exercise several times. Twice he pulled the tree out of the ground. We tied him to another. Finally, he stood with the shank loose, a little bewildered at the turn of events. Problem solved, at least for as long as he lived with me. For the rest of the ride, we tied him to the smallest of branches and he stood, albeit somewhat nervously. He did not want a tree to slap him again.

We had not counted on an early start in the morning. We suspected packing Bobby would be slow and it was. He lunged around the meadow hobbled and threw the panniers[80] on the ground several times before he gave up. Cody and our saddle horses stood

---

[80] Panniers are the pair of boxes slung one on each side of a packhorse.

quietly tied to trees for the *three hours* it took us to get the job done. Finally Bobby, packed with all we would need for an overnight at the cabin, walked calmly behind Don's horse. We rode out of the meadow and onto the trail up the mountain.

We did not reach the cabin. The old logging road climbed sharply from our camp. Light patches of snow turned to deeper ones. When we entered heavy forest, snow banks completely snuffed out the trail. Not wanting to give up, I made one last effort, slogging uphill through slushy banks leading Cody, until even Champagne refused to go any farther. I looked back at Cody, buried to his chin in wet snow and still valiantly trying to follow. We had to turn around.

Back at camp, I had an idea. Bobby had been on the trail for several hours so he should be tired, tired enough to be more agreeable. I was going to ride him!

Bobby, to his way of thinking, had had a tough day. Convinced that he would be unsaddled, fed and put away for the night, that his day was done with the removal of the pack saddle, he turned and *stared* when I reached for the western saddle. He didn't need verbal skills to communicate his dismay, horrified that another saddle was headed his way! I rode him around the meadow, across the creek and back through the water again. He did not flinch or spook. I called this trail ride "Educating Bobby."

Don and I headed for the trails again in June with four horses. This time *I* chose the trail, destination the mythical Blue Lake on the backside of Hunters Range out of Enderby. My hairdresser told me her father summered cattle on that range and there was a cabin. Perfect. We loaded Lady Di and a three-year-old gelding I was training. Bobby would once again be our pack horse and I chose a pretty, little three-year-old mare to soft pack.[81] Off we went.

It was June. This time, we thought, the trails would be open. We would ride to the top, graze the horses, stay in the cabin and go on to Blue Lake the next day. Right on the first count. Wrong on the second. Right on the third. Wrong on the fourth.

We found the corrals the hairdresser had told me about and parked the truck and trailer (in front of the chute—oops!), unloaded horses, packed, and struck out on a trail leading west away from the corrals. The faint trail disappeared in a large meadow but, with a

---

[81] "Soft pack" (*verb*) is the act of packing a horse with only a light canvas bag with pouches on both sides.

little wandering around, we found it again leading into the bush. When we started climbing, we were sure the trail was the right one.

We did not know how far it was to the top. One switchback after another of progressively steeper, rockier, trail led to more of the same. Fog settled in around us and, with it, an eerie stillness. To give the horses a break, we got off and led them.

"We will be at the top after the next switchback," Don predicted. We were not. A few minutes passed and he tried again.

"After this one." Wrong again. And so on. . .

When we finally emerged into a meadow, still in clouds of foggy dampness, patches of snow covered much of the ground. Where the ground was not snow-covered, vague paths wandered away from the trail we traveled into mist-obscured clumps of trees. We didn't know where to start looking for the cabin.

105. Don packing Bobby on the Blue Lake trail ride in June 1993.

"I think we should put up the tent before it gets dark," Don said.

"Let's look a little more because I sure would like to be inside tonight."

A few minutes later, I caught a glimpse of a building to the right. We had found the rancher's cabin.

The horses weren't so lucky. They didn't have shelter. Worse than that, they didn't have anything to eat. We had brought a little grain, but had counted on grass. We were wrong. With the snow not all melted, the only plant growing was skunk cabbage.[82] They would be unhappy, but it was too late to go back down the mountain. We hobbled two and left two loose.

Warm and comfortable in the cabin, I was concerned for our horses, especially since they were hungry, but we could not move until morning. At four o'clock, chewing on the walls of the cabin woke us. They had come back to complain. No choice but to pack up, saddle up, and ride down. Blue Lake would wait for another ride.

Don and I explored one or two other trails during that summer and, for the next few years, included trail rides in our schedule. I believed riding and packing my horses to be a necessary part of my training program. I rode and packed two-year-olds into the bush at least once before snow closed the trails. These colts were reining horses in training and their three-year-old year would be intense. The change of venue relaxed minds and bodies.

In 1994, I moved in with Don bringing my business and horses with me. Duchess, Tamarac, Shadow and Destiny relocated to MacDonald Road. I added Cody to my training string and Don entered him in the NRHA Futurity. As I revved up for a busy year riding, reining and trail riding, an accident brought my activities to an abrupt halt.

Thus far, I had been very lucky. The knee injury in 1980 was the worst injury I had had. In June, a riding wreck sidelined me.

I had hauled a two-year-old mare to a sale for a client and was riding her in an outside pen the evening before the sale, jogging along the rail completely relaxed, when horses ran up behind on the other side of the arena and startled her. Faster than I could tell it, she popped her head up and executed an airborne ninety degree turn to the left across the arena, throwing me off balance immediately. From his view leaving the barn, above low bleachers by the arena, Don could see me hanging out to the side of the mare. He said I was saying, "Oh, shit!"

The mare's next lunging jump drilled me into the ground behind the only other horse in the arena, another two-year-old, who kicked me. The whole episode took five seconds to happen.

Several people ran out to assist, including Don, who *caught the*

---

[82] Skunk cabbage is one of the first native plants to emerge through the soil in the spring. It is large leaved and smelly (hence, the name)!

horse while I struggled to a sitting position. Nausea engulfed me.

"I have to lie down again," I told the people around me. My stomach churned. My vision blurred.

I'm really going to hurt tomorrow.

One woman said she was a nurse, examined me, and told me she didn't think I had broken bones so, after a few minutes, I got to my feet. Don had passed the mare to someone and disappeared. I took the reins and got on, thinking she needed to be ridden. In the saddle, though, I was in so much pain I knew I should get off again. Don was back and he was angry.

"What good do you think you are going to do?" he said. "I went for my boots so I could ride her. Get off."

"I would but I can't." I didn't know how I got on. He offered to help, but my body hurt so much I had to control the situation myself. Drenched in sweat, I tried different positions in the saddle until, by adjusting my body to muscles other than the painful ones, I slumped to the ground. Sick to my stomach again, I gave the reins to Don and made my way to the truck to sit down while he rode her. Later, on the way back to the motel room, I mentioned that my collarbone was "clicking". We detoured to the hospital. X-rays revealed a broken collarbone and six broken ribs, and I spent the night in the hospital. The story circulated, of course, and the young mare did not sell. She was not at all nasty, just young, and sold later for the asking price.

With a futurity horse in training and clinics and lessons booked all summer, it was inconvenient to be laid up. We sent Cody to Vern Sapergia in Moose Jaw so he would not miss any training and picked him up at the Cardston Futurity (Alberta) in August, where I showed him. In July, I taught a clinic in the Kootenays, barely six weeks after the accident. I bought a special chair to sit in and didn't sit in it much. I had promised myself I would not get on any horses, but I did. It was a tough three days. I was thankful that Don was with me to drive home. By August, I was back to work fulltime.

In November, Don and I hauled Cody to Oklahoma City for the NRHA Futurity. Cody tried hard and made few mistakes. I, on the other hand, overspun in the first go for a zero score. I expected to bring home experience, not money, but I was still disappointed. However, to live, eat and breathe reining of that caliber was an enormous opportunity. I was a little fish in a big pond all right, but I had fast-forwarded two years by competing there. Reining was in my blood. There was no turning back.

106. Wild West Cody reining at the NRHA Futurity in Oklahoma City (November 1994). *Waltenberry*

107. The arena on MacDonald Road, Armstrong B.C.

In 1995, I leased part of Don's property for Wildwood and, for the first time in my life, had the use of an indoor arena. I was thrilled that I had a partner too, for companionship, support, and assistance in the operation of what now had become a more than full time occupation for one person. I opened the doors wide for training, coaching, clinics and workshops and Don and I both showed the reining horses in Alberta and B.C. Any spare time I had, usually nights, I spent learning computer skills to complement the business. These years were a very busy, very happy time in my life.

**108. MacDonald Road property (view from MacDonald Road). The
house is to the left backed up against the mountain.**

109. Wildwood on MacDonald Road. The arena.

A Life With Horses

Ponchita

*If you act like you've only got fifteen minutes, it'll take all day. Act
like you've got all day and it'll take fifteen minutes.*
~ Monty Roberts

Sometimes a single horse monopolized my time. Ponchita's
owner told me she had picked the good-looking, nice-
moving three-year-old Paint mare out of a herd in New
Mexico for a barrel racing prospect. She had not been ridden, she
said, and had run out with the herd all of her young life. Since she
was pregnant (the owner), she wanted me to start her mare so she
would be ready to ride after she had her baby.

The mare settled in nicely at my barn. Her ground manners were
decent and she was quiet. Most of what I could see, I liked. Over 15
hands and still growing, she looked athletic and strong. Smooth, fluid
bodylines and good bone certainly indicated she could be a barrel
racing prospect. What I did not like was Ponchita's eyes. They were
small and, though not flighty or angry, were not warm.

I started her education in the small round pen. She free lunged all
right, so I attached the line to her halter and sent her back out on the

rail. What happened next was so unusual I didn't know what to make of it. When she felt the line to her halter tighten, she had a full-blown anxiety attack, turning into the line and continuing to turn until she had wrapped the line around her body several times. I completely lost control and had to drop the line. Even then, she didn't stop until the entire length of the lunge line circled her body.

Not sure what she would do next, I carefully approached her, talking more calmly than I felt, and untangled the lunge line. Cautiously, I sent her out on the rail of the pen again. Again, she wrapped herself up. At that point, I decided a past negative experience had triggered her bizarre reaction. I unclipped the lunge line and went back to free lunging.

Now I was not convinced Ponchita had not been handled (or *mishandled*) before she came to me. I put her away for the day and repeated free lunging in the small round pen the second day. When she warmed up, I cautiously approached her with the saddle, blanket and snaffle bit. She offered no resistance to bridling and saddling. Apparently, she was comfortable with everything *except* the lunge line. Relieved to have the saddle cinched down, I gently urged her to take a step forward. That's when she told me what she really thought of my program. She tucked her head between her knees, rounded her back, propped her legs and bucked as hard as I have ever seen any horse buck in the rodeo arena. Each time she made contact with the ground, she grunted pure fury. As I sidestepped the wild plunging, I knew I had not been wrong about the look in her eye.

Eventually, Ponchita stood, heaving and tense, but her eye and body language told me she had not given up. I worked her a little longer, unsaddled her and retired to the house to think about how I should handle this mare. I knew only one way—deliver the *same* message the *same* way *every* day until she gave up bucking. For the next few days, I alternated between the round pen and the hot walker. She bucked every time. Finally, I could manage her on the lunge line in the big round pen. If I was very careful, I could keep her from tangling up in the line there, but she added a new twist. She flipped over backwards—seven times! I was not going to try to ride her until all of the nonsense stopped and she showed no signs of reforming.

Don was away on a fishing trip, so had not witnessed these first "works" with Ponchita. When he returned, I filled him in but, though he didn't say so, I could see he doubted my evaluation of the mare. I was leaving for a clinic the day after he got home and I issued orders.

"I know you want to help, but Ponchita isn't ready to ride. She's dangerous. Under no circumstances are you to get on her. If you wish, you can lunge her but nothing else." One word out of me. . .

The first evening I phoned home and asked if he had done anything with Ponchita.

"Yes," he said. "I lunged her and she seemed fine, so I got on."

"What? Are you crazy?" I was shocked, worried, and more than a little mad.

"I only got on, sat a few seconds, and then got off again. Right after I got off, she exploded. I've never seen a horse buck that hard. She's wicked!"

He had enlisted the reluctant help of a woman at the barn to hold the mare while he mounted. He said the woman looked like she wanted to be somewhere else. (She had watched me work Ponchita!)

Don did not get on Ponchita again while I was gone. Riding her had lost its appeal.

When I returned home, I returned with a plan—I would become her worst nightmare. Every morning I saddled her and chose one of the three training venues: round pen, hot walker or lunge line. If she bucked on the first (round pen), I worked her until she quit, took her back to the barn and tied her in her stall still saddled. An hour later or so, I took her to the second (hot walker). If she bucked there, I left her on the walker until she walked quietly. Back to the stall saddled. Still later, I advanced (?) to step three (lunge line). I continued the program until she did not offer to buck. It worked. I saw something new in her eyes—respect.

I had won that argument. Now she didn't buck every time I took her out of the barn. Now she allowed me to get on.

It was not over though. She had more in store for me. I couldn't ride in the indoor arena because she ran to the wall and tried to rub me off. In the large round pen, I had a better chance of keeping her away from walls. If she did get to the edge, I kicked—*kicked* and *kicked* until she moved forward. I rode with my hands forward all the time so she would not go over backwards. When I could control her a little, I rode in the field. I was winning. She had not bucked with me . . . yet! That's why we took Ponchita on a pack trip. She was the pack horse.

Remember the aborted pack trip to Blue Lake? We were ready to try again. We loaded Champagne, Destiny, Ponchita and Shiloh, a strong four-year-old in training with me. Destiny, only two, would carry a light pack.

110. Ponchita with pack saddle on the hot walker at home.

We had no problems packing Ponchita and we were not surprised. She had never been spooky about things on or around her. The trail ride was more adventure than we had counted on, however—such an adventure, in fact, that I wrote the following article, *A Reining Horse Adventure* for local newsletters and magazines:

"Don't tell me they're gone!"

"Okay, I won't tell you, but they *are* gone."

Docs Champagne Taste and Wildwood Destiny were lost in the wilderness and our mountain holiday was turning into a nightmare.

Don and I had been excited about our pack trip up Noisy Creek to the high country. As we climbed the steep, rocky trail, we talked mostly of exploring new territory and of what we might see. We sure were not thinking of using precious holiday hours searching for lost horses.

Two years earlier, we had packed up the same trail in June and there had been too much snow to continue on to Blue Lake. Now, in August, we planned to see all there was to see at the top.

We took four horses. I rode Champagne, a six-year-old reining horse, and Don rode Shiloh, a four-year-old in training. We soft-packed Destiny and let Ponchita, a three-year-old with an attitude, carry the rest.

Trail riding was a new experience for all the horses except Champagne, but our string accepted everything we asked of them. I was proud of them. When we reached the cabin it was almost dark, so we unsaddled the horses, stashed the grub, hobbled Champagne (the only horse broke to hobbles), and concentrated on educating Shiloh and Ponchita. Ponchita chose the hard way, fighting her hobbles and pulling a shoe. That's when we found out we had brought extra shoes but no nails or hammer.

The horses all grazed for a couple of hours, two hobbled and three belled, before we tied them where they were relatively comfortable and retired to the warm, dry cabin for the night. The next morning, after breakfast and camp chores, Don and I saddled Champagne and Destiny for a day ride to Blue Lake. Although I had originally planned to ride Ponchita, the loss of her shoe necessitated a change in plans. I was eager to ride Destiny anyway.

Saddlebags loaded with camera, food, drinks, etc., we happily

111. Ponchita, Destiny, Champagne and Shiloh grazing at the cabin.

set out to explore new territory. The trail led out of camp through trees and meandered upward to open meadows dotted with clumps of trees such as grow in high altitudes. The weather deteriorated as we rode and I pulled my oilskin around me as hail/snow pelted us. The sun peeked out to tease us, and then more snow.

At two o'clock, we stopped above Blue Lake to eat and warm ourselves over a fire. We stripped saddles and bridles off the horses, haltered both, and hobbled Champagne. They munched contentedly while Don built a fire inside a circle of trees and I joined him with lunch. Five minutes later, Don got up to check the horses, which were out of our view. They were gone.

I flew out of the trees.

"You look around here," Don said, "and I'll go down the trail."

He was already running.

I ran over knolls in several different directions and back to where we had pulled our saddles. No horses.

Champagne had slipped her hobbles. With her small feet and dainty way of inching forward for the lush grass, she had simply stepped out of them . . . and left!

I knew Don would follow the back trail, so I turned and struck out across the valley to the top of the ridge we had so recently ridden. Since the trail from the cabin doubled back, I could head the mares off if they had re-traced our trail. Don would be behind them. Then it started to hail, obliterating any tracks that could help us find our horses.

I peeled clothes as I scrambled up the incredibly steep incline on the other side of the valley, determined to be on the trail before Champagne and Destiny got there. Gasping for breath, legs wobbling, I scanned the ridge for any sign of my beloved mares. I saw only Don.

The full impact hit us then. From the ridge, we could view hundreds of acres of wilderness, some open, some heavily treed. Two very valuable, very special Quarter Horse mares were out there, Destiny dragging a long cotton rope shank guaranteed to get her in trouble. Our saddles lay where we had set them on the grass at lunchtime miles from the cabin. Shiloh and Ponchita waited at the cabin, but we could not ride either one of them bareback.

"I'll go back for one of the saddles," Don offered, and he walked off in the direction I had just come. While he did that, I looked around some more but didn't find a trace of our lost horses. I couldn't shake a terrifying image from my mind—Destiny's halter shank snagged by the underbrush. I knew it was not a question of *if* the shank would catch on something; it was a matter of *when* and *where*.

Don, exhausted, returned to the ridge with one saddle and bridle, but we were running out of daylight. With heavy hearts, we abandoned our search. Don had to talk me out of staying out overnight. I couldn't imagine not being there for my horse; I cried all the way back to camp.

The night loomed long and desolate. We lay awake listening but hope that they would return to camp dimmed with each passing hour.

Still in the dark, we silently prepared to continue the search. Of course, we had two horses but no saddles at camp, so we belled Ponchita and Shiloh and walked out of camp before the sun was up.

When we reached the saddle Don had carried part way, we put it on Ponchita.

"Don't get on this horse," Don warned me.

"You mean I'm going to walk leading a saddled horse?"

"The last thing I need," he said, "is to have two horses lost and you hurt." Don was going to cut across to the other saddle while I stayed on the trail and searched the top.

I walked off obediently leading Ponchita, as Don and Shiloh disappeared down the mountain. We had arranged a place to meet.

Ponchita was quiet and willing to go with me but, after a couple of miles, my legs reminded me of the exercise the day before. It just seemed crazy to be walking. I got on. (*I didn't listen to Don any better than he listened to me. . .*) My legs loved the ride and Ponchita didn't buck, but before I met Don, I got off again.

112. Search and Rescue: Ponchita and Shiloh over Blue Lake

"Who do you think you're kidding?"

"What do you mean?"

"I've already seen your tracks and there weren't any footprints. You rode Ponchita."

(*I guess we were even.*)

Don had had a brief glimmer of hope as they approached the spot we had unsaddled. Shiloh had picked up his head and whinnied. False alarm. Don did not hear or see anything. Wilderness had swallowed up our horses. Occasionally, I snapped a photo as we searched, but my heart was not in it.

"If anything happens to Champagne and Destiny, I don't ever want to see these pictures," I told Don.

At noon, we started to make our way back to the cabin, still detouring several times to search out new territory. Don took only a few minutes at camp to pack, then left me at the cabin with Shiloh to return to the truck with a now sore-footed Ponchita. He would hire a helicopter to fly the area. I reminded him to bring a gun in case he found a horse too injured to save. I couldn't lose the image in my mind of Destiny tangled in the brush.

Don left at one-thirty. I did camp chores for a couple of hours, then saddled Shiloh again. I would go back to the ridge where I could view the area we had lost the horses and let Shiloh graze, belling the gelding so the mares would hear the familiar sound. I took a few minutes mounting and talking to him because he wouldn't stand. Even after I mounted, he wanted to turn around. I twisted in the saddle to look behind. Out of the trees trotted Champagne and Destiny.

I was stunned. I had so given up I could not believe what I saw, but there they were! I don't remember getting off, but I stood beside Shiloh as they trotted up to me, tucked their heads to my chest, and breathed warm breaths on me. I stroked their foreheads, whispering my relief. Destiny's shank was gone, the snap dangling from the halter. She was rope-burned on a hind pastern, too, but otherwise both mares were fine. They still had their sliders on.

I had no way of getting in touch with Don, who arrived in a hired helicopter that evening, overjoyed to see three horses in the meadow by the cabin. Only later did the full ramifications of the adventure hit him—when he got the bill from the helicopter service!

I tied Champagne, Destiny and Shiloh behind the cabin, put bells on them and had a peaceful, uneventful night. Don returned the next day with yet another horse and we packed for the descent. As we rode, we discussed what we had learned. We felt more than a little stupid. Later, as we told our story to friends, we were not quite so hard on ourselves. Many had a tale of lost horses to tell, some with more grim conclusions, and the ones who pointed out or laughed at our incompetence were the ones who would never undertake such an adventure. We have since bought better hobbles.

I will not soon forget my feeling of helplessness staring over thousands of acres of wilderness at seven thousand feet for a glimpse of a bay and a sorrel mare and seeing only beautiful B.C. scenery. Nor will I forget how grateful I was to have them back unharmed.

113. Champagne and Destiny headed home after a night lost in the mountains (August 1995).

The trail ride did not change Ponchita. A month later, riding in the field (still could not trust her in the arena), loping a large circle with the reins bridged, I accidentally dropped the end (just the end, not the entire rein) on the right side. When I reached for it, she took advantage of my momentary loss of attention. pancaked me on the spot and kept bucking across the field with the stirrups slapping above the saddle.

I wrenched my back when she bucked me off. Even standing was painful, so I asked Don to take Ponchita to the big round pen, get on and walk her around so she would know she had not got away with anything. He did as I asked and mare did not buck.

The next day, muscles in my back spasmed with every step. I knew I could not ride Ponchita. I asked Don if he would ride her for me again so she understood work did not end because she had bucked me off. Reluctantly, he agreed. I was at the house when he phoned from the barn.

"I can't do this," he said. "I'm afraid and she knows it."

Ponchita two, Don and Sharon zip. I had to get the ball back in my court.

Since I was still hurting, I made a couple of phone calls for a rider. One man promised to come but never showed up. I gave my back two more days of rest, then took matters into my own hands.

Don helped me. In the indoor arena, we laid her down with ropes, covered her with a tarp and sat on her. We were not rough but sought only to humble her. Since she did not fear any kind of tack, she did not fight us. She may have been a little confused. When we let her up, I saddled her, rode out the gate and up the mountain—*fast*. Night approached as I left and Don was far from happy but, in the frame of mind to complete the task, I would not turn back. Ponchita was in a mellow mood when I got back. Don was not.

When Ponchita's owner (with a new baby) came to pick her up, we were getting along, but barely. I could not guarantee her mare to be dependable or safe, so I advised her to get someone to ride her before she did. She took my advice, but Ponchita never reverted to her old ways.

Before she left, she told me she had found out something that explained the Paint mare's bad behaviour.

"Two of Ponchita's full siblings are in bucking strings in the States."

In 1996, Don and I married and purchased his ex-wife's share of the property. Even more motivated to work the business, I spent long days "at the barn". Many of the horses I trained were not reining horses, but they contributed to my education. I continued to rein. I showed Cody, now fully trained, bought young stock to train and sell and bred a few of my own.

Don and I still found time for trail rides and still ran into some kind of a glitch on almost every ride. We searched for new trails and re-rode some old ones.

I was just getting started. There was a wilderness to explore on horseback. There were reining horses to train and ride. There were reining horses not yet born.

In the 70's and 80's I had owned a stallion and broodmares, breeding and selling the offspring. I was building a broodmare band again. It had roots in those early years but with a difference. Now I crossed my race-bred Quarter Horses with reining stallions. Tamarac, granddaughter of Duchess, had been the first, and she was producing—all fillies, all reining bred. These mares would be the heart of Wildwood Reining Horses.

Horses like Ponchita paid the bills, but I hoped one day to exclusively breed and ride reining horses. Destiny, first-born daughter of Tamarac, was the first step of that plan.

Destiny

*A true horseman does not look at the horse with his eyes. He looks at
his horse with his heart. ~ Author Unknown*

The two-year-old we lost on the trail ride to Blue Lake was
Destiny. The time would come when I would wonder why I
named her that. Was she destined for greatness or destined for
trouble?

I was still living on Grandview Flats when Destiny was born.
Tamarac foaled in the pasture in midday sun with no difficulty on
gestation day 366 (!), the birth normal, the little bay filly strong and
healthy. Nothing prepared me for the chaos to come.

The next morning I looked out the window, spotted Tamarac and
Destiny in the field below the house, jumped in my clothes and
walked down the hill to admire the baby I had waited for so long. As
I approached, she moved away from her mother and Tamarac's eyes
locked on the movement. Her ears flicked forward, and then flat
back. Eyes wild, mouth open, she charged Destiny and knocked her
to the ground. I scrambled to intervene as Destiny struggled to her
feet, but I wasn't fast enough. Tamarac body-slammed her newborn

again. Before she killed her baby in front of my eyes, I grabbed Destiny, now trembling and traumatized, and blocked Tamarac with my own body. Cradling the little filly between my arms, I pushed her up the hill to the barn, shoved her into a stall with Dutch doors that opened to an outside paddock and sank to the ground. Heaving from exertion, adrenalin and shock, I stared at Tamarac, who had followed. *How could you?* She could see Destiny over the bottom door but could only touch her with her nose. For the moment, the foal was safe.

114. Destiny born April 20, 1993.

My first priority to feed Destiny, I tentatively led Tamarac into the stall to see if she would allow her foal to suck. She did (Thank goodness Destiny still wanted to!), but still showed signs of running her down if she was in front of her. She could not be trusted alone with her foal.

That night I rolled out my sleeping bag on the straw in the corner of the stall and slept with Destiny, rising every two hours to feed. Between overseeing feeding and worrying, I didn't get much sleep but towards morning, I dozed off. The clout of a small hoof on my shoulder woke me. Destiny had it figured out. If she was hungry, she woke me up to get her mother.

I set up a routine to monitor feedings and maintain a connection between mother and baby, hoping they could be one day be turned out together. For a month, I brought Tamarac into the stall only to feed Destiny, beginning with two-hour intervals between feedings and extending to four. I slept in the house, getting up to bring Tamarac into the stall for Destiny to nurse. In a sleepy stupor, I dragged myself out of bed, stumbled to the barn, caught Tamarac, and slumped in the corner while Destiny sucked. Sometimes, I didn't remember any of it.

After three weeks, I led them both to the arena and tied Tamarac while Destiny played around her. When that went all right, I turned them together in the arena, praying Tamarac would not attack (she didn't), then finally in the pasture.

Though I had not heard of this syndrome before, I found out it is called "savaging" and there is not any explanation why mares behave this way. Tamarac didn't understand her foal running around her, especially if she was in front. It was a long time until I forgave her, a long time until I could forget Destiny shaking in fear of her own mother.

As Destiny grew up, a somewhat obnoxious attitude replaced that fear, almost certainly the result of too much human interaction at such an impressionable time in her life. Most importantly, I saved

115. Destiny (1 year) and I in August 1994.

her, great granddaughter of Duchess, first of a fourth generation. For that reason alone, she was special. She would carry Duchess' gene to the next generation.

Destiny was a charming addition to my herd. Just as her mother had, she watched me ride from behind the security of the arena fence in the pasture she shared with Tamarac and Duchess. She was always interested in what I was doing and would look for me. If I called to her, she lifted her head and whinnied a reply. Though pushy and bossy, she never laid her ears back or kicked, but she didn't have the respect she should for people. I understood. She was a survivor. She would be tested again. . .

When Destiny was ready to start riding, I was living with Don on his property. Since I had not rented the arena yet, I rode in the open fields of snow, so I tried to make the process as safe as possible by progressing slowly. She was easy to start. Like her mother, I rode her first bareback with a halter. True to her nature, she loved the attention and looked forward to our short schooling sessions. I saddled her and rode in the fields or down MacDonald Road. Her delightful personality blossomed with training. She loved her lessons and welcomed our time together. Not surprisingly after her shaky introduction to life, she was tough and unflappable.

"Usually when I put the bucket up on the tractor it spooks the horses. Not Destiny. She comes over and wants to crawl in it," Don said.

One day I was eating fig newtons when I saddled her. She turned around to me, ears forward. She thought I had grain.

"Okay," I said, "but you won't like it!" Wrong. She wolfed the cookie down.

She would eat anything I ate, but I rarely gave in to her obvious "requests", fearing her pushy attitude would get out of control. It did come in handy when I wormed though. She ran to get her wormer. It got to the point I had to tie her up to worm the rest of the herd. She would have been a great advertisement for a worm product.

Destiny's education intensified as the months passed. Always happy, she enjoyed schooling as much as I did. We circled, spun and stopped. In the small indoor arena, she counter cantered and changed leads any time and any place I chose. She loped naturally framed up, naturally "round", a huge asset for reining training. I loved her ability, but it was her personality that inspired me to write about her . . . or *for* her. In December 1995, she wrote the following letter to Santa Claus:

236

Dear Santa,

My name is Destiny and I'm only two years old. You don't know me yet, but all the horses in the barn said I should write a letter to you this Christmas. Actually, they voted me "Horse Most Likely to Get What She Wants", but I know they weren't being nasty. We have all tried to be good horses, so do you think you could leave a little something in front of our stalls when you and your reindeer fly over Armstrong on Christmas Eve?

Quite a bit has happened to me this year. My owner, who I call "Mom", calls herself a "trainer", and I found out what that meant in February, when she showed up at the barn with a saddle and bridle. Almost every day she rode me a little bit. At first I thought it was kind of fun—you know, playing in the snow, exploring the field. But she had definite ideas about where I could go and I didn't get to make any decisions! I went along with her plan 'cause it seemed like too much work to try to get her to see it my way. We went up and down MacDonald Road and around the field for a couple of months and if she hadn't gained all that weight in the winter, I might have bucked her off just for laughs. She has a great sense of humor! The most I could do was jump up in the air, and she didn't like me doing that either, 'cause she slapped me with the reins. Cody must have waited until she wasn't paying attention and bucked her off in a couple of jumps, but he was only playing, Santa. He didn't mean to hurt her. I'm kind of glad I didn't do that though, because after she healed up it seemed to me Cody worked longer and harder than any horse in the barn.

I really was a good horse all year, Santa, but stuff just kept happening to me that wasn't my fault, like when Mom had to pay the vet to sew up my eyelid after a teeny-weeny accident in my stall. I tried to pretend it was nothing, but she freaked when I greeted her at 6:00 A.M. with an inch of my eyelid hanging over my eye. It happened when I was checking out the stall door to see if there was any chance I could take a midnight stroll. I thought if I could just wiggle the door loose with my lips and use my head for a lever. . . I can't be blamed if I have an inquiring mind, can I?

Anyway, Santa, it seems all Mom talks about is REINING. I don't know what REINING is, but most of the horses in the barn are REINING HORSES, and they all talk about SPINNING AND SLIDING. I think Mom is training me to do that spinning and sliding stuff, too. She sure is getting more serious about my lessons lately and I find it hard to be serious. I'm just a child, you know. Isn't there a law about training a two-year-old? I wish you would look into that for me.

Oh, yes, I had an adventure in August that was really quite frightening. Mom and Don took four of us up into the mountains. Can you believe they used me for a pack horse? I guess Mom missed riding me, though, 'cause the second day of the trip they left two of the horses at camp and took Champagne and me for what they called a "day ride". It was all very interesting for a while, but I got a little tired. I was sure glad they stopped for lunch and took the saddles off. And, Santa, it really wasn't my idea to leave. I thought we were playing hide and seek. Then we got lost! I had a terrible time with that halter shank and Champagne was really sick of coming back for me when I got tangled up! I thought I was going to be bear bait if that shank didn't break, but Champagne and I figured it out and we got back to camp. Good thing we did, too, 'cause they weren't ever going to find us! Do you know they hired a helicopter to look for us? I don't think we should be blamed for the helicopter bill, though, because we came home as soon as we could. It was just a slight error in judgment leaving them in the wilderness that way.

So you see, Santa, my life has been pretty interesting for the past year, and I need all the help I can get in 1996. From the time I was born, Mom has been talking about a "futurity", and I think it has something to do with this reining stuff I hear so much about around the barn. I have to admit it sounds pretty neat, but I'm worried about my body. Reining looks like hard work and I've tried everything to change her mind—nuzzling and "soft eyes"—but she has tunnel vision about reining and futurities. Maybe you could leave me a book like "A Reining Horse's Guide to Coping with a Reiner" or any book written by a horse who won the NRHA Futurity. I hear that's the big show! I need to gain some perspective on Mom's plan. Also, I might need some liniment for my aching muscles and a new set of sliding plates. What do you have on your reindeer? Maybe I could impress Mom with the latest thing in sliders. If I can't change her mind about training me for a reining horse, I might as well be a star! My friends in the other stalls would all like more feed and less riding, please. Thank you, Santa. As for mom, you might try to encourage her to take up a hobby, like knitting. Yes, that's it. Get her a bag of wool. And maybe a book, too, a book stressing a less vigorous training program than the one she is currently using. AS I said, I'm worried about my body if she keeps this up.

116. Destiny celebrates Christmas.

Say hello to all your reindeer from all of us at Wildwood. We will be watching for you on Christmas Eve. There's lots of hay in the shed and I'll make sure Mom leaves the coffee on upstairs, so you can have a snack if you have time. Respectfully yours, Destiny

Not yet three years old, she had been savaged by her mother, lost in the mountains and had almost lost an eye. What was her destiny? Her problems were not over. In 1997, she writes another letter to Santa Claus:

Dear Santa,

My name is Wildwood Destiny. Do you remember me, Santa? I wrote to you two years ago. If you remember, it was my very first letter to you. I had had a very interesting year and I told you all about it.

Thank you for the extra goodies in my stocking Christmas morning, especially the fig newtons. I sure appreciate a change from hay and Tiz Whiz.

How are your reindeer? Did you try out any of the reining stuff I told you about? I heard a rumour about "reining reindeer" and I wondered if it was you? I'm sorry I didn't write to you last Christmas, but you'll understand when I tell you about all the things that happened.

Right after Christmas two years ago, when everything was finally going good, I had a pretty bad wreck. I was loping around the arena on a counter-canter (I can do that with my eyes closed!) waiting for Mom to tell me to change leads. I just took my mind off my work for a teeny-weeny second to peak at the nice dun gelding in the pen with me and I forgot about those pillars that stick out into the arena. The next thing I knew, both Mom and I were on the ground and the pain in my shoulder was so bad I nearly fainted. Mom was crying and Don was running to help! What a commotion! I tried real hard to pretend it didn't hurt, but it did, and my right shoulder isn't quite what it used to be yet. Let me tell you, I was on R&R for a while!

But I did everything I was supposed to do and even Dr. Denton said I was amazing!

It just seems like things happen even though I try to be good. Like what happened to my back leg. Do you remember about me being worried about my body with all Mom's reining training? She said it was going to be a lot of fun, but it seemed to me it was all work and no play. We all need to play sometimes, don't we Santa? Anyway, I was hoping you could find a book with a different training program for Mom. Do you remember Santa? I guess books like that are hard to come by, 'cause I didn't see any difference in Mom's training methods after Christmas. I was doing pretty good, too, until I hurt that leg. Mom said she couldn't ride me until I got better, so I had a great summer. She turned me out in the pasture and I finally got to play. I felt kind of sorry, though, 'cause Mom and I had so many plans, with the NRHA Futurity and all. I was just getting into this reining stuff.

My leg didn't get any better after a long rest, though, and the next thing I knew, the vet came to x-ray it. You know what happened then? Mom sent me to Dr. Crawford in Alberta for surgery. Now that was an interesting experience! Have you ever had to take any of your reindeer to the vet? I know you must have, 'cause if they're anything like us horses, things happen. Anyway, Dr. Crawford is apparently **the vet** to go to and I felt pretty important to be chosen. And Dr. Crawford's wife said she knew my great granny, Duchess, so we hit it off right away. I started to wonder if they knew what they were doing though, when I woke up after the surgery. I was doing better before, almost back to my old self. Now my leg hurt like crazy again. And there *were layers and layers of stuff on it. It was kind of neat though, 'cause the doc said I had three pins in my leg and after a long rest I would be fine. The girls in the barn told Mom I was good and they all liked me. You can check with them, if you want. After two weeks, Mom picked me up and took me home and guess what? After quite a few more weeks of bandages and such, Mom and I are back reining! Mom even took me and my sister, Kokanee, on a trail ride. I was real grown up, too, Santa, with Kokanee depending on me like that. You would have been proud of me.*

So, Santa, I've been a really good horse this year. I'm doing everything I can now to keep out of trouble and keep the vet bills down for Mom. I'm trying to take my lessons more seriously so I can be one of the crowd in the reining circle, and I'm teaching my younger sisters all I know.

My friends in the barn have all been good this year, too, Santa, and would like something in the stockings on their doors if you have time. We have lots of hay for the reindeer and Mom always has cookies and hot chocolate upstairs. Maybe you could make Wildwood your coffee stop on Christmas Eve. We'll be waiting.
Respectfully yours,
Wildwood Destiny

Destiny and I did not compete in the NRHA Futurity. With three pins in her left back to repair the ringbone, she was sound enough to compete, but she had missed her three-year-old year. I finally showed her at four with limited success. Although sound, I felt a stiffness that affected the stops. I bred her for a 1999 foal.

Destiny is one of four performing daughters of Tamarac I have retained for my broodmares. To date she has produced five fillies and one colt. I still own Wildwood Legacy Lace, named for Lace (her first filly) and Duchess (who died the year she was born). Legacy will carry the "legacy" of Duchess to the next generation, the sixth.

117. Destiny in 2007.

118. Destiny and I winning the reining at the Interior Provincial Exhibition, Armstrong B.C. *Diane C. Nicholson*

On a Path

As he knotted the reins and took his stand, the horse's soul came into
his hand, and up from the mouth that held the steel came an
innermost word, half thought, half feel.
~ Poet, John Masefield

Many horses left hoof prints on the property my husband and I owned on MacDonald Road. I raised a few babies, coached riders, started colts, trained reining horses, and showed in Alberta and B.C. At first, Don and I managed the business together and even took to the trail a few times. He went with me to shows and often showed in Non Pro reining classes on whatever finished reiner we owned.

Tamarac added to a future broodmare band. Year after year, she produced another filly. Destiny, the mare "destined" for trouble, was the first. Wildwood Kokanee, sired by Goldrush Kid Bonanza, was the second.

Where Destiny was always in some kind of drama, Kokanee was amazingly healthy, sound, and accident free. For the entire time I owned her, I did not have vet bill. Sorrel, as many of Tamarac's foals were, with a star in her forehead, she grew into a big, strong mare with athletic ability and a good mind. I started riding her in 1997. She was my demonstration horse for a "Start Your Colt" clinic.

Since the purpose of the clinic was to demonstrate how I start my colts, I turned Kokanee loose in the temporary round pen in the arena and started from the beginning, explaining the process into the microphone as I worked with her. I had picked the coldest weekend of the winter, -25° C with a wind! The spectators watched and listened from the heated viewing area, but I was not so lucky. Bundled up in Don's ski suit, I worked Kokanee through groundwork the first day, and again the second day. There was nothing contrived about the clinic. Kokanee was an untouched two-year-old out of the pasture. I progressed through lunging without a saddle, then bitting, saddling and bending exercises from the ground just as I would have done if no one had been watching. I planned to ride her the second day. At the end of the first session, she exploded into bucking complete with sound effects—grunts and squeals! I lunged her more and ended on a good note. By the end of the session the next day, I mounted and dismounted several times. She accepted my program so well that I walked, jogged and backed her up in the confines of the round pen. Kokanee had had her first ride.

My credibility might have been in question if she had bucked me off that day. I was careful for several months because Kokanee had showed me some fancy moves in the round pen. During her time with me, she bucked only once and by some miracle, I pulled her head up and stopped her. No one was around when it happened, though Don was in the barn. I almost never stay on a horse that bucks, my talent lying more in preventing bucking, so was disappointed he had not had seen my bronc ride. A year later, in the outside arena, Kokanee unloaded Don. I didn't see his bronc ride either.

I rode Kokanee in several competitions waiting for my other mares to grow up. She was my horse of choice on trails for riding or packing and she was excellent. I believed her value to be as a riding horse, not a broodmare, so never planned for her to remain with me. I sold her in 2001 to a Non Pro reiner who eventually sold her to another Non Pro. As it should be, Kokanee helped others learn the art of reining.

Tamarac's third filly was born early. I had not separated Tamarac from the other broodmares in the pasture, so finding the placenta and no mare alarmed me. I should not have worried. In a section of pasture removed from the other horses, Duchess was watching over mare and newborn. Don and I had set a date for our wedding—June 15, 1996—and I named the little sorrel filly for that occasion. I called her Wildwood Promise. At our wedding, the Master of Ceremonies brought me to tears when he read this poem:

I came one spring day
I came as a surprise
I came as a promise -
A promise of love
A promise of joy
A promise of honor
You gave me love
You gave me joy
You gave me honor
And you gave me privilege,
The privilege of your promise
To each other,
To your families,
To your friends.
It is now time
For me to return
The promise in your hearts.
I give you love
I give you joy
I give you respect
I give you understanding,
The understanding that with our hearts
We will ride and slide
All the way to Oklahoma.
With love,
Wildwood Promise

Promise and I did not go to Oklahoma for the NRHA Futurity. I trained her and showed her a little but sold her at four years old at The Western Horse Sale in Red Deer. She did not make the cut for my future broodmare band. Promise certainly was a good mare, but I thought she lacked personality. She was great to train and performed well, but there was no real connection between us. Though reluctant to sell a mare with a sentimental tie to my life, for once I was sensible. She sold to a ranch in Alberta and probably never had sliding plates on again, but the woman who bought her loved her.

119. Wildwood Promise sliding in the arena at home (1999).

Wildwood Whisperin was born in 1997, another filly for Tamarac sired by the hot new stallion in Alberta, Chics In The Male. Right from the beginning, she showed extraordinary ability. I planned for 2000. She would compete in the NRHA Futurity in Oklahoma.

As Duchess' family tree grew more branches, so did mine, the two intertwined. When my grandchildren visited, they rode. Cindy's daughter, Kendra, visited a few times every year and, from 1997 to 2002, progressed from Duchess to Tamarac to Destiny and Harmony (another Tamarac filly). We started in the small round pen when Kendra was five or six years old and Duchess over thirty. Duchess loved her job. She cared for her young rider too, always obedient and "catching" her if she lost her balance. Only once do I remember an out-of-control situation.

I believed Kendra rode well enough for a ride out of the arena so I, on Destiny, took her and Duchess into the big hay field near the barn. Since we did not own a child's saddle, Kendra rode in Don's cutting saddle. She could not reach the stirrups but had been riding well without them.

I opened the gate to the field and Kendra rode through, Duchess bobbing her head and pulling the reins away from Kendra a little. No doubt bored with arena, she looked forward to the freedom of the open field. I told Kendra to tighten her grip on the reins so Duchess could not pull them out of her hands, closed the gate and got on Destiny.

As we rode side by side around the perimeter of the field to the far corner, I watched Duchess and Kendra carefully for any signs of lack of control, but there were none. At the corner, we turned around to ride diagonally across the field and back to the gate. Duchess started to trot.

"You better slow her down," I told Kendra. "Pull on the reins."

Kendra's hands grasped the horn, the reins loose.

"Take one hand off the horn and pull the reins."

Kendra did as I asked, but Duchess had increased her gait to a very fast trot and Kendra bounced so much she didn't want to relinquish her grip on the horn very long. I had tied a knot in the reins, but it had slipped away from her and she held only the tail of the reins, so any half-hearted attempt to stop Duchess was ineffective. Duchess broke into a lope. Riding up beside her on Destiny would make Duchess would run faster, so I stayed slightly behind and continued to talk to Kendra.

"Hang on to the horn with one hand and pull on the reins with the other. Duchess will slow down if you pull the reins."

Duchess was running now. Kendra was screeching. The race was on, Duchess increasing speed and Kendra hitting a higher note with every stride. Her seat slid wildly back and forth in Don's big cutting saddle, but thanks to the hours she had ridden without stirrups, she kept her balance—with two hands glued to the horn! Every ten strides or so, she bravely took one hand off the horn to pull Duchess up as I directed, but with rein so long as to be useless, Duchess did not slow down. I imagined Kendra flying through the air at the closed gate, but I was helpless to stop the runaway. I should not have worried. Duchess took care of her young charge. As she neared the gate, she softened her stride, slowed, and stopped without turning. Kendra stayed on. The screeching stopped. I trotted up to them, sure Kendra would be crying or frozen with fear.

"Can we go back, Grandma?"

120. Kendra on Duchess.

Apparently, Kendra had enjoyed the ride and, judging by the satisfied look Duchess had on her face, I had the distinct impression she had had just as much fun as Kendra. Grandma had had enough excitement for one day.

Duchess also packed Adara and Larissa, Lana's daughters, for their first rides. Though the girls were not used to horses, Duchess must have inspired confidence because they were never afraid. One time, when I asked Duchess to lope in the round pen, Adara, only four, lost her balance. I could see her slipping to the outside. I ran to catch her, but Duchess was already slowing down. By the time I reached the pair, Duchess had stopped, Adara sliding down the offside stirrup. I reached under Duchess' neck to grab Adara's arm just before she connected with the sand. Adara, not frightened at all, asked to get on again.

121. Adara (3) on Duchess (32).   **122. Larissa (3) on Duchess (35).**

When Larissa was a few months old, I took her up on Duchess. I walked, jogged, backed up, and even executed slow spins with Larissa in my arms. It was the last time I rode Duchess. She was thirty-two. For three more years, my grandchildren rode her when they visited, until I worried she could fall. Although sound, she might stumble if her old legs tripped on something. Kendra graduated to Tamarac when she didn't have a foal and she rode Destiny a few times. In 2002, she wiled away the hours in the arena on Harmony.

As it should be, Duchess and her family introduced mine to the wonderful world of horses.

I had been active in reining associations for a few years. In 1997, Don and I were briefly embroiled in an upheaval in the existing reining association that resulted in the organization of a new one with a slightly altered name, British Columbia Reining Association. I was elected President and on the Board of the local "chapter", North Okanagan Reiners. NOR bravely hosted the first annual Okanagan Summer Slide in 1997 and cast the die for one of the best reining shows in B.C. By 1999, the show had outgrown the small club and NOR passed the reins to the parent club. Either way, I was deeply involved in the planning and hosting of Okanagan Summer Slide for nine years. The show was a huge success but we had created a time-eating monster. Okanagan Summer Slide consumed my summer, and because volunteers were scarce, I could not step down. I served on the BCRA Board and Show Committee and edited the newsletter, *Slide Trax,* all in addition to the responsibilities at home.

In 1998, Tamarac gave me Wildwood Harmony, a beautiful sorrel filly sired by Peeping Bo Badger. In 1999, she added Wildwood Soul O Silk. I now owned six fillies from Tamarac. About this time, I started calling Duchess' family "The Dynasty".

In the fall of 1998, I received a call from a woman in Ontario who expressed an interest in reactivating Reining Canada. She knew I was on the Board of the national association, now in hiatus, and wanted me to help. I called the former president and got the ball rolling. By January 1999, Reining Canada was up and running again. I served as Treasurer for a year and edited another newsletter.

At one Reining Canada meeting, the Board of Directors expressed an interest in a database to track Canadian reining earnings. The idea appealed to me, but Reining Canada's budget could not handle a custom designed program. When I could not find a program to fit the budget, I investigated other possibilities. I already had Microsoft Access (a database program) on the computer, so I bought books and, over the next two years, developed a program to track reining statistics. My laptop went everywhere with me, even to the mountains, while I worked on the program. Then I hassled show secretaries from coast to coast for results of reining shows. The result was a compilation of Canadian reining statistics from which reports of earnings of riders, owners, horses, get of sires, etc. could be generated. I sold CanStats in 2003 complete with five years of Canadian reining results.

What does CanStats have to do with my life with horses? Quite a bit. Horses were the reason I pursued programming and horses were the reason CanStats spawned several other programs. I used ReinShowTrak to manage Okanagan Summer Slide and sold the program to other shows. I also developed ClubTrak for British Columbia Reining Association, BarnTrak to manage my business and HorseTrak for Wildwood horses. I customized all of these programs to fit the needs of the user.

Up to 1999, I started, trained and showed all my horses. I decided that year to exercise caution and common sense. I hired a young man to ride Whisper the first times. I did all the groundwork and when I thought she was ready, I asked him to come to the arena. I lunged and otherwise warmed Whisper up; then he stepped up on her. He wasn't there long. She promptly bucked him off. I could see he didn't "safety up" at all, so we discussed that and he got on again. This time he took a deeper seat, but Whisper bucked and lunged across the arena several times, dropping her front end each time she turned at the wall. He was on the ground again. I was glad it wasn't me.

"What happened?" I asked.

"I just sort of got tired and fell off."

She wanted to buck and she learned it worked, but we eased her into a better way by keeping her on the lunge line for the next ride. After a couple of days, I took over.

Whisper advanced remarkably fast in her training. She changed leads naturally, circled with her head down and had the prettiest run down and stop I had ever seen . . . and she loved to stop!

In keeping with my new plan to slow down, I sent Whisper to Shawna Sapergia in January 2000, to finish her training and show her. I questioned my decision—Whisper was the best reining mare I had had since Tamarac—but Don encouraged me to make the transition from "trainer" to "owner". Shawna showed Whisper to a Canadian Supreme championship in Canada and hauled her to the NRHA Futurity in Oklahoma. For the first time, I *watched* my horse compete from the stands.

Whisper did not perform at the level required to win at the Futurity and she needed a rest. I took her home, rode her lightly during the winter, and planned for the next year. I showed Whisper for several years thereafter and always enjoyed her. It was a great feeling to run down the pen and *know* she would always stop.

123. Wildwood Whisperin and I competing at Okanagan Summer Slide (August 2001). *Sharon Latimer*

I was training Wildwood Harmony in 2000 when Whisper was with Shawna. I liked the mare, the fourth daughter for Tamarac and the most like her. A gentle soul with a gentle heart, Harmony was easy to train and easy to ride. I had only to show her what I wanted and she tried.

I missed Harmony's birth. I had driven to Calgary to visit my new granddaughter and hoped Tamarac would wait until I returned. I was reluctant to leave home for that reason and another. In my absence, my black gelding, Shadow, was to be euthanized. The navicular[83] disease in his feet grew worse every year. I could not see him suffer any longer. Before I left, I slid on him bareback with a halter, loped him across the big round pen with soft footing, my legs hugging his warm body. Gently, I asked him to change leads and just

---

[83] Navicular is a medical term for degenerative changes in a small bone in the horse's foot (navicular), navicular bursa and deep flexor tendon.

as gently, he did. I remembered the gift of confidence he had given my students and me. Shadow would not be there when I returned.

124. Tamarac and Wildwood Harmony May 9, 1998 (3 days old).

On the day the vet euthanized Shadow, Tamarac, pastured in the field under Don's watchful eye, was not due to foal for several days. Under Duchess' *more watchful* eye, she foaled out Harmony in the trees behind the house. It seemed poignant to me that Harmony arrived the same day I lost Shadow, so I wrote this:

In His Shadow

On May 6, 1998, I said goodbye to a good and faithful friend. Wildwood Shadow, my big, kind Quarter Horse gelding, was laid to rest under the apple tree overlooking our arena. Shadow—show horse, teacher, companion, friend, and always a perfect gentleman. I will miss him.

A few hours later, a short distance from the apple tree, the newest addition to Wildwood was born, a beautiful sorrel filly. Wildwood Harmony entered a world of Okanagan sunshine and love. Her mother, great grandmother, (thirty-two years old) and her yearling sister welcomed her. She will never know Shadow but already shows signs of becoming a trusting, kind, quiet and loving horse as he was. Did Shadow leave a legacy of his wonderful disposition to her? Was it coincidence or providence that Harmony was born on the day he died? Either way, his passing was made a little easier by her arrival.

It seemed as if Harmony took Shadow's disposition. She loved people as he had. When she developed a chronic pneumonia and I treated her for a few weeks, I walked up to her in the field with a syringe of sulfa solution, opened her mouth with one hand and squirted it down her throat with the other. I never haltered to give her the medicine.

I had changed the name of the business from Wildwood Training to Wildwood Reining Horses, which more suited my goals. Wildwood horses grazed the fields on our property and entered the show pen. Wildwood horses sold to new homes. My husband and I enjoyed good health, good horses and a good life. Our days were full but always full of life, animal and human. Our children, married with children of their own, visited regularly. We enjoyed our grandchildren and introduced all of them to the horses, especially the foals. There were always several foals in the pastures because we boarded and foaled out broodmares for customers. The kids loved the babies.

I trusted in a happy future. I had no reason to think otherwise.

A Life With Horses

Losing Lace
24

I'll lend you for a little while my grandest foal, HE said.
For you to love while he's alive and mourn when he is dead.
It may be one or twenty years, or days or months, you see,
But will you, till I take him back, take care of him for me?
He'll bring his charms to gladden you, and should his stay be brief,
You'll have treasured memories as solace for your grief.
I cannot promise he will stay, since all from earth return,
But there are lessons taught on earth I want this foal to learn.
I've looked the wide world over in my search for teachers true.
And from the throngs that crowd life's lanes, with trust, I've chosen
you.
Now will you give him total love? Not think the labor vain?
Nor hate me when I come here to take him back again?
I know you'll give him tenderness and love will bloom each day,
And for the happiness you've known, forever grateful stay
But should I come and call for him much sooner than you'd planned,
You'll brave the bitter grief that comes, and someday, understand.
~ Author Unknown

I do not accept the death of one of my horses well. I've lost a few, of course. I grieved for each. I learned from each. There was Cheetah, for whom I made a choice I regretted. There was Shadow, whose painful steps left me no choice. There was Duchess, still with me in 1999, whose time would soon come. There would be others.

I was particularly vulnerable as I waited for Destiny to foal. I had a huge emotional investment in the baby, a new generation of Duchess through Mahogany and Tamarac. Destiny had overcome adversity over and over again. Now she was in foal. I couldn't wait for this special baby. Rod Jeffries had given me the service to his stallion, Hot Pretense, admittedly not a reining cross but a very pretty, very talented, bay stallion. He was as anxious as I to see the offspring.

I pastured Destiny by herself in a field by the house and watched her closely as her time approached. On April 18, 1999, I jumped out of bed at five o'clock to check her from the windows, but she was not in view of the house. As I walked down the driveway, a haze hovered over the grass as the spring sun warmed the earth. The air was fresh and cool. I heard only morning sounds—a few contented, sleepy, chirps from birds, the distant muffled highway hum. Suddenly, movement on the wooded slope to my left caught my attention. I looked up into the trees. Three does had been grazing the hillside but now stood quite still, intently watching. I was not the object of their interest; something in the trees ahead of me held their attention. I followed the direction of their gaze to a large spruce . . . and Destiny. Alert but motionless, dirty but quietly proud, obviously exhausted, my resilient bay mare rested beneath craggy evergreen branches. Under her sweat-encrusted neck, on unsteady, quivering legs, stood her first-born. The fourth generation of Duchess had arrived.

125. Destiny and Lace, an hour old, April 18, 1999.

"Destiny has a filly," I yelled to Don, startling him out of a sound sleep as I burst into the house.

The filly came with colour and chrome—sorrel with a star, strip and snip and four white socks! Where did that come from? Sire and dam are bay. Could it be a throw back to Doc Bar, Destiny's grandsire?

Lace was a beautiful filly—healthy, strong, pretty. After two or three days in the barn, I turned her and Destiny back in the field where she was born. I watched them every day. Destiny was a good mother, Lace sassy and full of life.

126. Destiny and Lace May 9, 1999.

On May 12, I packed to leave to teach a clinic. I saw Destiny and Lace at the fence around the house in the morning and noticed Destiny dripped milk from her udder. I did not investigate further. Later, when I went to the barn to meet the farrier, I checked the filly again and this time I knew she was sick. She had not been sucking. Head down, she did not want to move. Frantic now, I could think of only one thing to do. I must get her to the barn. Since no one was home to help, I pushed and pulled Lace ahead of her mother out of the field and into a stall. She was extremely ill and could barely breathe. I ran for the phone but could not reach a vet and I knew time was running out. I grabbed Ventripulmin in a desperate attempt to clear her lungs and help her breathe, but when I went back to the stall, my beautiful filly lay dead in the straw. I sank down beside her.

Devastated, inconsolable, I blamed myself for Lace's death by my neglect. When the farrier arrived, he found me sobbing into Lace's soft sorrel neck.

Lace died of a lightning-quick, extremely deadly form of pneumonia, confirmed when the vet sent samples to be tested. He told me he could not visually detect signs of pneumonia in her lung tissue.

To say the next few days were difficult would be an understatement. I buried Lace under the apple tree with Shadow and tried to bury the memories with her. I didn't think I could teach the three-day clinic, so I phoned the woman organizing the clinic, told her what had happened and tried to cancel. She talked me into going.

I took the image of Lace's last moments with me everywhere. I could not accept that I did not do enough to save her. I heaped guilt upon myself. Music has always been a part of my life and I stopped listening. Certain music connects to events, people and animals in my life and particular pieces deepen the emotion of particular events. They all reminded me of Lace. Eventually a few hours, then a day, would go by when I did not relive the tragedy, but I never played my music.

I could not talk about my loss and my friends knew not to. I did not tell my own children, now grown and gone. I kept the tragedy locked inside myself for a time, a long time as it turned out. For many months, I could not bear to watch the video of Lace running in the field with her mother. When I did watch, the Randalls sang, "You took the flower, but you stole the seed." in the background on the tape deck in my truck. I wept again.

I immediately sent Destiny away for breeding, an impulse decision I later regretted. Not ready to go through another loss if it should happen, I wished I had not bred either her or Tamarac.

I thought a lot about Duchess' family, the Dynasty. Something was missing, something besides little Lace. It was time to bring Mahogany home.

I had sold Mahogany ten years before and she had resold at least once. I did not know where she was, or even if she was alive, but I started looking. With the help of the internet, AQHA, and the phone, I located her in northern Alberta and bought her. When Don and I drove into the yard, she stood in a panel pen in the yard. I walked over and spoke to her. Her eyes flickered for an instant, and then tentatively she walked to me and touched my hand with her nose. Mahogany remembered.

Although she had a good home then, Mahogany had suffered some bad times. She was not sound and showed evidence mentally and physically of abuse. She had recently lost a foal and, if I had not made that call, her life was going to end. Don and I hauled her home to her family and turned her in the pasture with Duchess and the others. She was probably happier than she had been for a long time. She and Duchess bonded almost immediately and thereafter were never far apart. I planned to breed her the next year but, for now, I allowed her to heal. She knew she was home.

Several months later, Mahogany again showed me she had not forgotten me. I didn't intend to ride her again, but one day I couldn't resist. When I bridled her, she fussed with the bit, expecting it to hurt. I hopped on bareback and played a little with the reins. She pulled back on my hands; she didn't think there would be any release. I lifted my hands and lowered them when she "gave" to the bit even a little. Her head lowered and stayed there. She remembered . . .

I felt tears welling up in my eyes. How wonderful that this beautiful mare, abused by uneducated and cruel hands, could forgive! We jogged and loped around the arena collected and correct. I even spun her slowly. I had trained all my life, but never, until that moment, did I truly believe my own words. A horse does not forget a good training program.

I would like to say I started to heal too, but I have never really accepted Lace's death. I know the fault was mine. I pray another horse of mine does not pay the ultimate price for my negligence.

In the spring of 2000, I discovered a tool to soothe, if not heal, the ache in my heart. I developed the area around the graves of Shadow and Lace. I fenced the plot, hand digging every post in and railing it myself. A wild rose bush had sprung up at the head of Shadow's grave and I planted a white spirea at the head of Lace's. I rocked around the shrubs and mowed the grass. That fall I added crocus and tulips and every spring thereafter, life sprang from the earth covering the horses I loved so much. Working over their graves provided comfort for me and for the rest of the time I lived on the property, I kept the site pretty.

Maybe Destiny needed time to heal too because, though she checked in foal, she did not carry a foal in the spring.

*****

127. The gravesite under the apple tree.

Part 5

Riding Full Circle

*No ride is ever the last one. No horse is ever the last one
you will have. Somehow there will always be other horses, other
places to ride. ~ Monica Dickens*

Riding into the Millennium

*"The essential joy of being with horses is that it brings us in contact
with the rare elements of grace, beauty, spirit and freedom."*
~ Sharon Ralls Lemon

When I was a child, I wondered many times where I would
be and what I would be doing at the turn of the century.
As the date drew nearer, I knew I wanted to celebrate with people I
loved in a place we all loved. Most of all, I wanted to make a
memory. I did not look far to find what I was looking for. My
granddaughter, our dogs, two of our horses and my husband and I
welcomed 2000 on top of the mountain behind our house.

The "Millennium Adventure" required advance preparation.
Before snow fell, Don and I rode up the mountain to choose a
campsite. A week before Christmas, Don and Kokanee packed in a
tent, stove, hay and firewood. Don set up the tent, arranged cedar
boughs for a bed and built a temporary corral for our horses.

On New Year's Eve, we packed Kokanee with food, clothing
and sleeping gear, saddled Destiny, added saddlebags stuffed with
extra clothes and hot chocolate and walked away from the barn

leading the horses. Don shouldered a "day pack" with emergency supplies, I carried a 35 mm camera and Kendra, eight years old, packed party favours in her own backpack. The Millennium Adventure on the Mountain had begun.

"I still think you're crazy!" our chore girl called as she videotaped our departure.

Not too crazy though. I usually rode trails in sliding plates. For this trip, I chose unshod horses even though two conditioned three-year-olds stood in the barn, but with sliders.

Don and I immediately felt the effect of slogging uphill through deep snow in winter clothes. Our legs and lungs burned; our hands sweated inside our mitts. I unbuttoned my jacket and stuffed my toque in a pocket. Kendra, in her pink snowsuit, trudged through the snow in front of us, the safest place since the horses would not run uphill away from home if they got loose.

Heading up a mountain through the snow was not Destiny's idea of the best way to spend New Year's Eve. She jumped around until she threw my video camera out of the saddlebag and when I got on, she reared, turned on a slippery slope and almost fell. I pushed her up the mountain ahead of Don and Kendra until she behaved. When they caught up, we rested for hot chocolate, and then continued the steady climb with more control.

Kendra toughed it out, but her little legs tired after an hour of hiking uphill in snow, so I boosted her on Destiny. As Kendra told her mother later, "Destiny was bad with Grandma, but she was good when I rode her."

When we arrived at the already-erected tent, I remembered what I had forgotten—the truffle cake! Darned if I would let 2000 arrive without that cake! I climbed on Destiny and rode back for it while Don and Kendra unpacked.

The tent was warm and cozy when I got back. Fox and Kirby (the dogs) had made themselves at home and Kendra was housekeeping already, deciding who would sleep where and hanging her outside clothes on the temporary line down the ridgepole. I pulled the saddle off Destiny and turned her with Kokanee in the pen Don had fashioned from white electric fencing tape. Snowflakes salted their backs as they buried their noses in hay.

Having Kendra with us lent unexpected charm to our adventure. She helped Grandpa gather firewood and fetch water (the creek was still running so we didn't have to melt snow), chattering a mile a minute. She had an opinion on everything.

"Kokanee carried the luggage, didn't she, Grandma?"

"Kirby and Fox are going to sleep with me."

She attacked the adventure with eagerness and wonder, but after a hearty meal of steak, potatoes and cake, she couldn't keep her eyes open. I promised to wake her at midnight, and she snuggled into her sleeping bag with a dog on each side. Don and I sat on blocks of wood by the fire and talked. Firelight dancing on fat flakes of snow bejeweled the nightscape, setting the scene for the much-anticipated moment in time, a moment none of us would forget.

A few minutes before midnight, I set the video camera on the tripod and woke Kendra. With Kirby and Fox at our sides, Destiny and Kokanee watching from behind their enclosure, the three of us counted down the seconds to the magic hour. We toasted the new millennium with funny little hats, noisemakers and champagne by a crackling fire on a snowy mountain. Wilderness touched settlement as coyotes barked in the shadows and fireworks popped in the valley below. Then a deep stillness that is at the same time ethereal and eerie wrapped us in peace.

128. Destiny, Sharon, Kirby, Kendra, Don, Kokanee January 1, 2000.

It snowed all night. First light of a new century fell on a "marshmallow world". Evergreens bowed under the white blanket and the mares shook snow off their backs. A hush had settled over our meadow on the mountain with the heavy snowfall. Time slowed. In the snug closeness of the tent, we didn't want to leave. Only after a pancake breakfast and multiple cups of camp coffee did we stir enough to organize for a photo in front of the tent, a memory of a special adventure shared with special people on a special day. When I look at that photo, I can easily imagine our ancestors in a similar scenario, not by design but by necessity, on January 1, 1900.

Tamarac gave me a colt for the first time in 2000—Wildwood Badger, a full brother to Harmony. I found him in the stall a few minutes after he was born, a big, muscled colt. He had not been up yet but appeared strong and healthy.

Two hours passed before Badger stood up—too long. When he did, he was slightly "over at the knees", but many newborns are that way. The next day, one leg bent over at the fetlock and the vet treated Badger for contracted tendons, but I suspected more than mild angular limb deformity. I hoped stall rest would give his coltish legs a chance to straighten and strengthen but, worried, added massages to his recovery program. Twice daily, I sat in the straw with him, extended each leg and gently massaged the tendons. Sometimes, I lay down with him with my head resting on his flank. He welcomed me into his life and loved the attention.

Sadly, the diagnosis of hypothyroidism was not made until two weeks later and his knees had sustained permanent damage. Only surgery could save Badger. When I told Don I was going to send him to the best veterinary surgeon, I could see he was going to veto the idea.

Don't try to change my mind!

He opened his mouth to say something and closed it again. Later, he told me the look on my face told him I would ignore anything he had to say. He was right. After losing Lace, nothing was going to stop me from giving this foal a chance to live.

Badger tolerated his operations and postoperative care with grace. Always a delight to work with, he showed no resentment for all the pain we inflicted on him. He always met us with his ears up.

Dr. Denton Moffat removed the pins from his legs after the surgery. When I arrived at the clinic, Badger was in the aisle. Denton disappeared for a second, came back with a brush and started brushing Badger.

"He likes to be brushed, you know," Denton said.

Yes, I knew.

I sold Badger for a breeding stallion. I lost a ton of money, but I saved him. I hope I made up a little for not doing everything possible for Lace.

129. Badger loved to be massaged (May 2000).

130. Badger May 2001.

A Life With Horses

Riding B.C. Trails

Know the peace of open country
Shared with a faithful friend.
You'll leave with spirit lifted
Until you come again.
Let your horse be your companion
And your Maker be your guide.
As you set your pace to His
On this, your lonely ride.
- Sharon Gates from the poem "Lonely Ride"

I started taking to the trails by myself in 1997, not entirely by choice but because, most of the time, Don was not available. I did not let going alone stop me—I still wanted to explore much of B.C. on horseback—but the nature of my business made *planning* trail trips impossible. Excursions to the mountains tended to be impulsive. If all was running smoothly at home and the weather was good, I loaded and left.

Information about B.C trails seemed to be hard to come by. I quizzed a few riders, but many did not trail ride or stuck to closer, easier ones than I had in mind. I looked for books for B.C. trail riding. No luck there either. Finally, I researched maps, chose a destination and headed out on my own. The dearth of information had spawned an idea—to ride the trails, document them with video, photos and notes, and publish a trail riding book. Thereafter, I always packed cameras, GPS, a notebook and pencils in my saddlebags. I am still gathering material for the book.

In August, I loaded Cimarron (Colonel Poco Sugar), my current three-year-old reining trainee, and drove to an area just past Keefer Lake in the Monashees. I targeted the Barnes Creek Trail, relying on B.C. Forest Service maps for directions. The Barnes Creek ride was not entirely successful.

The day started well. I drove until the road ended at a creek I hoped was named "Barnes", parked, saddled Cimarron and looked around. *More than one way out of camp and no signs.* My sketchy maps indicated Barnes Creek Trail would take me to a view of The Pinnacles by way of Vista Pass, so I chose an old forest service road that looked like the most direct path to those Monashees peaks and rode away—*up*—from the creek and my outfit. An hour later, the trail convinced me it was the wrong one. I returned to the trailer, tied Cimarron to a tree and made myself comfortable in my living quarters just as it started to rain.

At least I don't have to sleep in a tent.

Cimarron, usually patient, was not. From my warm bed, I heard him fidgeting and fussing. After a couple of hours of fitful sleep, I got up and loaded him. For the rest of the night, he kept me awake stomping around in the trailer.

In the morning, I slipped cameras in plastic bags and rode out on another old road under a grey, overcast sky. This one took me to the top of the mountain and, after a dead-end detour, to an identifying sign by a creek, Barnes Creek trail.

The atmosphere was gloomy, almost spooky, with heavy fog and a light drizzle. Hoping for a break in the clouds, I crossed the creek to follow a distinct trail over a lightly treed knoll. When it disappeared into a stand of tall timber, I stopped. The prospect of riding into the obscurity of a forest I was not familiar with did not appeal to me. Besides, would I be able to see anything if it came out in the open? To Cimarron's relief, I turned around.

When we returned to the trailer, camp was not what we had left.

We had company. Two lively groups complete with quads and chainsaws were setting up camp two hundred yards from my trailer. Peaceful solitude shattered, I decided to move in the morning. The Barnes Creek trail ride would wait for another time. (In 1998, I rode here again. The shaded forest trail opened up to a panorama of subalpine splendor—verdant meadows, clear tarns and a *spectacular view!*)

The next day, I drove to another part of the Monashees I had learned about first from a map, then from an employee at the Forest Service office. Again, I parked by a creek and this time Cimarron and I were alone. Cimarron even had a small corral, which I assumed belonged to the rancher who ran cattle on that range. Two rough roads from the parking area led to hiking trails not accessible to horses but to more scenic views of the Pinnacles. I rode both of them.

I had only just begun. I would be back.

131. Cimarron and I in the Monashees in August 1997 (Pinnacles behind).

For my first solo *pack trip*, I chose a trail I had ridden before with Don, a trail off Ashnola River to Joe Lake. Good corrals at the trailhead appealed to me. I would not worry as much about my horses.

I arrived at the corrals in time to settle Destiny and Kokanee for the night, built a fire, and watched the October moon rise over the mountain. Relaxed, content, and confident, I retired to my bed in the camper and slept soundly.

The next morning promised clear skies, but sunlight struggled to touch the bottom of the narrow valley and my camp. Frost whitewashed every blade of grass. A thick layer of transparent ice covered the mares' water. I blew on my hands and slapped them together while I built a fire.

After bacon, eggs, and plenty of coffee all cooked on the campfire, I haltered my mares and tied them to the trailer. Since I planned only a day ride, I didn't need a pack horse, but I light-packed Kokanee, two years old, as practice for both of us. I had not packed her at home, so departure from camp was slow but with no wrecks (unlike the experience with Bobby). Proud of myself, I mounted Destiny and, leading Kokanee, crossed Ewart Creek, which ran by the trailhead. From there, the trail meandered through golden-leaved poplars above the creek for a few kilometers. Filtered sunlight danced over us, not at all warm but at least cheerful.

Destiny, with her usual down-to-business approach to life, clip-clopped down the well-worn trail. Any time Kokanee stopped, she pulled her along. On one particularly rocky, twisty climb, Kokanee refused to lead and I dallied to my saddle horn. When Destiny, uphill from Kokanee, tried to drag her, she yanked her off balance and the lead shank swept me out of the saddle over Destiny's rump. I fell backwards on the rocks between the mares. Unhurt but slightly alarmed, I vowed to be more careful. If I had hit my head on a rock, I could have lain there for a long time before someone found me.

The trail crossed Ewart Creek again, this time on a bridge. The four-foot wide wood structure suspended several feet above churning water and not railed could have ended the ride, but Destiny matter-of-factly clomped across and Kokanee, seeing no reason not to, followed. Crossing Juniper Creek was a bigger event. Deep, swift water boiled over good-sized, slippery rocks. *Go for it*, I thought. I pulled my video camera from my pack, turned it on and, with reins and shank in my left hand and camera to my eye in my right, asked Destiny to step into the creek. Kokanee followed at first but changed her mind midstream, stopped, jerked my arm, and blurred video. I hastily dropped the halter shank in favour of saving my camera and myself from a dunking but kept the camera rolling. The resulting footage of rapid, roaring creek viewed through Destiny's ears and, when I turned in the saddle, Kokanee sloshing through with halter shank dragging, is at least creative.

The trail climbed sharply and steadily from the creek, first through more poplars, then up the long, open, yellow-grassed slope to cabins built for wildlife specialists studying Bighorn sheep. I unsaddled both mares at the top for a rest and grazing. Kokanee, exhausted, did not eat, but Destiny and I took advantage of the break to grab a bite and, for me, to open my thermos. Coffee never tasted better. I stared into hazy mountains many miles away and sipped. I had re-discovered the benefits of riding alone.

132. Kokanee (2) and Destiny at Sheep Cabin October 1997.

In June 1998, Kokanee (now three years old) and I set out to find another trail, a hiking trail in the Monashees that interested me. Again, I chased views of the Pinnacles, which maps indicated I could access from several different directions.

The forest service road was passable, a blessing because it was new to me. Thus far, I had been lucky. I had pointed my truck and trailer up a mountain road and no huge rocks, washed out bridges or dead ends had stopped me. Maybe I should have made one trip with the truck before I hauled my gooseneck two-horse with living quarters up a new trail. . .?

Since I had never driven the road, I did not know the distance to the trailhead. When I thought I had climbed far enough, I investigated a spur off the road and decided I could park there. (Don accompanied me on a later ride here and couldn't believe I turned the rig around in that tight spot.)

Kokanee spent the night tied to a tree, but early the next morning I belled and hobbled her so she could graze the small grassy area. I crawled back into my camper bed and, lulled by the clang of her bell, went back to sleep for an hour. After breakfast, I saddled, stuffed saddlebags with maps, cameras, GPS and lunch, and cautiously asked Kokanee to lead with the load. Not comfortable with saddlebags slapping her flanks, she crow-hopped[84] in a wild circle around me, so I led her for a short distance up the trail before mounting.

133. Kokanee and I in the Monashees in June 1998.

Squirrels chattered objections to anything and everything as we entered their world. Resident birds trilled a chorus of greetings and announced the presence of an intruder to whatever animals watched from the cover of trees. Crisp morning air scented with pine and the musk of heavy forest filled my lungs. My spirits soared.

Kokanee's ground-covering walk ate up the steady climb to the trailhead, which turned out to be three or four kilometers from my camp. Just before the trailhead, out of dense forest, a gentle stream

---

[84] Crow-hop is cowboy slang for a half-hearted buck. (Can also be used as a verb.)

276

trickled across the trail from one of several patches of snow. Kokanee dropped her head to the water. I listened as she drank. . . only a mountain melody—birdcalls, marmot whistles, and gurgling water! A few steps later, in a flattened area that no doubt had something to do with logging, a sign marked a hiking trail, the one I planned to ride. With the rest of the day ahead, I reined onto the path.

There is no trail riding experience quite like riding a trail for the first time—the anticipation of a view, a lake or animal, a glimpse of a peak around the next corner or over the next rise. I was ready for adventure.

The trail was not ready. I had ridden less than a kilometer when snow banks too deep for Kokanee to wade through forced me to turn back. Disappointed but not discouraged, and with so much daylight left, I retraced our steps down the mountain to trail heading *down*.

At least I won't be stopped by snow.

The trail was pretty. It had once been a logging road, but six-foot high poplar and willow grew on both sides now. Only a narrow trail remained. Riding east into the warm morning sun, I videoed a backlit peak in the distance and hooked the camera over my shoulder, anticipating wildlife shots. Since bear signs were everywhere, I hoped to see one.

The trail wound down into a deep gorge to a creek. Almost at the bottom, around a bend to the right, I snatched the reins and pulled Kokanee up. A huge square head stared at me from the willow on the right side of the road, a grizzly. Kokanee froze, more fascinated than frightened. I scrambled for the video camera.

I have to get this footage before he disappears into the bush.

I framed the shot through the lens. Black. I had not taken the lens cap off. All thumbs now, I flipped the cap off and brought the camera to my eye again.

Oh, oh. . .

The bear I had been sure would crash through the bush in his haste to *run away*, walked out onto the trail (leaving no doubt it was a grizzly) and I could read enough animal language to understand his message: ***This is my territory and I want you gone!***

No problem, Mr. Bear. I will be leaving.

Kokanee, thus far, had not spooked. That could change at any moment. As calmly as possible under the circumstances, I turned her, walked back around the corner, and looked over my shoulder. I was sure that would be the end of it.

It was not. The bear had followed. Either annoyed or curious (I didn't ask!), he stood up, snapped his jaws and lunged. The time for *walking* away was over. I yelled and booted with both legs. Saddlebags flapping, I charged up the trail, knowing we could not outrun a grizzly uphill, "feeling" the powerful grip of legs and jaws on my horse's rump, *on my back*, as we ran. I thought I would die.

He never touched us and I did not see him again. I stayed in my camp overnight but not without reservations. Was he mad enough to follow? I woke up several times listening.

I do not have video or photo of the magnificent grizzly standing on his hind legs with every silvery tip of every hair glinting in golden morning sunlight, but the scene is etched in my mind. I must be content with that . . . and my life!

Trail riding alone had its own rewards. I knew a peace and harmony in the mountains not possible anywhere else. Because my business was home based, I could not escape *unless* I left home. A couple of days on the trail brought me back to center and ready to work again. I squeezed in time for trails whenever I could. Sometimes I talked my husband into accompanying me, as I did for repeat rides of the Monashee trails in July. I was excited to be able to show Don the beautiful mountain areas he had not yet seen. Since I had not completed either trail, much would be new to me as well.

We parked by Barnes Creek again. This time, I knew how to access the trail and we wasted no time reaching the point I had turned back. From the sign at the creek, the trail wound through the trees following the contour of the forested terrain. Briefly, it opened into a small meadow, where we searched for markers, then back into the trees. Don rode Destiny. I rode Kokanee.

The ride would have been better without bugs. Huge horse flies were the worst, attacking the horses twenty or so at a time. Kokanee and I coped with them; Don and Destiny did not. Between Destiny stomping and shaking her head and Don yelling at her, I considered aborting the Barnes Creek Trail ride again until we popped out into open subalpine. The trail vanished beneath our horses' feet, replaced by fragile alpine plants and wildflowers. It was very, very quiet, almost otherworldly. Side by side now, Don and I skirted two small lakes with our sights set on a ridge that promised a view. (The battle of the bugs had abated.) A few evergreens dotted the gentle slope to the crest. Behind the ridgeline poked the craggy tops of The Pinnacles. We picked up a faint trail again and, silent now, weaved around trees and rocks to the top . . . and gasped!

134. Destiny and Kokanee, Vista Pass in July 1998.

From our rocky vantage point, the ground dropped off sharply into a deep valley. Across the valley, rugged peaks towered into a smoky blue sky. Each stony projection reaching for a cloud, fingers of snow on granite walls touching gentler, greener slopes, The Pinnacles stood in full, impressive glory.

The view more spectacular than we expected, Don and I stared. . . until our horses impatiently pulled at us, aware of a change in the weather. A cold wind pushed us back from the edge. Dark clouds slid over the peaks. Hail bounced off the rocks. We hobbled the mares, dug out sandwiches and coffee from the saddlebags, and ran for cover under the nearest scraggy evergreen. Destiny and Kokanee turned their backs to the weather as we huddled in our koolahs[85] and tried to convince ourselves Vista Pass was exactly where we wanted to be.

The squall ended as quickly as it started . . . and improved my photos! Grey-black storm clouds now partially shrouded the craggy peaks; ambient light softened harsh lines. I snapped a few shots and, as I rode away, spotted another photo opportunity too good to miss. I stationed Don with cameras and Kokanee and I walked down the ridge with the Pinnacles behind us. The scene had all the charm of a western movie, but while the video captured the moment, the

---

[85] A Koolah is an oilskin slicker.

135. The Pinnacles viewed from Vista Pass.

resulting photo did not. Maybe that was impossible. We returned to the trailer, loaded the mares and moved to the second trailhead for further investigation of the "snowbound-in-June" trail.

In the morning, we saddled Destiny and Kokanee and quickly rode to the point in the trail where I had turned around earlier that year. The snow was gone and the trail open, but there were a few surprises: a log to jump, a steep ascent and a treacherous descent. The hundred-foot drop over rolling, slippery rocks challenged but did not defeat us. For the safety of all, we led the horses down the winding, rocky trail. In the beautiful meadow at the bottom, Don tightened one shoe and reset another. Both mares wore sliding plates, not ideal for that kind of terrain.

From the meadow, an easy, relatively level trail over open alpine took us to a view of two tiny lakes nestled between mountains. The lakes, fed by melting snow, gleamed azure blue in the spring green alpine. Rocks poked through the water. Clumps of stunted evergreen dotted the boulder-strewn slopes rising above the shores. We tied the mares to spruce at the top and walked down the long slope to the little lakes. When we returned to the horses, it was raining.

In late July, I rode the trail again, intending to camp at the lakes. I drove directly to the trailhead, a steep climb but with more area to park and turn around, and unloaded Kokanee and Promise.

Since Promise, my pack horse, was only two years old, I packed light. She had never packed, so packing up would be a slow process, especially since I was learning too, but the day was bright and sunny and I could think of no reason to hurry.

I laid all my supplies out on the ground, divided items for each side and quieted any rattling with towels. Then I hobbled Promise, set the video camera on a tripod, turned it on, and prepared to take whatever time necessary to pack my green pack horse.

Promise, understandably apprehensive, cautiously accepted pack saddle, breeching and the soft canvas pack, but I had not quite muffled every sound in my supplies. The jangle of pots and pans unnerved her little. As is always the case with horses, patience is the best training tool. Before long, she graciously carried tent, sleeping bag, utensils, a little grain and food. I hooked the halter shank to the horn of Kokanee's saddle, picked up my camera and looked through the lens. Distant snowcapped Monashee peaks framed my mares. It was time to ride.

With big sister leading, Promise good-naturedly tolerated her role and when she dragged on my arm, I dallied up to encourage her. On one very steep, twisted trail up a brushy slope, the lead rope slipped under Kokanee's tail. I hastily dismounted to diffuse a potential wreck and, from the ground, pulled the shank out.

I wasn't sure how to negotiate the steep, rocky grade Don and I had led our horses down earlier that month. I couldn't lead the horses side by side on the single file trail, and Promise would probably not follow if turned loose. No choice. I must ride down leading Promise.

Once started, I ran out of options. As Kokanee picked her way through the rocks one careful slipping, sliding, grinding step at a time, her front end dropped away form me. Left hand on the reins guiding, Promise's shank clasped in my right (braced on the swells of the saddle), I sat back and let my mare find her way through the rocks, stopping only when Promise balked. In the meadow

136. Promise and Kokanee at the bottom of the steep drop.

below, I checked shoes. As our horses had for the first trip, both mares wore sliding plates. After I videoed scenery, I focused back on the horses.

"Yes, Scott we have all our shoes." (Scott, my farrier, admonished me several times for trail riding in sliding plates!)

The day was very hot and the mares thirsty, so when snow crisscrossed the trail, they buried their noses in the icy granules. A half hour later, we looked down the winding trail to the lakes. Promise stopped. Tired and probably muscle sore, the prospect of inching down the twisty, rocky path was too much for her. She refused to lead. I dropped the shank and asked her to follow, but she rooted to the spot. I rode off anyway down the trail to the lake, turning in my saddle and calling several times.

"Come on, Promise. Come on, girl."

Kokanee dipped her nose in the water and I looked back at Promise, sky lined on the hill where I left her.

"Don't make me go back for you!" *Or worse yet, turn around and go home.* I started to question the wisdom of riding away.

Promise did not want separation from me any more than I did from her. Bravely but tentatively, she placed one foot in front of the other to edge herself and her now *lopsided* load down the trail. Several times, she stepped on the excessively long lead rope even

though she held her head to one side to manage it.

I'm glad there's not any experienced packers to see this.

I felt sorry for her. She was tired.

With the horses tied and quiet I unpacked and set up camp, Later, they would graze in hobbles but for now they were more than willing to rest for a couple of hours.

I put up my little blue tent (which blew across the lake once before I got it staked), started a fire, cooked dinner on it, and ate watching the moon rise above the peaks and over the water. *What could be more perfect*, I thought.

137. Kokanee and Promise slurping snow in the Monashees in July 1998.

138. Kokanee and I leading Promise (2), Monashees. (July 1998)

The evening here rates as one of the best in my life, a summer night alone in the alpine with my horses.

The next day I walked to the top of the mountain to the north of the lakes and discovered the cell phone (almost never in range) worked. I phoned Cindy to wish her a happy birthday. Then I had an idea. I called Don to ask if he would join me for the second night and the ride back. He agreed.

The weather was just as good the next day when Don arrived on Destiny. We spent time with the horses; we relaxed and talked around the campfire. I began this ride alone and ended it with company. I hope Don enjoyed it as much as I did.

The three mares were Tamarac's first three fillies. (I planned to repeat this ride with her next three fillies—Whisper, Harmony, and Silk—but never did.) The mares enjoyed camp. They grazed, slept in the sun and waded into the lake for a swim . . . hobbled!

After one more night by the lakes, Don and I packed Promise and returned to both trucks and trailers parked at the trailhead and home. At the trailhead, we met hikers preparing to hike the same trail. They did not look pleased that horses had been on "their" trail. Later, one gave Don a "Leave No Trace" book. I suspect we were blamed for fire rings and burning. In fact, we used an existing fire ring. Because of this, though, I have not identified the trail. They may have been right. If trail riders used this trail often, there would be significant damage to the alpine.

In the fall of 1999, Don accompanied me on the Joe Lake trail. Destiny and Kokanee had both been on the trail. Now it was Whisper's turn.

Whisper, fourth daughter of Tamarac, followed in the slide tracks of her mother and sisters. She was a reining horse, possibly the best I had raised since Tamarac herself. There were reining futurities and derbies in her future, but since I believed my horses should taste as much of the real world as possible before spending most of their time in an arena, I included packing experience in her program. Whisper would be our pack horse.

139. Destiny leading the way for Whisper (2) over Ewart Creek bridge (October 1999).

Don and I rode Destiny and Kokanee, leading Whisper into creeks, up the mountain, over logs and through rocks to arrive at the cabin with the first few flakes of snow. When the snow deteriorated to a "horizontal white-out" as we unpacked, our horses may not have been impressed with us, warm and dry in the cabin while they were cold and wet. Whisper, always a bit of a prima donna, turned her back to the driving snow and hung her head, the picture of despair. What a way to treat my best reining prospect! The horses were fine, of course, just a little hungry and cold. When we hobbled them and turned them loose to graze the next morning, Destiny immediately found the trail back to the trailhead. With short, quick, hobbled steps, she boogied down the slope away from the cabin and Don ran to catch her. We may have been as grumpy as the horses packing up, but we left snow behind long before we reached the truck and trailer.

By 2000, Don seldom rode with me, but I promised myself several Millennium trail rides. I loaded strong, dependable, experienced Kokanee for every one.

May 25, 2000: Joe Lake

With Promise and Kokanee in the trailer, I headed for the Keromeos area and the Joe Lake trail for the first of several rides I had planned to celebrate the new century. I hoped to ride to the cabin when I reached the trailhead. Promise had not been in the mountains much, so I wanted to ride her this time and pack Kokanee. Weather had been a problem. A cool spring had slowed the melting of snow in the high country (everywhere I wanted to ride). Winter plans already askew, I gambled on this trail because earlier warm weather in southern B.C. bared the mountains sooner.

140. Ashnola pack trip. Promise (saddled) and Kokanee (packed) at Ewart Creek Trailhead (May 2000). Photo taken with timer on tripod.

I arrived at Ewart Creek trailhead in the early afternoon under a sunny sky but, after turning the horses in the corrals, I altered plans. I could have ridden as far as the cabin, but the mares were comfortable, so was I, and after all, this was my holiday. I would stay until morning.

I was *almost* alone at the trailhead. A man was working at the creek. I felt sure he would leave soon and I was right, but before he did, he walked to my camp to visit. We discussed my plans, the water levels of the creeks (which turned out to be his job) and the snow levels in the mountains. He was a little in awe of what I was doing.

"I envy you," he said. Score one for the Millennium Trail Rides.

The next morning dawned bright but within an hour changed to drizzly and wet. I held out for sun and, by noon, the skies had cleared so I packed Kokanee and saddled Promise. The mares were fresh, having stood in the rain, Promise wide-eyed.

Might be interesting crossing Ewart Creek.

We stepped into the water. At least, we did with quite a bit of urging on my part. Three quarters of the way across, Promise dropped a front foot into a deep channel. For an instant, she thrashed around, while I reassured her and scrambled to hang on to Kokanee's shank.

Only two minutes on the trail and I have a boot full of water.

A few minutes later, I untied my slicker. The drizzle had started again. I contemplated waiting for sun but, packed and on the trail, going back seemed foolish. I wondered how high Juniper Creek was.

I'll ride that far, assess the weather situation, and see how difficult it's going to be getting Promise across the creek.

Juniper Creek, though swift and rocky, was not overly deep. Promise crossed like a seasoned trail horse. The wind howled as we climbed the long, open grade above the creek, and I buttoned up. I had been on this trail in better and worse weather. With Promise in tow, Kokanee bowed her head to the wind and her back to the task. She, too, had traveled this trail before. Still, I started to feel just a bit vulnerable alone with horses in the wilderness.

As soon as I reached the cabin, I tried the key a friend had given me in the door. I had brought a tent, and the A-frame cabin just beyond the cabin was probably empty, but this is where I wanted to stay. The key turned. I untacked, unpacked, and hobbled and belled the horses. Promise hopped around in the hobbles, though, so I tied her and gave her one of the feed blocks I had brought. Not interested.

After a tasty fried chicken dinner (not fast food) and potato baked in foil on the pot-bellied stove, I turned Promise and Kokanee in the roughly-fenced pen in the trees below the cabin, sat on the porch for a spell, then prepared for bed. I was just a little bored. Maybe I should have ridden farther on the trail to Joe Lake. . .

"Hello!"

What was that?

"Hello!"

Definitely a human voice. I opened the door. Two men on horses leading a pack horse stared back at me.

"Who are you?" one of them asked.

"Sharon. Who are you?"

We filled in the blanks. They were more than a little surprised I had packed in by myself. All set to do the "man thing", tough it out in the wilderness, they find a woman *alone* in the same area. They had come to hunt bear (not a passion of mine). We compared lifestyles and stories over their dinner, broken only by "Your horses are loose." when Promise ran by the window. She had escaped from the pen and thereafter I tied her.

Ewes and lambs grazed by the cabin at dawn the next morning and I dashed out with cameras. When I returned, the men had breakfast ready.

Sure didn't think I would be served breakfast at four thousand feet when I headed out on this trail ride, especially by a man!

After pancakes, the men assured me I should not leave on their account and left for their hunt. They had told me the trail to Joe Lake was still under snow in places, but I wanted to see new country, so I saddled Promise, led Kokanee unpacked, and rode off to see how far I could go. The wind was still blowing, the sky dark and threatening.

The trail immediately climbed, and as I rode higher, the wind raged more. Maybe it would snow . . . been there before! The higher I climbed (Remember the Hog's Back?), the more awesome the view and storm clouds over the mountains enhanced it, but the frigid wind spoiled the ride. I rode as high as I could in a vain effort to call home on the cell phone, snapped photos and returned to the cabin. About noon, I packed up and started riding down the mountain. I had had enough of the incessant, bitterly cold wind.

At the bottom, in the shelter of trees, the mares and I escaped the gale, the remainder of the ride pleasant. At Ewart Creek, I lay on my back on the bridge while the horses rested under the trees. Beneath me, the creek churned over rocks and fallen trees; above, filtered sunlight cast warm rays on my chilled body. I was *alive*.

When I mounted Promise again, I turned Kokanee loose to follow. Fifteen minutes from my truck and trailer at the trailhead, a cinnamon-coloured bear sunned himself just off the trail. I jumped off Promise and scrambled for cameras. Neither horse saw the bear, but Promise jittered, not because of the bear, but because Kokanee walked past us and continued down the trail. The bear did not leave, and for a brief instant, I thought of moving closer. He yawned and sat down. Bored or contented?

Better leave well enough alone before I get myself into trouble.

I wondered where the bear hunters were.

Promise stepped into Ewart Creek at the trailhead without a second thought this time, no doubt anticipating a more comfortable night in the little pens at the trailhead than in the barbed wire pen in the trees below the cabin.

141. Kokanee and Promise grazing a slope to Joe Lake (May 2000).

July 9, 2000: Galloping Hills

For my second Millennium Ride, I loaded Kokanee and headed for Galloping Hills in the Monashees where vast space, masses of wild flowers and panoramic vistas await those who brave the road to the top. Don and I had ridden the high plateaus a few times. Before I left, we discussed the last five kilometers. We had always unloaded horses and pulled up empty. He reminded me now that he had bent axles on the trailers every time he had driven up *without horses*. We were well acquainted with one particular boulder and I wasn't sure how I would handle it. I should have worried about more than a rock.

The huge rock was still embedded in the road. I stopped, considered all possible ways of dealing with it (not many options), lined up truck and trailer, and listened for a sickening scrape as I inched the rig over. No sickening crunch. . .! I had bridged the rock! Confidence surged through me . . . for a few minutes. Then I realized there was more and more snow on the road. How far to the top?

I may have got myself in a real mess.

Visions of camping on the road until the snow melted replaced dreams of a relaxing ride in the mountains. If I couldn't go any farther forward, I couldn't back down either and turnarounds were non-existent. Concern changed to alarm.

I had to know what lay ahead. On the first level spot, I unloaded Kokanee, saddled and rode to the top. Thankfully, the road, though snow-covered in many places, was passable.

Galloping Hills was more peaceful than usual, as if the clock had turned back to spring. Water ran everywhere, many times under snow banks, and only early blooming wildflowers dotted the bare patches. Without doubt, I was the first person in Galloping Hills that year.

It rained off and on most of the next morning, so I studied database programming in the relative comfort of my camper. After lunch, I saddled for a short ride. After standing out in a cool night, Kokanee humped her back under the double-rigged saddle and saddlebags. She hopped around the trailer but, once we struck out away from camp, she leveled out to her usual flatfooted walk. With Mount Scaia my destination and the entire afternoon to get there, I was in no hurry, but the farther we walked, the more snow lay on the old logging road until, at the base of the mountain, a solid bank a few feet deep blocked us. I asked Kokanee to flounder through and she tried, but I had to turn around (I turned around a lot on the trails!). On the return trip to the trailer, I checked the Lightning Peak route. Though the ground was very wet, the first portion of the trail was open. I would ride there the next day.

I was out of camp at eight o'clock in the morning, having planned a long day of riding. Leaving camp at a long trot, I turned up the trail through patches of forest. Walking now, Kokanee zigzagged the slope to the top. In the open space of Galloping Hills, I picked up the trail to Lightning Peak . . . when I could find it! Snow obliterated much of the trail. Kokanee skirted patches or waded through until we came to a deep draw, followed by another draw, both leveled. By riding down the slope, we crossed both through running water, and scrambled up again. As we traveled further, more and more times we had to go around—way around—a snow bank or boggy ground. Many times, I had difficulty finding the trail again after a detour.

I stopped for lunch beside a small lake and stretched out on the damp ground. For a few minutes, I existed absolutely in the present. Dark, ominous clouds swirled and changed above me; cool, sweet earth rooted me to Galloping Hills, to the wilderness, to aloneness.

This is why I do this.

142. Lunch break with Kokanee in Galloping Hills in July 2000. Small lake behind. I ate my lunch here and stretched out on the grass beside Kokanee for a few minutes. Note snow banks.

I rode until, after one long detour, I could not find the trail. A four-point buck bounded into a clump of trees, surprised he was not alone, I think. I pulled out the camera and rode around the trees, not really expecting to see him again since most bucks in Galloping Hills are "hunter spooked", but I glimpsed a tawny hide motionless in the bush. He did not run. He knew I watched him, but we had an unspoken truce—if I did not bother him, he would not leave.

Finally, the snow so deep I lost the trail, I had to turn around. The return trip gave me an opportunity to learn more about my GPS. I had marked waypoints as I rode, not because I thought I would get lost but for practice with the instrument. I reversed the route and tried to follow the waypoints.

Kokanee was not patient with GPS 101. She was "going home", and every time I reined her up to read the GPS, she stood for only a few seconds, and then jittered. At one snow bank, she pulled to the north as I struggled to figure out where we had crossed. Eventually, I followed the line to the waypoint . . . north to Kokanee's tracks through the snow! She had been telling me all along where to go!

143. Galloping Hills looking north (July 2000).

I had another experience like this on Silk a few years later. Zigzagging back and forth across channels for six kilometers of rocky riverbed to an obscure, unmarked trail out of the river, I repeatedly corrected Silk when she changed course. She pulled on the reins, wanting to stay to the left. Suddenly, I stopped.

"We have gone too far," I said to my companion. "We have missed the spot to get out of the river." Daylight fading, we did not have much time to locate the path leading out of the river. I looked at my GPS. I had taken many waypoints, but, with so much trouble

getting into the river with the pack horse, I had not taken a reading there.

Concerned now and not wanting to spend the night in the riverbed, I knew I had made a serious error. I had not trusted Silk, who had been veering left for a reason! If the choice is GPS or horse sense, listen to the horse!

Luckily for all of us, I spotted the muddy bank and the trail from the middle of the riverbed. Silk had given up "telling" me where it was.

"You figure it out," she might have said.

144. Galloping Hills looking south over Granby (photo taken on another trail ride in August when wildflowers bloom.)

Although Kokanee would have preferred to hurry back to camp, I rested one more time. On a knoll rising out of a particularly difficult section of the trail, I dismounted and pulled out notebook, cameras and coffee. Overhead the sun graced me with its warmth; in the distance, dark clouds threatened a change in the weather. The vastness and the isolation of the Galloping Hills and all that I could see from where I sat overwhelmed me.

"I feel like such an insignificant part of this," I wrote as I sipped lukewarm coffee.

145. Kokanee and I in Galloping Hills (July 2000).

I didn't get anywhere near Lightning Peak, but it didn't matter.

August 15, 2000: Earl Grey Trail

The Purcells beckoned. I had driven back roads in that area the year before and had marked several trails on my Forest Service maps for exploration. One trail, especially, I wanted to ride—the Earl Grey.

Earl Grey Pass divides the trail into two distinct sections—east and west—and two terrains. The west side of Earl Grey is not open or accessible to horses; the east side is. Since hunters on horseback frequented the area, I expected to find good trails through the bush.

Due to a highway delay, I arrived at corrals about a kilometer before the "official" Earl Grey Trailhead late in the day. A truck and horse trailer was parked beside the corral, but I saw no people or horses. Alone and loving it, I saddled to investigate further. I knew, from my research, that the Earl Grey cabin (built by Earl Grey, of course) stood only a few kilometers in. A short ride to the cabin was just what we needed before dinner. We disappeared into the trees.

A mostly-level path wound westerly through the bush to a sign identifying the Earl Grey Trail (Why is it trailhead signs are posted *after* I am on the trail?) and, a few minutes later, a lush meadow. At the top of a long slope to the north, late day sun bathed logs of an old building in red-gold, the Earl Grey cabin. Kokanee and I climbed the hill to explore the ruins and, while she grazed, I recorded location with GPS, photos and video. For a moment, I imagined myself in the Earl's shoes in 1909 when he built the cabin. He must have felt as I did now—peaceful, tranquil. Regretfully, I returned to the trailhead and turned Kokanee in the outfitter's corrals for the night. After a satisfying meal of vegetables from my garden at home, I slept to the steady hum of Toby Creek.

The sun rose in a cloudless sky as I embarked on the new trail beyond Earl Grey cabin. Heeding warnings of numerous friends, I had belled[86] Kokanee. This was grizzly country! It was the first time I had belled my horse on the trail and the bell would scare off wildlife (hence, no photos), but it was the safe thing to do. I packed

146. The Earl Grey Cabin (Purcells).

lunch, cameras, GPS and basic survival items and rode off into unknown territory (unknown to me, that is) with the constant clang of the bell in my ears.

The trail was easy to follow. After I crossed the meadow beneath the cabin, the forest swallowed me up, but I popped into another meadow. This was the pattern for the ride—trees, meadow, trees. . .

I had checked the maps before I left and knew the trail followed

---

[86] To "bell" a horse is to tie a strap with a bell around the horse's neck.

Toby Creek but that I must cross Pharaoh Creek. Mount Earl Grey and Pharaoh Peaks towered over me to the north. Other mountains I could not name. Kokanee waded through Pharaoh Creek, then back into more forest, the trail following a marshy area along Toby Creek. There we met the owners of the horse trailer—three bearded bushmen with five pack horses! The "boss man" introduced himself simply as "Joe" and told me I could ride to Earl Grey Pass but may not have enough time to get there and back. He said they were repairing bridges, supplying camps, etc. for hunting season. Again, it amused me to meet men on the trail who obviously didn't expect to find a woman alone in the bush.

Toby Creek still on my left, the men behind, I pointed Kokanee down the trail again. The unmistakable sound of rushing water indicated we must be near McKay Falls. We popped out of the forest

147. Kokanee along Toby Creek (August 2000).

into a meadow, Kokanee swishing through tall, dry grasses bent over the worn horse trail. Ahead, in Toby Creek, I couldn't miss the waterfall, intriguing but completely inaccessible by horse unless approached by a route I didn't know about. I loved the sound, though, so I stopped for lunch.

Strange. The meadow grass appears untouched in spite of resident wildlife.

Sprawled in the grass under a tree, Kokanee beside, I opened my notebook.

"Kokanee and I are here by special permission," I wrote.

After following Toby Creek through sometimes-boggy ground,

the trail climbed out of the valley via a long, steep slope overlooking Toby Creek drainage. In the distance, another waterfall—Toby Falls? When we climbed up in the trees again (we were climbing all the time now), I checked the time. I wondered how far I could ride and still get back to camp in daylight. I estimated the location of Earl Grey Pass, surely a lot farther away than it looked. I pressed on through rooty, boring trees always with the anticipation of what I would see when we came out the other side. We crossed a creek, Kokanee drank and I considered turning around. Just a little further. . .

I rode nine hours that day, returning a little saddle sore, very hungry but completely energized!

"Next time," I told Kokanee, "we will go all the way to the Pass."

148. Toby Creek drainage.   **149. Kokanee under Pharaoh Peaks.**

Most trail rides were solitary ones in the next few years. My friends were concerned for my safety riding alone, but I went anyway. I chose experiencing life over reading about it.

"When I am old and sitting on the porch in my rocking chair, I'm going to have memories," I told them.

Smooth As Silk

"Hers is a power enhanced by pride, a courage heightened by challenge. Hers is a swiftness intensified by strength, a majesty magnified by grace. Hers is a timeless beauty touched with gentleness, a spirit that calls our hearts to dream."
~ Author Unknown

Only a handful of the horses I have ridden would I class as favourites. On that list are several with remarkably similar characteristics. Rocky, Cheetah and Seco were all small in stature, big in heart, courageous, full of fire, power-packed and fast! I would have another like that.

Silk was born in 1999, the sixth foal for Tamarac. Her sire, Dox West Gray, is a proven cutting horse with a gorgeous head, expressive eyes, classic ears, and a deep-in-the-ground stop I particularly like. Best of all, he is grey. For years, I had wanted a grey mare.

Silk was everything I had hoped for *except* colour. For two years, I looked for grey hairs. Almost all of Dox West Gray's foals inherited the grey gene, but Silk did not. She had taken her mother's colour. She is sorrel.

Colour is a small thing when everything else is perfect. With those Dox West Gray ears and big doe eyes, her head was about the prettiest I had ever seen. Tiny, dainty, delicate, she appeared fragile . . . until I looked into her eyes. Steely resolve glinted back at me. "I'll give you all I've got," those eyes said. I shivered. We had connected. When she rocked back on her hocks, snapped around and floated away, I named her.

"I'm calling her Silk, and I can't wait to ride her!" I told my husband. Goosebumps raised on my arms when I watched her run and play. I could *feel* the ride. I named her Wildwood Soul O Silk. If she was as smooth inside as she was outside, she was perfect.

It was a difficult year. Lace, Destiny's first born, died when Silk was a few days old. My husband's commitment to the business and me waned. My workload increased as he backed away and I retreated to the emotional safety of my horses, who welcomed me into their lives. It was a subtle change I was not fully aware of at the time, a gradual shifting to a deep, spiritual connection with my horses. Silk shared my journey.

I registered Silk in my name only, not jointly with my husband's as I had always done. At the time, I didn't know why, but now I think I did not want to share her. The little sorrel mare had wrapped herself around my heart.

150. Duchess, Silk, and Tamarac, May 1999.

When Silk was a yearling, we bought two Gallo Del Cielo (Rooster) mares the same age from Wisconsin. The barn names for these two were Prima (She would always be first!) and Skye (The sky's the limit!). In 2001, I started riding the three fillies. Silk and

Skye started well, but Prima developed a neurological problem whereby her hindquarters were uncoordinated. I worked my own brand of physical therapy with her daily, the first time since Tonka I "played" with a horse. I moved her around with my hands, walked her over obstacles, lunged her over rails, slipped on and off her back, and taught her voice commands. I encouraged her to use her hindquarters any way I could think of, even spinning with me on the ground. She performed 360-degree spins from my signals. I stood at her shoulder, dropped the halter shank and stepped toward her crossing my legs one over the other just as she should to spin. She learned the exercise so well I had to run around the outside to keep up with her!

I suspected Prima was afflicted with equine protozoal myeloencephalitis, caused by a parasite. The expensive drug my vet brought in from the States halted further damage, but I would not be able to show Prima, a huge disappointment. I continued to ride her throughout the summer but bred her to Listo Pollito Lena and transferred the embryo to a recipient mare.

151. Peppy Del Cielo (Prima).

I continued to train Silk and Skye for reining futurities. Neither mare bucked, but they were very different. Skye, steady and strong, did all I asked with a minimum of fuss. Silk, though willing, was chock full of raw energy. On one of the first rides in the open field in the spring, a bicyclist pedaled down MacDonald Road and Silk saw him out of the corner of her eye. Every muscle tensed for flight. I thought she might bolt as Cheetah had so many years before, but I kept control. When I knew her better, I loved the "ready for anything" feeling, but that day she unnerved me a little. Later that year, on a snowy trail behind our property, she scared me again when we happened upon a llama and a sheep. The llama ran to us and Silk turned inside out. I got off. Riding it out on a slippery mountain slope was not to my liking.

In 2002, as three-year-olds, Silk and Skye competed in futurities. Where Skye was steady and quiet, Silk was hot. They showed first in

Armstrong at Okanagan Summer Slide. Skye performed well for both runs, placing in the aggregate, but Silk's first run was not good. The judge knew she was "on the muscle" for the entire run and, of course, he penalized heavily even though she performed the maneuvers.

"She has a big motor, doesn't she?" he asked when I dismounted for the bit check.[87] It was more of a statement than a question.

However, Silk and I had another run, the second go, and that time she delivered. She circled, she spun and she nailed every stop. As we lined up for the rundown to the last sliding stop of the pattern, confidence surged through me.

I'm having a run!

152. Silk and I at Okanagan Summer Slide, August 2002. *Sharon Latimer*

The score of the first go spoiled the aggregate score, but I was pleased with Silk, so pleased I post entered[88] her into the Cardston

---

[87] A "bit check" is an inspection by the judge to check for legal bit and/or abuse (Rider must dismount and remove bit from the horse's mouth.).

[88] A rider can "post enter" a competition after the closing deadline, usually with a penalty payment.

South Country Slide In, where I was showing Skye. It was a mistake. Silk could not handle more mental pressure, the only time I remember her losing the "try". I read the signs in time and did not ask any more. She let me know she could not give me what I wanted at that time in her life.

In October, I showed Silk and Skye in the Saskatchewan Stakes and Futurities where I was happy with the performances of both. While I was at the show, I received a call I had been dreading but which I knew would come some day. Duchess was dying . . . and I was not with her.

I remembered her 35th birthday party the year before, the memory box I had made for her 36th birthday. I thought of all the years she had been with me, all the joy she had given me. I called the vet and asked him to send her home gently. My grand lady would die as she lived, with dignity.

153. Duchess and I at her 35th birthday party, May 12, 2001

Duchess, Mahogany and Tamarac had all shown in the arena I entered that evening. Competing on Silk in the Golden Mile Arena in Moose Jaw, Saskatchewan on the day Duchess died seemed somehow fitting.

This one is for you, Duchess, I thought as I walked my beautiful little sorrel mare, great granddaughter of Duchess, to the middle of the pen to start my reining pattern.

On October 17, 2002, my neighbour buried Duchess, age thirty-six, under the apple tree with Shadow and Lace. She shared my life for thirty-four years. I still miss her.

When the 2002 show season was over, I knew I *had* to see a doctor. An agonizing pain in my left shoulder had rendered my arm and me almost useless. I could not ignore the inevitable any longer. I needed surgery. I planned to attend to the arm in the winter and be back strong and healthy for the 2003 season.

It didn't quite go like that. I had surgery in April. All winter I rode Skye with a dysfunctional left arm; other riding was on hold while I waited for surgery.

Since I was not riding Silk, I used my downtime to send her to a Working Cow Horse trainer. I had long ago become interested in the event, and thought Working Cow Horse to be a natural extension of reining for horses bred to work cattle, which Silk certainly was, but Don and I did not own cattle nor did I have any experience. In February, I sent Silk to Cayley Wilson for two months to see if she had "cow" and if he thought she would make a Cow Horse. He phoned me almost immediately.

"Yes, she's a cow horse," he said.

Cayley worked cattle and buffalo almost every day he had Silk in his barn but never ran down the fence or circled a cow as is required in the event. He was confident all the "try" I wanted would be there when the time came to compete. Cayley's wife had a different idea about Silk's abilities.

"She'd make an awesome barrel horse," Jeanie said.

She was right, but I wanted to show Working Cow Horse and I had the horse to do it. In May, I hauled Whisper, Skye and Silk to a reining show on Vancouver Island and entered Silk in two Cow Horse classes.

I was still learning rules for the event, which affected my confidence. I was very nervous. I rode Silk in a snaffle bit, legal headgear for a four-year-old. Handling the reins with two hands (legal with a snaffle) was, theoretically, an advantage. I wasn't so sure. Two minutes before I entered the pen, Silk, feeding off my energy, felt like a runaway-in-the-making.

I shouldn't have entered. I should have used a different bridle.

Too late to back out. Too late to change bits. Silk and I walked into the pen and opened a door we would never close.

Silk *was* strong on my hands for the reining portion, but I eased her through the pattern by asking and releasing. If I had pulled hard on the reins, she might have run through the bit.[89] When the cow entered the arena, all thoughts of bits left both our heads. The years dropped away. I was back on the Community Pasture controlling a cow! Some things are never forgotten—never taking eyes off the cow, the deep seat in the saddle, asking, *expecting* instant response from the horse. Silk was there for me with all the determination and grit she had promised the day she was born. Working Cow Horse was an adrenalin rush for both of us. We were addicted.

If not spectacular, the run was at least complete and we posted a score. The internal excitement more than the physical effort left Silk foaming, but she walked from the arena on a loose rein, completely relaxed and totally satisfied with herself. If she could have talked she could not have told me more clearly, "This is what I was born to do!"

I didn't have cows at home to work, but I entered two or three Working Cow Horse classes a year for the next three years. One of the most exciting runs was at Prince George in 2003, the second competition for Silk and me. Many of my fellow reiners had not seen me in this event, so did not know what to expect. Our reining pattern, only average, left spectators and competitors bored, but everybody came alive for the cow work. When Silk and I shot down the fence and slam-dunked the cow, the crowd exploded. Two turns on the wall, two circles and we finished . . . except I could not hear the whistle over the screaming and cheering! I knew enough to continue working until the judge blew the whistle, but he whistled three times before I heard and pulled Silk up.

Cayley had not seen my first Cow Horse event on Vancouver Island and watched this one with interest. He met me at the gate when I rode back to the rest of the competitors. His eyes danced with excitement.

"Seventy-four, you scored seventy-four!" he shouted over the din in the arena. He was talking about the score for cow work portion of the class; the reining score was not as good. I thought how nice it was that he was so happy for my success (Or maybe Silk's success?) His wife again had a different view.

"Wasted on cows," she said. "Should be a barrel horse."

---

[89] "Run through the bit" is a phrase describing the action of a horse that does not heed pressure from the bit. Similar to hard-mouthed.

Silk's speed impressed everyone and it seemed as if someone chose our cows to highlight that quality. It was tradition. Give Silk and Sharon a fast cow and watch Silk run . . . or watch Silk and Sharon run. We both loved the game and it showed. One man said, "What do you do for fun? Ride bulls?"

Another commented, "You are just crazy, woman!"

"I haven't competed in this event before," I said, "but I've worked a lot of cattle on the range. They didn't usually get away from me."

"I can see why," he said.

The day after the Prince George competition, a man asked if I would sell Silk.

"She's not for sale," I said.

"Too bad. I was going to offer you big money."

No money would buy Silk.

154. Silk and I Working Cow Horse, Chilliwack , July 2005. *Tracey Eide*

As I did with all of my horses, I took Silk on the trails from time to time. When she was three, I convinced my husband to go with me on Skye for an overnight in the Purcell Mountains even though he had told me he did not want to ride any more. Both mares needed a break between the Armstrong and Cardston shows. Silk was as brave on the trail as she was in the arena, always eager, always willing. In later years, she and I rode the Barnes Creek trail and a weeklong ride in Height of the Rockies. On Joffre Creek trail in Height of the Rockies, she led younger barn mates through a rockslide that I will never ask a horse to walk through again. I never packed her, though. I couldn't pass up a chance to ride Silk.

155. Skye, Silk and I in front of Earl Grey Cabin in August 2002.

156. Silk and I in Height of the Rockies Wilderness in September 2006. Pack horse is Wildwood Magic Miss out of Destiny.

157. Palliser River in Height of the Rockies. Silk and I rode this trail in early September 2006.

I competed on Silk in several reining shows up to 2005. With each year, she gained confidence. She had always changed leads, but the changes improved as she relaxed. Though she struggled with spins, circles were beautifully correct and stops deep and hard. Silk's overall performance, though correct, could look out of control when it was not, and judges sometimes penalized her. Her higher neck carriage and wide eyes did not look relaxed. Her manner and way of going suited more the style of the Cow Horse, but she performed well enough in the reining pen to earn a few championships. Silk's performance career is not over. I hope to be able to show her for a few years. We love working cows.

Almost no one rides Silk but me. When I "allow" someone to step on her, reaction varies from "I love her." to "She makes me nervous." I understand. Power and agility combined with barely-contained energy is unsettling. Sitting on Silk is exactly that—*sitting on silk!*

One of my students once commented, "I've seen you ride a lot of horses, but the one you look most part of is Silk. You ride as one." I think she said it best.

I bred Silk to my own stallion (more about him later) in 2007. Three months before she foaled, I woke with only one thought:

Silk's going to have a filly and I'm going to name her Sapphire.

I keep a list of names and that name was not on it. On May 16, 2008, under a setting sun, Silk foaled a sorrel filly that looked exactly like her. I called her Wildwood Sapphire.

158. Wildwood Soul O Silk (May 1999).

159. Wildwood Sapphire (May 2008)

A Life With Horses

A Misty Moment

*When God created the horse, he said to the magnificent creature: I
have made thee as no other. All the treasures of the earth shall lie
between thy eyes. Thou shalt cast thy enemies between thy hooves,
but thou shalt carry thy friends upon thy back. Thy saddle shall be
the seat of prayers to me. And though fly without any wings, and
conquer without any sword. ~ The Koran*

On a bright September day in 2005, I learned a life-changing
lesson from a little black mare.

The day started as any other. I fed the horses at the barn, ate
breakfast, did some housework, rode two horses and went to the
house for lunch. It had rained the day before, but the sun was drying
the outside arena quickly. I hoped to be able to ride the more trained
reining horses in the afternoon. Misty was one of those.

Misty had come to me in the spring as a three-year-old. Only
14.1 hands high but with a huge heart, she soon endeared herself to
everyone at the barn and became one of *my* favourites. Always alert,
always poised for action, the little black mare exuded energy and joy.
Wide-spaced, dark eyes shone with intelligence. Short, perky ears

and flaring nostrils didn't miss a thing. When she ran in the field, silky black mane soaring, thick black tail sweeping the ground, she snorted a passion for life. Misty was just about the cutest horse I had ever seen.

160. Misty (Players Miss)

Under saddle, Misty's extreme athleticism impressed me. Bred to cut, Misty had the "sting" of a cutting horse—quick and precise movement. I liked that. So did her owners, Rick and Cindy, but although they liked cutting, they felt the best place for Misty was with me. They thought the intense training of cutting would shatter her confidence.

"Your quiet method is what she needs. See if she will rein."

For several months, I worked with Misty to gain her trust. If I could do that, she would be happy. I discovered she took comfort in knowing the program, knowing what I expected of her.

Each time I introduced a new step or added speed, she stressed. When she knew the exercise, she relaxed.

"Misty likes to know what the plan is," I told Rick and Cindy.

Short, small boned and dainty, Misty rode like a much bigger horse. I never felt I didn't have enough horse for the job. She circled with confidence and a great deal of presence, spun like a top, and stopped every time. From the first ride, I liked everything about her, but it was when I taught her lead changes that I *loved* her ability. Flat, fluid, effortless changes were Misty's strength. I didn't need to school her on lead changes; instead, I practiced *not* changing leads, which is exactly how the accident happened that September day.

I had just enough time to ride Misty before my student, Jill, arrived for a lesson. I warmed her up with suppling exercises, jogging and trotting, extending the work area to the outside arena and checking the ground for muddy spots as I rode. Since Misty did not slip, I asked her to lope. Following my usual daily schooling routine, we loped straight lines down the sides of the arena and circles on each end. Then we loped diagonally across the arena in the left lead to counter canter the circle in the outside part of the arena. Three quarters of the way around the circle, I asked her to change leads, which she did, but when her right legs extended into the right lead, both legs slid to the left and she fell flat on her side. My right foot, *still in the stirrup,* dropped to the ground with her.

161. Misty and I loping the arena as we did the day of the accident. This photo, taken another day, is just ahead of the spot where she fell (August 2006).

A lifetime of experience had taught me to kick my feet out of the stirrups if a horse fell, but I didn't have time. I knew my stirrup would connect with the arena sand with my foot in it. Even as Misty was going down, I was thinking about how I could get my foot out of the stirrup when she jumped up again, as I was positive she would. I wondered if my boot would come off but didn't think so; I might be able to throw my body around to untwist the foot in the stirrup, but I doubted that was possible. I knew jerking my foot loose was paramount to my survival. If I didn't, Misty would drag me to my death when she got up and ran. There would not be much time.

My mind still churning out strategies to save my life, Misty pinned me to the dirt with my leg twisted at the ankle in the stirrup. I prepared for a gigantic effort on my part when she scrambled to her feet. Then she granted me a reprieve. She didn't get up.

Trapped under her, I could not see for a moment how that helped my plight. With my right leg, hip to foot, nailed to the ground by her torso, I had almost no maneuverability. I lay on my stomach sprawled out at right angles to her back. My own body trapped my right arm and shoulder under me, and I could only partially turn to the left. The immobility of my body restricted movement of my left arm even though free. I tried to wiggle the leg under Misty. I tried to pull it out. It would not move an inch.

How can such a little horse be so heavy?

I could only wait for her to get up. When she did, with my foot completely turned around in the stirrup, she would drag me in wild circles around the arena and barnyard. An incredible calm settled over me.

I guess this is it. I am going to die.

In the next few seconds, I wished three wishes: (1) *I hope Rick and Cindy don't blame Misty for killing me.* (2) *I wish I had changed my will* (not changed after the separation). (3) *I hope this doesn't hurt too much* (cement feeders at the end of the arena).

Misty raised her head and neck as if to rise.

"Whoa. Whoa." I said softly. She put her head back on the ground.

Suddenly, I knew what to do.

I have to undo the saddle.

By twisting my upper body to the left, I could reach over the saddle and Misty's body with my left hand. If the cinch was not too tight, I could work it loose with one hand.

"Whoa. Whoa."

Fortunately, I used a single rigging and no breast collar. With surprisingly steady fingers, I worked the tongue out of the hole in the latigo, talking to Misty at the same time, and pulled the latigo wrap by wrap until the cinch was completely undone. I sank back on the cool sand, sweating, heart pounding. The saddle and I, now separated from Misty, would remain on the ground when she got up.

For a moment, I reflected on what had just happened. I had always feared death, had always believed I would be frightened in the face of my own demise, but instead I had felt only calm acceptance. I loved life, had many things I still wanted to do. How or why had I felt such peace? There were many more unanswered questions . . . but the immediate situation needed attention.

My right ankle and knee started to hurt. I couldn't feel my right arm at all. It was time for Misty to get up. I turned to her head again. I loosened the rein. I even slapped her a little with a rein. She didn't move.

I wonder when Jill will get here. I lay my head down in the sand again.

I'll wait for Jill.

Five minutes later (Was it really five minutes?) Misty, with no preamble, in one fluid motion, rose to her feet and stood quietly, a little bewildered, the saddle and I still on the ground. I dragged myself out from under the rigging, walked a few steps to the cement feeders I had imagined would be the instrument of my death and slumped to the ground with my back on them.

"Sharon?"

Jill had walked in the arena. She could not make sense of the scene.

"Saddle on the ground, Misty just standing there. I didn't even see you at first," she said later.

I told her what had happened as she led Misty back to her stall.

"I think you need a cup of tea," Jill said, which, whether I needed it or not, is exactly what I had before I taught Jill her lesson.

I thought a lot about the incident in the next few days. Why didn't Misty get up immediately? Traumatized by the fall? Confused? Hurt? I checked her over thoroughly for injuries and soundness, but she showed no signs of soreness, except for a large swelling on her right side. My spur, at right angles to her body, had been digging into her belly the entire time she lay on my leg!

My daughter, Cindy, offered one explanation.

"She knew."

"What do you mean, 'she knew'?" I asked.

"She knew it was you. All your horses bond to you. You have been riding her, caring for her all those months. She knew she would not hurt you."

My son-in-law asked me if I had prayed.

"I never thought of that," I said. "I figured if I got myself into the mess I should get myself out."

As He has done all my life, He looked after me anyway.

Misty stayed with me for another year, until I moved from the Armstrong property. I loved to ride her. She reminded me of Silk in many ways—the attitude, the look, the fragile exterior and tough interior. At her first show, she amazed me even more. I thought she might be anxious in a show atmosphere, but she walked into the reining pen and performed as she was trained to do. She knew the plan.

Misty, like Silk, was born to be a Working Cow Horse, but I did not have cows. At a clinic with Cayley Wilson, I introduced her to cattle. When the cow entered the arena, Misty's eyes fastened on her. The cow stopped. Misty froze. The cow moved. Misty leaped.

"That's a cow horse," Cayley said.

You think? I was glad I was still on top. . .

Misty had one more talent she had not shown me. I was cleaning stalls at the barn, Misty in a large pen at the other end of the arena. A long lane connected the barn to the pen and the cement feeders I envisioned my head whacked on if she dragged me by a stirrup. As I rolled the wheelbarrow out of the barn, Misty, for no apparent reason, jumped the feeder from a standstill and tore down the lane to the barn. Who knew she could jump?

By a twist of irony, Jill owns Misty today. She has competed in reining classes with her, has started working buffalo and cattle, and has recently added jumping to her list of accomplishments.

Wildwood, Broodmares and Babies

When a horse greets you with a nicker and regards you with a large and liquid eye, the question of where you want to be has been answered. ~ Author Unknown

Tamarac was the only broodmare I owned when Destiny was born in 1993. Though breeding was a very small part of Wildwood Reining Horses, I bred Tamarac every year for the next several years with an eye on the future. As the granddaughter of my beloved Duchess and the first "bred-to-rein" mare I owned, Tamarac had earned a place in that future—to carry good genes forward to the next generation.

Breeders of quality horses sometimes overlook the importance of the dam, crediting the sire for the offspring's conformation and disposition. I believe the dam is *more* important than the stallion. To that end, as Tamarac produced filly after filly, I considered each for a broodmare. Mare power would be the focus of my breeding program.

Pedigree and conformation was not enough. I trained and showed my mares for first-hand knowledge of each mare's disposition and talent. Each earned a performance record. I planned to breed proven mares to proven stallions.

Though Tamarac and her fillies formed the foundation of my future broodmare band, I could not let sentiment overrule good breeding practices. I needed to introduce new bloodlines to Wildwood Reining Horses. I had always loved Gallo Del Cielo, a bay stallion by Peppy San Badger making a name for himself in the States as a sire of reining horses. After Don and I saw him in Oklahoma in 1999, I was more determined than ever to own a "Rooster" (barn name for Gallo Del Cielo). We purchased Rey Del Cielo and Peppy Del Cielo (Skye and Prima respectively) in 2000. Prima's unsoundness (Chapter 27) was a huge disappointment given her obvious talent, but she would play an important role in my breeding program. She lives with me still.

Raising quality horses was important, but the real reason I bred may have been the babies—the waiting, the wonder. For all my life, wherever I lived, the foals tugged at my heart.

My perspective to breeding, broodmares and foals had changed through the years. On the Diamond Dot, mares foaled in the hills. My parents did not plan to attend births, so rarely saw a foal born. Occasionally, they found a dead foal or a mare without a foal that should have had one, but most times a herd check revealed the addition. Sometimes days passed before they knew if the new foal was a filly or colt.

As a teenager, I wanted to know more about the foaling process. I rode out into the fields every day to check expectant mares, but since Dad turned the stallion with the mares in the pasture the year before, I had no way of knowing the breeding dates or the expected foaling dates. I could only observe the mare's physical appearance, habits and demeanor. I tried to predict the births and hoped to see a mare foal but never did. I learned then most mares did not want me to know when they would foal and could go to great lengths to accomplish that.

When Garry and I bred Quarter Horses in the 70's, I kept records for each mare. In the beginning, we pasture bred too, so still did not have exact breeding dates, but when we live-covered the mares in our corral, I wrote down a "due date". That's when I found out the date could vary—a lot! I needed more information. I watched closely, took notes for each mare and recorded the gestation. (I have recently entered these handwritten records into my database program.)

The mares still ran out, but in a small pasture close to the house. As I monitored more mares, I learned more and, with breeding dates and histories, usually knew when my mare's time was near. I still did not try to be on hand for the foaling. My parents' foaling philosophy ("Let nature handle it.") stuck with me. I may have even believed foaling went better without human interference. For whatever reason, I checked the mares often but did not bring them to the barn or sleep with them at night. I do not remember witnessing any births during these years either, but the broodmares taught me another foaling fundamental—Mother Nature is not entirely in control! After seeing many mares through pregnancy and birth, I discovered the mare, to some degree, decides when she will foal. She can speed the process up or slow it down. Kitten did.

The year we moved to Crooked River, Kitten was due to foal in early April, too early for the northern climate. All her life, she had foaled outside. This time, I stalled her and she was not happy. She waddled around the stall, irritated, agitated, and begged me to let her out every time I checked her, which was often because the baby was overdue. Kitten did not intend to foal in the barn. When the weather warmed, I turned her out and went to the house, whereby she must have foaled as soon as I left. She waited until she was alone and where she wanted to have it—in the field!

Another year, Kitten played a part in a foaling scenario of a different kind. If this had not happened to us, I may have questioned the validity of the story.

Although I liked to be home when the mares foaled (I wouldn't think of being away now!), I left Garry in charge when I hauled to a rodeo on the last weekend of April 1974.

"Cameo is close," I told him, "so watch her." Cameo, with the other broodmares in a small field, was a maiden mare and the possibility of foaling problems was greater. I wanted Garry to be extra vigilant.

I phoned home the next day.

"Did Cameo foal yet?" I asked my husband.

"Yes," he said, "and so did Kitten and Searra."

"Three!"

He told me how it happened. When he got up, he checked Cameo and she had not foaled, so he fed at the barn, milked the cow and went back in for breakfast as he always did. When he went out again, *an hour later*, three foals had arrived!

There was a little confusion about which foal belonged to which mare, Garry said, since Cameo had no experience with motherhood, but he soon sorted it out by the process of elimination. Kitten and Searra claimed their foals.

We will never know for sure but guessed Cameo foaled first and the other mares, having had foals before, decided to make it a party.

My commitment to my broodmares and their babies deepened with each passing spring. For the last few years in Saskatchewan, working a horse breeding/training/selling business, the mares received my undivided attention at foaling time, but I still missed many births. For a few years after I moved to B.C., until I bred Tamarac, spring came and went without even one new foal. When Destiny arrived, even with the extra care she needed, I knew spring would never be as bright without the babies. Though an overwhelming responsibility, foals had stolen my heart. I needed a "foal fix" every year.

Foaling can turn from miraculous to devastating in a matter of minutes, as with Lace, but sometimes from a tragedy comes a miracle. One spring in Armstrong, two local breeders captivated me with this story:

Louise had lost a foal the day before her neighbour, Leah, lost an aged broodmare. The veterinarian had delivered Leah's foal by caesarian section. Two weeks premature and stressed at delivery, the little buckskin filly struggled to breathe, but when caregivers wrapped her in a blanket, she nickered and tried to rise to her feet. Since only truck lights illuminated the pasture where she had been born, they transported the wee thing by wheelbarrow to a brightly lit spot under the yard light. There the vet served up her first meal—colostrum from Louise's foal-less mare tubed into her stomach.

Louise and Leah had an idea—baby needed a mommy and Louise's mare needed a baby. Hoping the grieving mare would take the orphan foal, they rolled her down the road and up the driveway to Louise's barn in the wheelbarrow, no small feat since by now she was trying to stand up. Everyone held their breath as they pushed her into the barn. The mare whinnied softly. From the wheelbarrow, the filly answered. Cautiously, they opened the stall door and lifted the baby out of the wheelbarrow. *Immediately, the mare licked her.* On shaky legs, that newborn filly wobbled to the mare's udder and nursed. The way Louise related the story to me, there wasn't a dry eye in the barn.

Understand. . . This is not my story, not my mare, not my foal. I did not see the bonding in the barn that day. The tale so touched me though that, on lunch break for a clinic, I started to tell the group the amazing tale of the orphan foal and her adoptive mother.

"Just a minute," I said. I picked up a newsletter on the coffee table. Louise had published her story. "I can read this article."

I started reading. As the words came, so did the emotion, until I *lived* the story I read. My voice thickened. My eyes watered. I was going to cry.

"I'm a goner," I admitted, and gave myself up to the inevitable. Tears washed down my cheeks as I read the last line, "Smoothie accepted that little premature baby as her own." I looked up. The women's faces glistened; the men turned away and found something else to do.

Losing Lace in 1999 and nursing Badger through his afflictions in 2000 had taken a toll on me. Up to that time, by coincidence, good management, or sheer luck, the foaling horror stories I had heard or read about had not been mine. Lace and Badger jolted me out of complacency into reality. Although I had always taken great care of my broodmares and foals, I was no longer confident I did enough. I resisted investing emotionally in the foals, a futile attempt to protect myself from the grief of losing one. Still, in 2000, I bred more mares—Tamarac, Mahogany and Destiny—and risked more heartbreak.

Tamarac, for the first time, did not conceive, no doubt in part due to the interruption in her life caused by Badger's surgeries and the travel involved. Destiny produced a beautiful bay filly, Breeze, a sister and replacement for Lace. This time Destiny raised her foal to weaning without incident.

I had bred Mahogany to Peeping Bo Badger, hoping for another Tamarac, since the bloodlines were so similar, but it was not to be. She gave me a bay colt with white socks on his hind legs. I slept in the barn to watch Mahogany the night Boots was born but missed his birth by a few moments. Barefoot and clad in a white flannel nightgown, I kneeled down beside him as his mother heaved herself to her feet. He was the busiest newborn I have ever seen. He scrambled to get up, sucked on the sleeve of my gown and whinnied at the same time!

From the six fillies Tamarac had birthed I kept Destiny, Harmony and Whisper for broodmares. Silk, in training in 2001, would not ever be for sale, and would someday join her sisters in the broodmare band.

162. Wildwood Magic Miss in August 2002.

Listo Pollito Lena, a sorrel stallion sired by Smart Chic Olena, had attracted my attention. I watched him rein at a few shows and I liked his easy way of moving, his effortless execution of each maneuver. He had already earned a performance record and I thought he would cross well with my mares. In 2001, I booked Destiny and Prima to him, shipped semen for Destiny, and hauled Prima to Alberta for breeding and an embryo transfer. Both mares conceived and the transfer of the embryo to a recipient mare was successful. Tamarac carried a Chics In The Male foal.

163. Wildwood Champagne in August 2002.

Mahogany lost her filly in January, but in the spring of 2002, three beautiful healthy fillies arrived: Diva for Prima, Champagne for Tamarac and Magic for Destiny. Diva, born to the recipient mare, required round-the-clock attention after she was born May 1st because the mare, a maiden mare, would not let her suck. By May 3rd, mare and filly were bonded and I could get a good night's sleep. Before I left the barn, I checked Tamarac in the field (at gestation day 364). She had to come in. I was almost positive she would foal that night but exhausted, asked Don to get up, check her at one o'clock, and switch stalls with the recipient mare and Tamarac if he thought Tamarac was going into labour. I fell into bed and deep sleep.

The phone jolted me awake. I knew it would be Don at the barn.
"What is it?"

"Not sure," he said, "but it's up, dried and sucked!"

Tamarac's sorrel filly, Champagne, had arrived unassisted in the smaller stall. Tamarac had everything under control. I love the old broodmares.

164. Wildwood Diva in August 2002.

In 2002, five generations lived with me: Duchess (at 36, the grand matriarch), Mahogany, Tamarac, Destiny, and her new filly, Magic. "The Dynasty" had added another to the next generation.

I showed at as many reining shows as I could in these years. Whisper was a top reining horse, noted mostly for her pretty rundown and stop. I showed her in Derbies and open reining classes in 2001 and 2002 with success and a whole lot of fun. I did not get Harmony shown in her three-year-old year (2001), but in 2002, I post entered her in the Reining Alberta Sire and Dam Maturity for which she was eligible and she surprised everyone by winning it! Always a kind, gentle mare, my granddaughter, Kendra, rode her that year in the unfenced, outside arena at home. Though Kendra had almost no experience with horses, I turned them loose and Harmony looked after her.

165. Kendra on Harmony in the arena at home (2002).

I hauled Whisper with the three-year-olds, Silk and Skye, in 2002. Showing three horses by myself was a marathon, but I was excited to be riding Wildwood horses. It had been my goal for several years to walk in the reining pen on Wildwoods.

It was not all good, though. At one show, I came to terms with an issue that had bothered me for some time—abuse.

I was schooling Whisper in the warm-up pen. I was not entered in the class running at the time but I was in earshot of a speaker blasting scores of the class. The last competitor had scored 142, quite a decent score. As I loped circles on Whisper, he entered the warm-up area from the arena, ran down the fence and rolled back several times, spurring hard at each turn.

Must have had a problem with a roll back, I thought. Then I saw the blood. On both sides of the mare, a crimson line trickled over the palomino hair. I stopped working Whisper. I studied the man and his horse, the whole ugly scene. I had witnessed abuse before, but this time was a defining moment in my reining career. I had to accept what I had not—competitors that abused horses sometimes *won.* My thinking organized now, I laid out the facts to myself, still sitting on Whisper in the middle of the pen:

- In some twisted way, rough training like that worked.
- I could not and would not train that way, so. . .
- I could (1) quit reining or (2) be content to place lower than some of those who abused. What was my choice?

There, in that warm-up pen, that day, I came to terms with the issue. Just as I promised myself a few years before not to push a horse to perform maneuvers he cannot, so I resolved that day to compete according to my goals only. From that day forward, I did not feel an overwhelming need to win. I wanted to be proud of my horses and I usually was. Moreover, I hoped a horse would come along some day that would win "my way". Maybe I'm getting close. At a show with my three-year-old stallion, a man, a reining trainer himself, gave me one of the biggest compliments of my life.

"I see a lot of riders spurring and jerking in that warm-up pen, but very few horsemen. You are the latter," he told me. He probably doesn't know how much I needed to hear that.

I had three nice mares to show—Whisper, Skye and Silk. I showed in B.C. mostly, but also traveled to Alberta for a couple of shows. Skye and Whisper were good "open" horses, but Silk was not as steady. Reining shows in B.C. offered Working Cow Horse classes, though. She excelled in those.

166. Rey Del Cielo (Skye) Canadian Supreme. *Sharon Latimer*

In January of 2003, I lost Mahogany. Don found her in distress at feeding time in the morning. I immediately went to her with blankets and drugs, but she was gone. She died where she wanted to be—at home with me—and she lies where she belongs—with Duchess under the apple tree.

My business thrived. I accepted as many training horses as I could manage and coached riders. For the first time in my career, I hired a girl part time to ride and clean stalls. I liked to feed, and would if I could, but she filled in when I traveled to shows. I was very particular about who rode my horses and fortunate to find great help. She rode for me two or three times a week. That took the pressure off.

Wildwood Reining Horses had established a presence in the reining world.

In August of 2004, my husband, unhappy and uncommitted, moved out, leaving me alone on our big property, which we would have to sell but which for now was home to my horses and me. Financial security threatened and the emotional safety of a supportive partner gone, I stumbled, but struggle ultimately led me back to my horses, whose needs did not end because my marriage did. They provided a stable beginning to a new piece of my life.

I had bred mares to performing stallions, sold a few and trained many. I had slowly built up my herd. I had returned to Listo Pollito Lena four more times. Destiny had added a gorgeous bay filly, Legacy, in 2003 and Tamarac a handsome sorrel stallion, Eagle, in 2004. When Don left, Prima and Destiny carried Listo Pollito Lena babies.

Prima and Destiny were not the only mares expecting foals the following spring. I had bred Tamarac to Shawn O Lena and Harmony to Sonita Oakolena. Four babies would arrive in the spring. Nothing would change that. That alone may have saved my sanity in the next difficult months.

I have to be strong for my mares. They will need me.

I could not fall apart. Who would look after my horses, especially the new foals?

There is something especially healing about time spent with horses. They judge not; they play no games; they play fair. The connection deepened. In the spring, I was at each mare's side as she foaled. Four new arrivals confirmed my faith in all things good, an outstanding crop of foals destined to excel. I named them for qualities I needed to believe in. Honor sold at nine months to a Non Pro reiner who will have her trained and shown. Courage, undeniably a stallion prospect but now gelded, is in training for a Working Cow Horse. His trainer reports he has talent to burn and expects him to compete at a high level. Splendor, also Working Cow Horse material, I still own. She is athletic and pretty. The fourth of the 2005 foursome may ultimately leave the biggest mark. Running With Wolves is the Listo Pollito Lena colt out of Prima.

Oddly, the four foals sensed my emotional dependency. They attached themselves to me in an almost protective way. They never failed to greet me when I walked into their field. They checked in to see how I was doing and then, satisfied I was all right, wandered back to their mothers. I thought they needed me (and of course they did), but they knew I needed them more. They gave me a safe place to fall.

167. Courage, Wolf, Splendor, Honor and I, August 2005. *Dave Harley*

Added to the stress of the baggage that comes with an imminent divorce was increased responsibility and work. Luckily, I had never put the farm management skills I learned in my years alone to bed. I would need those skills and more.

First, I registered Wildwood Reining Horses in my name. The next order of business was the horses, which Don readily agreed to include in my part of the settlement, as he had no interest in them. I felt much more comfortable when I was the registered owner of the business and the horses. Wildwood Reining Horses was mine and I was ready to work.

168. Peppy Del Cielo births Running With Wolves, April 26, 2005.

Though I kept part time help for barn chores, I added many tasks to my list. I honed my tractor driving skills emptying the manure spreader, plowing snow in the winter, and moving sand around for the arenas. Fanatical about the ground in my inside and outside arenas, I harrowed often to keep the ground in the best possible condition for all kinds of riding, but especially for sliding stops.

I accepted as many training horses as I could manage, boarded a few horses and coached riders to bring in income. Wildwood Reining Horses ran like a well-oiled wheel for my remaining time at the facility on MacDonald Road. My clients, both boarders and owners of the horses I trained, were wonderful. If people are happy, horses are happy and the barn atmosphere is happy.

I sold horses too. Skye went back to the United States to a Non Pro reiner in California. She has an excellent home. Champagne, Tamarac's last filly, sold to a Non Pro reiner in Alberta. I also sold weanlings and yearlings.

After Don left, I developed a new marketing strategy for Wildwood Reining Horses. I chose a theme—the wolf. I had always liked the wolf, possibly because of his wild nature but probably because of how he lives his life, with loyalty. I would incorporate wolves in promotion for Wildwood Reining Horses every way I could.

I designed a logo with a wolf head and a horse and used it on business cards, statements and the web page, but I was looking even farther ahead.

Breeding my mares with shipped semen was expensive. With financial constraints and a move to somewhere possibly less accessible to veterinarians and airports, I needed to own a stallion again and I had one—Running With Wolves.

In November of 2005, after I weaned Courage, I called my vet. The inevitable could be delayed no longer. I must let Tamarac go. I brought her into the barn and spent an entire day with her. I washed her thin mane and tail and rubbed her ears. We talked.

The vet had arrived and I was not ready. I stood in front of Tamarac and pressed my forehead to hers. Her ears caressed my hair; her warm breath mixed with mine. In one hand, I clung to a sheet of photos encased in plastic, pictures of her ten foals.

"These will go with you. They are your legacy. Let them comfort you."

She stood with me only yards away from her final home under the apple tree. Huge cancer-ravaged patches blotched her once-silky sorrel coat. A few flaxen strands of mane trailed over her scabby, wrinkled neck. I wrapped my arms around her for the last time.

"My beautiful girl," I whispered. "Run again with Duchess, Mahogany, Shadow and Lace."

The last year my horses and I resided on the facility on MacDonald Road in Armstrong was 2006. In the preceding demanding two years, I had set Wildwood Reining Horses up for the future. I was still on a path with horses on it, but the path led to another area. The property sold and my horses and I moved in the fall.

A Life With Horses

30 *Peace*

The hooves of horses O'Witching and Sweet
Is music Earth steels from iron shod feet
No whisper of love, no trilling of bird
Can stir me as hooves of the horses have stirred.
They spurn disappointments and trample despair
And drown with the drumbeats the challenge of care.
With scarlet and silk for their banners above,
They are swifter than Fortune and sweeter then Love.
On the wings of the morning they gather and fly,
In the hush of the nighttime, I hear them go by,
The horses of memory thundering through
With flashing white fetlocks all wet with the dew.
When you lay me to slumber no spot can you choose,
But will ring to the rhythm of galloping hooves.
And under the daisies no grave be so deep
But the hooves of the horses shall sound in my sleep.
~ William Ogilvie

Sagebrush, sand and solitude. The land is all of that and more. It's silver green juniper dotted with smoky blue berries. It's wolf willow and prickly pear cactus, red willow and rabbit bush. Saskatoon berries and snowberries. Bald eagles, chickadees, finches, and hummingbirds. Deer, moose, cougar, lynx, wolves and bear. Aspens so golden they rival the sun. Salmon as red as the Chilcotin sunset in a river so turquoise it does not seem real.

A rustic log house overlooks that river. Below the house, trails mapped by wild animals zigzag steep forested grades to the river flat. Behind the house, several giant firs and a few aspens shelter a secluded yard. Two small hilly fields, also dotted with fir and aspen, pasture several mares.

A young sorrel stallion peers between the grey timbers of a dilapidated round pen. A trio in an old arena grown up to rosebushes fascinates him—a woman, a dog and a horse.

The woman leans back on an old fence board, the dog at her side. She rests her hand on the soft white head, and closes her eyes. She hears the shuffling and snuffling of horses in their morning feed, cheerful chirpings of birds in the aspens and firs above and in the distance, the steady hum of the river. She inhales the dewy freshness of spring mixed with the sweet scent of new life. Finally, she opens her eyes and drinks in the peaceful, perfect, pure scene before her.

A beautiful bay mare nuzzles her new foal, sprawled in front of her. He is wet and shivering but alert and eager. He shakes his head, stretches a leg, wiggles his body into various awkward positions. The mare sniffs him and licks him, then stands over him. He is five minutes old.

Breathless wonder has replaced the pang of apprehension the woman always feels before a foal is born. This birth was normal, the woman present to offer words of encouragement and assist if necessary, but the mare did not need her. Quite aware of the woman's presence, she trusts in it and takes comfort from it.

A squirrel jumps from one tree to another and the mare, senses keen to the slightest movement or sound, jerks her head up, eyes and ears on the underbrush. She circles her newborn, bobs her nose to him every few seconds, assuring him of her presence and her protection.

A few minutes later, the foal tries to stand, awkwardly splaying his front legs in front while he tries in vain to gather his hind legs under him. He falls, of course, but tries again. He knows he will have to stand to suck. The mare knows that too and allows him to try.

169. Peppy Del Cielo (Prima) and Walking With Wolves May 6, 2007.

170. Little Wolf (Walking With Wolves) struggling to stand.

Idly, the woman strokes the dog and observes the new life, somehow symbolic of hers. She reflects on the trails she has taken that have led to this place, the paths she has followed and roadblocks she has stumbled into and over. She remembers the child lying in the grass by a creek so long ago dreaming of a life with horses.

She is exactly where she wants to be.

171. Up at last!

Epilogue

My horses, my dog and I live on the Chilcotin plateau of British Columbia now. We nurture life, animal and human, on ninety-three acres of semi-wilderness. My horses graze northern bunch grass and drink from the Chilcotin River. They scramble up steep, sandy banks and learn how to avoid prickly pear cactus.

I live in an old log house overlooking the river and my horses. I still grow my own vegetables, bake all my bread and sew for myself. I cleared three-foot high rose bushes for a large outdoor arena and almost every day, I ride there. In the new little barn, fenced pastures and railed pens stand my horses, many descendents of Duchess. I brought four great-granddaughters and three great-great granddaughters of Duchess to my new home. Prima, Running With Wolves (Wolf) and a Poco Easter Lena moved with me as well.

In 2007, Walking With Wolves (the foal in Chapter 30) joined us. In 2008, the first foals sired by Running With Wolves arrived. Four more foals arrived in 2009, three sired by Wolf.

In 2008, I showed Wolf successfully in three-year-old reining futurities in B.C. and Alberta. In 2009, I showed him in derbies and Silk in Working Cow Horse. I am training Walking With Wolves (Little Wolf) for futurities in 2010. The same year, I will start riding Sapphire. I don't know how many more years I will show, but there is always another good horse to ride, another colt to start. Horses are the constant that define me.

I am a gentler person now. I find peace and contentment in the present. I watch hummingbirds at the feeder, chipmunks and chickadees vying for sunflower seeds on the lawn. I laugh at goslings bobbing down the river; I am in awe of a bald eagle perched on the tip of a Douglas fir. And I spend time with my horses. My day truly begins with soft nickers around the yard when I leave the house in the morning. Joy is a mare talking to her newborn, a foal nuzzling my hand.

From my earliest memory to present day, horse love has surrounded me. In my happiest moments and in some of my darkest hours, my horses protected and comforted me. Horses were just *there*, the thread holding my life together—familiar, stable.

As I wrote *A Life With Horses*, one thing became clear. Many beautiful, talented horses have enriched my life and, yes, *loved* me. I doubt I will ever live without horses. I am certain I will ride until I can no longer get on. My horses will be my legs, my eyes, my ears. My horses will not see an old woman but a friend. They will whinny for me, run their noses up and down my body, and breathe warmth into my soul. My horses will carry me and I will thank them. The view is best from the saddle.

172. Running With Wolves and I at the Canadian Supreme, October 2008. *Sharon Latimer*

173. My mares, Kirby and I in the Chilcotin in August 2007 (house behind). *Verna Allinson*

174. Enjoying a moment with Destiny and Kirby at my new home in the Chilcotin, August 2007. *Verna Allinson*

Notes

Part 1: Growing Up With Horses

1. Open range—unfenced grazing for cattle, expansive, mostly unimproved land of which a significant proportion of the natural vegetation is native grasses.
2. Dugout—an excavation "dug out" in a location to fill with water when the snow melts in the spring.
3. Runoff—snow that melts and "runs off" the ground, usually into sloughs, lakes or dugouts.
4. Fireguard—wide trails bladed through the hills by graders to aid in controlling a prairie fire should one occur.
5. Stone boat—a flat sled on skids turned up in front so it will slide and used for moving stones, firewood, manure, etc.
6. Slough—small lake formed by the runoff water in the spring.
7. Cutting out—separating specific animals from the rest of the herd.
8. Buck brush—erect, loosely branched shrub ranging from 1-3 meters high.
9. Threshing—separation of the kernels of grain from the straw and chaff.
10. Chaff—seed coverings and other debris separated from the kernels when the grain is threshed.
11. Sheaves—bundles in which grain is bound after reaping.
12. Unsound—lame.
13. Sound—not lame in any way.
14. Hard-mouthed—insensitive to pressure from a bit.
15. Grulla—colour of horses in the dun family, characterized by smoky, mouse-coloured hair.
16. Leg up—method of mounting a horse where the rider uses a hand of someone on the ground for leverage to propel himself up on the horse. (can also mean to condition a horse)
17. Snubbing post—large post, usually in the middle of a corral, used to tie a horse, especially if the horse is wild or not trained to a halter.
18. Ear (*verb*)—cowboy holds an ear of the horse and pulls steadily. The horse does not usually fight if he is "eared".
19. Herd bound—not comfortable away from other horses.
20. Sack out (*verb*)—process of systematically rubbing or flicking a sack or blanket on every part of a horse's body to desensitize him to objects on or around him prior to saddling the first time.
21. Pony—lead a horse from another horse.
22. Green horse—untrained horse.
23. Dally up—wrap the lead shank around the saddle horn.
24. Prairie wool—wild grass native to the prairies.
25. Matador—a very large Community Pasture southeast of Kyle, Saskatchewan.

26. Match race—a race between only two competitors.
27. Cold jawed (*verb*)—became insensitive to pressure from a bit.
28. Leg of race—one portion of a race.
29. Swathed—a field of grain that has been cut into rows in the field.
30. Black points—mane, tail and bottom portion of legs are black.
31. Snubbed—dallied to the saddle horn or post with a very short rope.
32. Cream can—large metal can for shipping cream.
33. Long two-year-olds—horses in the fall of their two-year-old year.

Part 2: Family and Horses

34. Catch colt—a term given to a foal that arrives unexpectedly from an unplanned breeding.
35. Remuda—a herd of horses from which a cowboy selects his mount
36. Jingle—round up the herd of horses for work that day.
37. Dry field—field for animals without calves (steers and/or heifers) or who will not be bred that year.
38. Pair up (*verb)*—match the calf and the calf's mother.
39. Cinch-sore—a sore in the girth area caused by the cinch of the saddle. (Can also be a verb)
40. Flat race—a horse race.
41. Jackpot—competition where competitors each contribute a set amount of money to compete. Total of all money is the purse for the race.
42. Goat Tying—an event for women whereby a goat is staked in the arena and the competitor rides to the goat, dismounts, wrestles the goat to the ground in some way and ties three legs together so the animal stays on the ground.
43. Rescue Race—a race with two people per team, one riding and one standing at another spot. The rider runs to the person on foot, who mounts behind the rider and both race to a finish.
44. Pony Express Race—a race with two people, both on horses. One rider carries a bag of mail to a predetermined point, returns to the second rider, passes the bag, and the second rider rides the same route.
45. Approved—eligible for association championships.
46. Dropped shoulder—horse fails to keep his shoulder upright, which results in leading into the turn with the shoulder and a loss of correctness.
47. Grade horses—horses not registered with any recognized breed association.
48. TAAA—a rating of speed by the American Quarter Horse Association (i.e. A, AA, AAA, TAAA).
49. Polled—without horns.
50. Face up (*verb*)—horse stands facing the animal with the rope tight after the rider has roped the animal.
51. Gather—round up cattle.
52. The plant—abattoir for horses.

53. Hot—too much energy.
54. Rate (*verb*)—prepare for turning by transferring weight to the hindquarters.
55. Go (*noun*)—short form for go-around, one barrel racing run at a rodeo with two or more runs.
56. Over-reach (*verb*)—hind foot strides too far forward to hit the back of the front foot.
57. Purse—total prize money for the event. The purse usually includes a given amount (added money) plus part or all of the entry fees.
58. Finals—deciding performance of top competitors determined by previous competition at that show.
59. Reverse seeded—a term for the order of go for a performance— reverse order of riders' standings. i.e. tenth placed rider goes first, first placed rider goes last.
60. Through the rider's hands—horse ignores direction from the rider through the reins (bit).
61. In the money—won money at a rodeo.
62. Scratch (*verb*)—cancel entry.
63. Riding double—phrase for two riders riding one horse, one rider in the saddle and one behind the saddle.
64. Take up the slack—gather up rope between the horse and the post by pulling as it loosened.
65. Half hitch—a knot or hitch made by looping a rope around an object, then back around itself, bringing the end of the rope through the loop—usually used with a second half hitch.
66. Coming three—phrase to describe a horse who is not three years old yet, but will be soon.

Part 3: Horse Training in Saskatchewan

67. Round-pen (*verb*)—a term for working a horse in the confines of a round pen.
68. Tying up—a medical condition characterized by profuse sweating, rapid pulse, stiffness of gait, and tense muscles, associated with exercise after a period of rest.
69. Run through the stop—the horse completely ignores rider's requests to stop and continues to run.
70. Pinned his ears—a phrase used to describe a horse laying his ears back in anger or defiance.
71. Cow-kick (*noun*)—cowboy slang for a forward, sideways kick from a horse's a hind leg. (Can also be used as a verb.)
72. War bridle—a halter fashioned from a rope, used to sharpen a horse's response by putting pressure simultaneously on the nose, chin and poll. Should be used by experienced handlers only.
73. Bushed cattle—cattle that will not leave the trees or bush.

Part 4: Horses and Training in B.C.

74. Fence (*verb*)—to run the horse in a straight line to a fence and allow the fence to stop the horse. This is a training exercise for reining horses.
75. Warm-up pen—an arena for "warming up" the horses for competition.
76. Magic cross—a term for the best cross of stallion and mare. i.e. for the best foal.
77. Turn-arounds—spins.
78. Bute—a short form for Butazone, an anti-inflammatory drug.
79. String—the group of horses that one rider is responsible for or rides.
80. Panniers—a pair of boxes slung one on each side of a pack horse.
81. Soft pack (*verb*)—the act of packing a horse with only a light canvas bag with pouches on both sides.
82. Skunk cabbage—one of the first native plant to emerge through the soil in the spring. It is large leaved and smelly!
83. Navicular —medical term for degenerative changes in small bones in a horse's foot (navicular bone), navicular bursa and deep flexor tendon.

Part 5: Riding Full Circle

84. Crow-hop (*noun*)—cowboy slang for a half-hearted buck (can also be used as a verb i.e. the horse crow-hopped).
85. Koolah—oilskin slicker.
86. Bell (*verb*)—to tie a strap with a bell around the horse's neck.
87. Bit check—an inspection by the judge to check for legal bit and/or abuse (Rider must dismount and remove bit from the horse's mouth).
88. Post enter (*verb*)—enter a competition after the closing deadline, usually with a penalty payment.
89. Run through the bit—a phrase describing the action of a horse that does not heed pressure from the bit. Similar to hard-mouthed.

Reference of Horses

List of Photographs